D-DAY

D-DAY

THE UNHEARD TAPES

GERAINT JONES

WALL TO WALL MEDIA LTD

This book is published to accompany the documentary series
D-Day: The Unheard Tapes, produced by Wall to Wall Media Ltd,
in association with the History Channel, and in partnership
with The National World War II Museum and The Imperial
War Museums, for the BBC and The Open University.

MACMILLAN

First published in the UK 2024 by Macmillan
an imprint of Pan Macmillan
The Smithson, 6 Briset Street, London EC1M 5NR
EU representative: Macmillan Publishers Ireland Ltd, 1st Floor,
The Liffey Trust Centre, 117–126 Sheriff Street Upper,
Dublin 1, D01 YC43
Associated companies throughout the world
www.panmacmillan.com

ISBN 978-1-0350-4963-9 HB
ISBN 978-1-0350-4964-6 TPB

1 3 5 7 9 8 6 4 2

A CIP catalogue record for this book is available from the British Library.

Map artwork © ML Design.

Typeset in Adobe Garamond by Jouve (UK), Milton Keynes
Printed and bound by CPI Group (UK) Ltd, Croydon, CR0 4YY

Visit **www.panmacmillan.com** to read more about all our books
and to buy them. You will also find features, author interviews and
news of any author events, and you can sign up for e-newsletters
so that you're always first to hear about our new releases.

CONTENTS

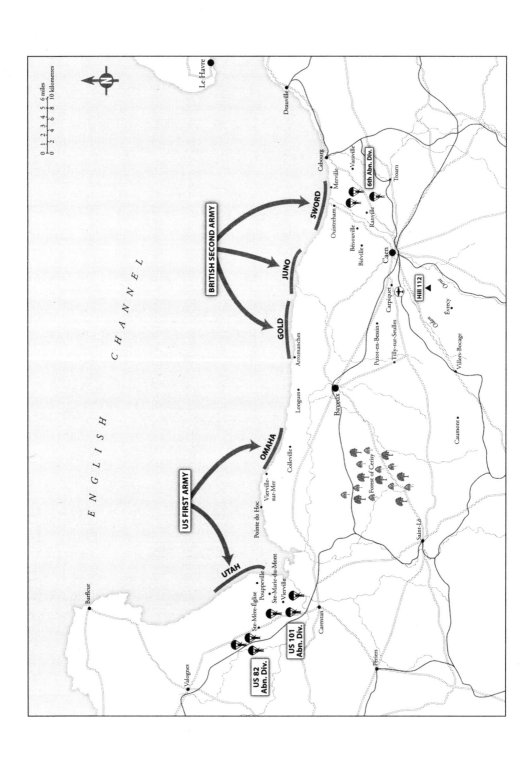

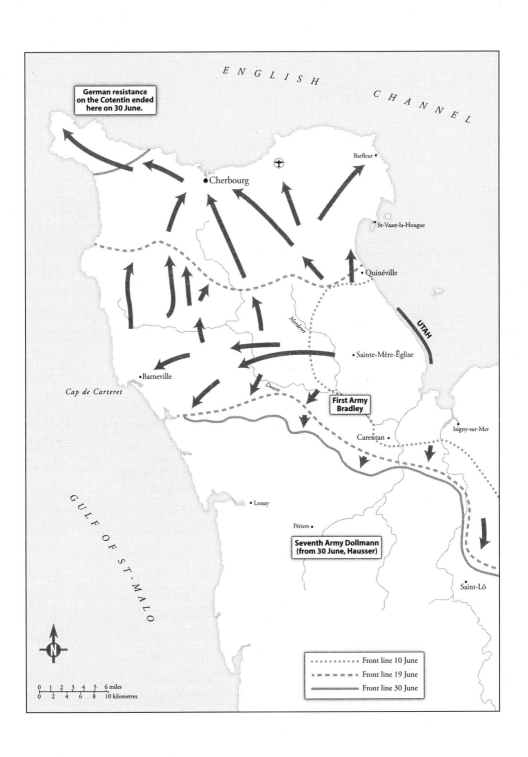

ENGLISH CHANNEL

German resistance on the Cotentin ended here on 30 June.

Barfleur •

⊕ Cherbourg •

St-Vaast-la-Hougue •

Quinéville •

Merdent

UTAH

Sainte-Mère-Église •

Barneville •

Cap de Carteret

Douve

First Army Bradley

Carentan •

Isigny-sur-Mer •

Lessay •

Périers •

Seventh Army Dollmann (from 30 June, Hausser)

Saint-Lô •

GULF OF ST · MALO

N

0 1 2 3 4 5 6 miles
0 2 4 6 8 10 kilometres

••••••••• Front line 10 June
– – – – – Front line 19 June
———— Front line 30 June

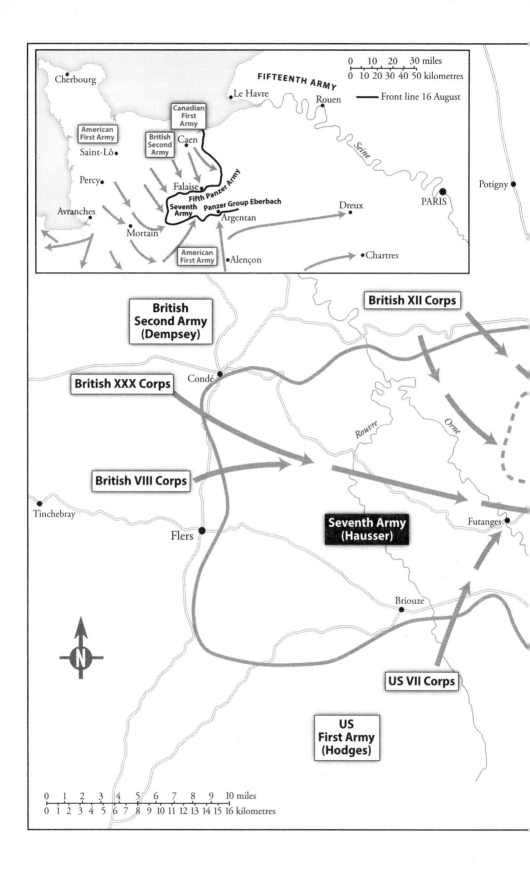

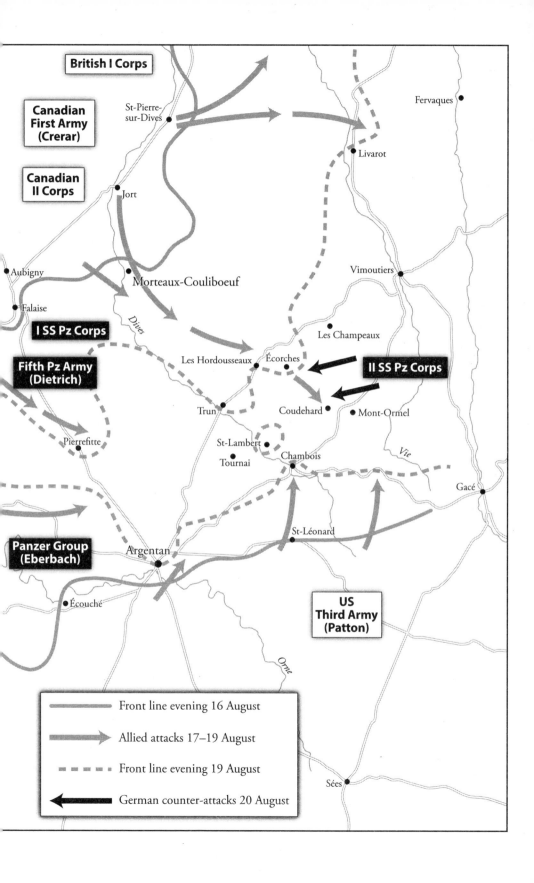

British I Corps

Canadian First Army (Crerar)

Canadian II Corps

St-Pierre-sur-Dives

Fervaques

Livarot

Jort

Vimoutiers

Aubigny

Morteaux-Couliboeuf

Les Champeaux

Falaise

I SS Pz Corps

Dives

Les Hordousseaux

Écorches

II SS Pz Corps

Fifth Pz Army (Dietrich)

Trun

Coudehard

Mont-Ormel

Pierrefitte

St-Lambert

Chambois

Vie

Tournai

Gacé

Panzer Group (Eberbach)

Argentan

St-Léonard

US Third Army (Patton)

Écouché

Orne

Sées

Front line evening 16 August

Allied attacks 17–19 August

Front line evening 19 August

German counter-attacks 20 August

D-DAY: INTRODUCTION

On the morning of 6 June 1944, a British landing craft carrying US Army Rangers ground ashore on Omaha Beach.

'The Germans opened fire with machine guns practically down the throat of the ramps,' Captain John Raaen remembered. 'Anyone who tried to go down the ramp died.'

The slaughter on Omaha was so terrible that some Allied soldiers on the beach thought the invasion would fail and yet, two months, three weeks, and two days later, Aircraftman Frank Collins bore witness to the destruction of the German army as it retreated from Normandy. 'I saw people coming out of burning tanks with their bodies alight, their clothing alight. And for me, I think that was possibly the worst part of the war.'

Every day of the Normandy campaign brought fresh horrors for the men who killed and died to establish, and then expand, the Allied beachhead in Western Europe. D-Day, and the Battle of Normandy, are rightly recognized not only as a turning point in the Second World War, but as one of the most significant events in our history. As such, the campaign has been written about extensively, which prompts the question: why another book about D-Day?

I believe that there are more than two million reasons, for this was the number of Allied soldiers who took part in the campaign. Add to that the French civilians whose homeland was turned into

1

a battleground, and the Germans who stood against the Allied landings. Each of their stories deserves telling, but tragically, most never will be.

Some of these stories were lost in battle, when men were cut down in their youth. Others were taken to the grave. How common it is to hear that 'My grandad was in the war, but he never talked about it.' It is exceptionally difficult to relive the worst days of one's life, and while compiling this book, watching and listening to interviews with veterans, I saw many tears, and heard many voices crack or trail away.

'You are the last person to talk to me about World War Two,' tank driver William Gast told his interviewer. 'This is the end.'

The reason why men like William told their stories was not because they searched for any kind of glory for themselves, but out of duty to their comrades: they did not want them to be forgotten, and they hoped that future generations might learn the lessons of history.

The recollections of William and John were made available by the National World War II Museum in the United States. The remarkable archives of this institution, which includes the Eisenhower Center Peter Kalikow World War II Collection, University of New Orleans, and of the Imperial War Museums in Great Britain, have provided the basis for this book. Both are home to thousands of oral histories, across rank, division and regiment, creating a lasting historical record. I am incredibly thankful to them for that, and for their tireless dedication in documenting the service of our veterans. The Juno Beach Centre's Legacy of Honour Video Collection also proved an invaluable resource. Any mistakes are, of course, my own.

I am also grateful to authors who have told the story of Operation Overlord, as the Battle of Normandy was known, from a strategic and a tactical level. The movements of the armies, the battles they fought, and the interplay of the commanders has been written superbly in several volumes. Other authors, such as Stephen Ambrose, Roderick Bailey, and Giles Milton, have helped to bring the individual's experience to the fore.

George MacDonald Fraser served as an infantry soldier in the Second World War and wrote, 'With all military histories it is necessary to remember that war is not a matter of maps with red and blue arrows and oblongs, but of weary, thirsty men with sore feet and aching shoulders wondering where they are.'[1]

So while there is some 'signposting' in this book to give readers a general idea of who was where, and when, its primary concern is with the experiences of the weary, thirsty men with sore feet and aching shoulders. It is an accompaniment to the groundbreaking BBC and History Channel documentary series *D-Day: The Unheard Tapes*, which has given new life to the voices of some of those who were part of this massive moment in our history by telling the stories of those who experienced D-Day first hand, in their own words, from all sides of the conflict. The book seeks to build around those powerful documentary interviews, with more than a hundred and fifty contributors from different nations and military branches. I have tried, wherever possible, to find additional complementary stories that have not been extensively covered in other works. While there may be crossover in some key moments in the Battle of Normandy, such as those pertaining to the important accounts of Major John Howard and the men of D Company at Pegasus Bridge, I hope that everyone who reads this book will also come across material that is as unfamiliar as it is moving.

Of course, it is beyond the scope of this book to give a voice to every man and woman, every unit, and every battle that took place in Normandy. Instead, in keeping with the documentary series with which this book is connected, I have tried to bring together voices that shine light on a certain personal aspect of the campaign. What was it like to fight in the hedgerows of the Normandy bocage? What went through the mind of a tank crew in a battle with superior German panzers? What was the experience of working in a field hospital, and dealing with a constant stream of wounded?

Throughout the text I have referred to people by their first name, and have generally dispensed with rank. I have tried to tell the story chronologically when possible, but some accounts have been moved to lend their voice to others. Where possible I have added the recollections exactly as they were spoken, but at times a word has been added or changed for clarity.

I have used the term 'recollections' for several reasons. First, because what you recall and what actually happened can differ in the best of circumstances, let alone when you're tired, afraid, and fighting for your life. Secondly, many of the interviews used in this book were given sixty years or more after the events took place. Time has a way of distorting our memories, as described by Captain John Raaen.

'There are certain brilliant flashes of memory, things that you will never forget. Things that were usually caused by trauma or great delight or some great event. They are short, they are very precise. They probably do not change over your entire life. Surrounding those important memories are a collection of other supporting memories. These supporting memories gradually fade. For a while you have memories of the memories, and then finally you develop a legend of memories, as I apparently have, about those brilliant, sharp primary memories. The legends very satisfactorily fit in with those primary memories and explain them.'

What we retain most strongly is *feelings*. Terror when a shell hits your tank. Disgust when you smell a rotting body. Joy when you reunite with a friend. War is perhaps the most extreme set of circumstances that human beings can find themselves in. Many who have seen it say that it brings out the best and the worst in mankind. It lays a person bare.

Many of the men who fought in Normandy were not soldiers until circumstance compelled them to be. When the war was gone, they tried to return to peaceful lives. I say try, because many carried the weight of what they had seen, and done, for the rest of their lives. These men abhorred war in a way that only those who have seen it can. They lived with memories of friends lost, and enemies killed. No soldier came back to his home the same man that had left it, nor was any family ever again whole after losing a loved one. We owe it to them all to listen, to learn, and to protect the peace for which they paid so much to give us.

Geraint Jones

CHAPTER ONE

The Eyes of the World Upon Them

The Men Who Fought on D-Day

'I don't think there's anybody closer than the man that you've got to fight with. You go through hell for them. And they go through hell for you.'

James 'Jimmy' Wilkinson,
9th Battalion, Durham Light Infantry

In February 1944, General Dwight D. Eisenhower, the Supreme Commander of the Allied Expeditionary Force, began drafting a message that would be delivered to the 'Soldiers, Sailors and Airmen' under his command. On the eve of D-Day, 175,000 copies of this 'Order of the Day' were distributed to those about to take part in one of the greatest operations in history.

'The eyes of the world are upon you,' Eisenhower told them in one of the many compelling passages. 'The hopes and prayers of liberty-loving people everywhere march with you. In company with our brave Allies and brothers-in-arms on other Fronts, you will bring about the destruction of the German war machine, the elimination of Nazi tyranny over the oppressed peoples of Europe, and security for ourselves in a free world.'

As Eisenhower told his troops, D-Day, and the Battle of Normandy, were an international affair. They were fought in the homes and the fields of the French people. The defenders were German, their own ranks including Soviet Russians, and Asiatic peoples. In the air were pilots from Australia, New Zealand, and Czechoslovakia. There were commandos from Hungary and tank crews from Poland. Canadian volunteers in their tens of thousands. American GIs from the Big Apple, Chicago, Los Angeles, and hometown USA. British soldiers from the Highlands, Cornwall, and everywhere in between.

Some of these soldiers, sailors, and airmen had been serving in their nations' armed forces before the war, but the majority were citizen soldiers. Some volunteered, others were conscripted. The pre-war occupations of these servicemen were as varied as their wartime roles: the miner who drove a tank onto the beaches; the office boy who flew a fighter bomber against panzers; the movie star who became a commando. Some grew up wealthy, others were dirt poor. They came as an army, but they were all individuals with different pasts, different futures, different dreams, and different beliefs. Now, in the summer of 1944, the threads of millions of lives were woven together for a common purpose: the invasion of France, the liberation of Europe, and the unconditional surrender of Nazi Germany.

'Overpaid, oversexed, and over here'

While the war in which they fought was a global event, many of those involved knew little of life outside of their own towns and cities before they began their military service. When the Japanese attacked the Pacific Fleet in Hawaii, a common question amongst the American population was: 'Where the hell is Pearl Harbor?'

There was no such confusion about their reaction to the attack, and the next day the lines outside recruiting stations were hundreds, even thousands of men long. For many, the road to Normandy began on 7 December 1941. By the eve of D-Day, more than 1,600,000 US service personnel were based in Britain. In some respects, it was a world away from the homes they left behind.

In the 1940s, the town of Athens, Texas, had a population of around 5,000 people. It was the kind of place where faith and football formed the cornerstones of the community.

'It was a great place to grow up,' said Frank Denius. 'Everybody knew each other. When I was twelve years old, in a family that was really dominated by my grandmother and my mother, all of my family, including my uncles, thought with the likelihood that World War Two might come along that I needed the discipline of attending a military school.' Frank graduated from the Schreiner Institute, and following the attack on Pearl Harbor he enlisted in the army at seventeen years old. Frank served in the artillery, and came to Britain aboard a troopship carrying 11,000 men.

'I went through Ranger training in England. And then in late April of '44 I joined the 30th Infantry Division as a forward observer. You went on marches and training almost 24/7. It was very intense.'

Harry Parley served in the 116th Regiment, 29th Infantry Division. Born and raised in the Bronx, he was recently married when he was drafted into the army at the age of twenty-three. After sixteen weeks of basic training in Texas, Harry was sent to New Jersey to board a troopship to England. The 116th were carried aboard the *Queen Mary*, and disembarked at Greenock on 2 October 1942. The *Queen Mary* played a vital role in WW2, carrying a total of 810,000 troops.[1]

Harry's first impression of Britain was that it was 'a fortress'. He spent the time leading up to D-Day in Wiltshire, Devon, and Cornwall, and other parts of the UK training as a member of an assault team in the 2nd Battalion. 'We were called E Company or Easy Company . . . They had been originally from a National Guard in Virginia, and the regiment or the division was made up of National Guard officers from Virginia and Maryland.

'We went to special schools. We went to assault training school. We went to flamethrowing schools. We went to commando courses. We were taught how to shoot from the hip. It's different shooting at a moving human than it is at a target. Actually shooting at a target allows you to regulate the sights of your weapon. But in combat, you seldom do that. It's what they call snap-shooting.'

Because they had been picked for special duties, and were given a large amount of training as a result, Harry and his comrades in Easy Company received little leave. When the Jewish men in the battalion were invited to a Passover Seder in Birmingham, Harry and about half a dozen other soldiers saw a chance to remedy the situation. 'They picked up other Jewish boys from other battalions, a truckload, I would say about sixteen. We got to Birmingham, went into the temple, out the other door, and went drinking. Time was short.'

While many US soldiers were training in Britain and awaiting the invasion of France, others were already engaged in combat.

Bruce LaRose grew up in a steel town in Pennsylvania during the Great Depression, his memories of which were 'hunger, for one. Eating a lot of onion sandwiches. Eating sugar on bread. Ketchup on bread, as the meal. And wearing shoes with holes in them that my brother wore out, or the two brothers before him.'

Bruce enlisted in the army in 1940, when America was still at peace. That all changed in December 1941.

'I heard about Pearl Harbor, as did all of us. The world got real close around us. We were in more intense training, and eventually we ended up going overseas.' Bruce's division, the 1st Infantry Division (better known as The Big Red One), was destined for Tunisia. 'We went to England on the *Queen Mary*. Shortly after that, we sailed for Africa, and did a beach landing at Arzew, where the African campaign began for the 1st Infantry Division.

'The landing wasn't a bad landing at all.' Bruce came ashore with B Company, 16th Infantry Regiment. In Africa he saw a comrade killed for the first time.

'We saw a group of men outside one of the houses, just standing there with shotguns. So we sent a scout forward to see what they were up to. They seemed harmless. Our scout's name was Kazmerkowitz. Kazmerkowitz got right up to them. We couldn't hear what they were saying, but one of them pointed his rifle up. There was a lot of birds flying around. But when they pointed up, Kazmerkowitz looked up, and one of them put a shotgun under his chin. Pulled the trigger and blew his head off. All three of us then zapped them.'

It was the first of countless actions for Bruce. Over the course of the Second World War he participated in the North Africa campaign, the invasion of Sicily, D-Day, Normandy, the Battle of the Bulge, and the Hürtgen Forest. Bruce was awarded the Silver Star and the Bronze Star for his bravery, and spent twenty years as a covert operative for the CIA.

While some of the American troops had lived through the Great Depression and were no stranger to hard times, Britain was very much a front line against Nazi Germany, and the GIs – as the American soldiers were known – were often shocked at conditions in their ally's home.

Walter Ehlers and his older brother Roland joined the US Army together in October 1940. As soldiers in the 18th

Regiment, 1st Infantry Division, they were about to embark on their third campaign of the war, having already fought in North Africa and Sicily. When they were recalled to England in December 1943 to prepare for D-Day, the Ehlers brothers got a chance to visit London.

'We weren't prepared for the chaos that we saw in London . . . It was unbelievable to see all the destruction . . . just building and block after block of town completely destroyed. It was just unbelievable. You just couldn't imagine it until you saw it.

'They had a raid that night.' As the air-raid sirens wailed, Walter and Roland took cover in an underground shelter with some local civilians. It wasn't long until the bombs started to explode. 'The English sat there . . . like nothing was happening. We were shaking in our boots, practically. We didn't know what the heck to do. Pretty soon they got an all-clear sound, and we came out. We followed the English out, and they went out about their business as though nothing had happened. Then we suddenly realized they'd been doing that for over three solid years . . . it was moving, very moving, to see them do that. We gained a lot of respect for the English when we saw that happen.'

John Witmeyer was a twenty-three-year-old from New Orleans, who arrived in Liverpool in April 1944. He'd had a regular boy's life, playing in the streets with his friends and doing his school work at night. He then worked as a roofer until the United States went to war. He enlisted the day after Pearl Harbor.

'I tried to join the Marine Corps, and I didn't pass their physical on account of my vision. They suggested I went to the navy.' John was then rejected a second time because of his eyesight. 'So I joined the army.'

The clubs and pubs of Britain were often busy with American servicemen. They were better paid than their British contemporaries, and as many of the latter were deployed in other theatres of war, that left a surplus of young women eager for companionship. This inevitably created some tension with the locals. 'We were moving to some area and some kid about thirteen years old . . . he was walking next to me . . . and starts spitting at me. So I promptly took him by his warm coat and hung him on a six-foot-high steel fence.'

John recalled an intense rivalry with the British servicemen. 'So being in the infantry we were always a little bit cocky about the air force. I was at a dance after a parade in England, and it was mostly RAF. I checked my coat at the coat check and she hung it on the rack at the end of a table, and I happened to go back there and go to the restroom, and there must have been thirty people must have spit on my coat. RAF guys, you know. They always had that old thing, overpaid, oversexed, and over here I think the British used to say. So I stopped the dance and wanted to know who did it. Who was big enough to come up and say who did it. Course nobody did, and then we started the music again. Started jostling one another. Started bumping one another.' Inevitably, things escalated. 'And we all ended up being locked up in the firehouse overnight because they didn't have enough jail space in that town for the American soldiers.'

In Normandy the Allies would be relying on each other to survive, but until that time came, soldiers would be soldiers.

An Army of Volunteers

Of all the national armies that took part in the Battle of Normandy, only one was composed purely of volunteers. Though the National Resources Mobilization Act initiated nationwide conscription across Canada in 1940, only the willing could be sent to fight overseas. Some 250,000 Canadians were active in Europe at the time of D-Day, from a population of around 12 million.

It can be argued that Canada's 'D-Day' losses actually began almost two years prior to the Normandy landings. On 19 August 1942, Operation Jubilee was launched against the French coast. Better known as the Dieppe Raid, Jubilee was intended to capture and hold a port for a short time, gather intelligence, boost Allied morale, and perhaps most importantly, demonstrate to the Soviet Union that the Allies were serious about opening a front in Western Europe. Nearly 5,000 Canadian troops took part in Jubilee, supported by around 1,000 British Commandos and 50 US Rangers, with support from the Royal Navy and RAF.

The operation was a failure in almost all respects, and was called off after six hours of heavy losses. Jubilee did, however, provide some important lessons, perhaps the greatest being that the liberation of France could not begin in 1943. More men and materials would need to be built up in Britain, and the Luftwaffe's capability would need to be degraded significantly.

A heavy price was paid to prove these points. Over 4,000 of the 6,086 men who landed at Dieppe were wounded, killed, or captured.

The sacrifice of Canadian soldiers on European soil was nothing new: 66,000 were killed during the First World War. From their first major battle, in 1915, to the close of the war, Canadians were recognized as some of the most ferocious and dependable troops, and often chosen to spearhead assaults. In his letter to Canadian forces on the eve of D-Day, General Crerar, commander of the First Canadian Army, told his troops that 'as Canadians, we inherit military characteristics which were feared by the enemy in the last Great War. They will be still more feared by the time this war terminates.' He went on to tell his army: 'The plans, the preparations, the methods and the technique which will be employed, are based on knowledge and experience bought and paid for by the 2nd Canadian Division at Dieppe. The contribution of that hazardous operation cannot be overestimated. It will prove to have been the essential prelude to our forthcoming and final success.'

One of the soldiers involved in that success was Jim Parks of the Winnipeg Rifles.

'I was just a young guy . . . we thought war was an adventurous thing. We went overseas on a banana boat called the SS *Orbita* and we landed in Liverpool about the 16th September 1941. We got on a train and went from Liverpool down to . . . Aldershot. We did a lot of training there, a lot of what they called anti-invasion exercises. We were stationed along the coast of England and there was always a threat that the Germans might invade.'[2]

Patrick 'Bill' Lewis grew up in Newfoundland, and was seventeen years old when war was declared in Europe. '(I felt) like John Wayne. I wanted to join up straight away and be a hero.' Bill tried to join the navy, 'but they told me to clear off and get back to school.' It was a temporary setback, and Bill joined the army the following year.

Though Newfoundland was at that point in effect a British dependency, and did not become part of Canada until 1949, its soldiers served in the Canadian army during the Second World War. This led to some tension between the troops.

'I look back and laugh now,' said Bill. 'But at the time it got on your nerves a bit to be constantly badgered by what you were. A Newfoundlander.'

There are two things that have bonded soldiers across the ages: a common 'enemy' and alcohol. Bill and his comrades found the first when trying to enjoy the second, as they were pitted against the military police who enforced Canada's strict drinking laws.

'The MPs would come and grab you with a gun out, believe it or not. That was very upsetting, to lose your bottle of whiskey. We decided that they had to be taught a lesson. So we grabbed them up one night, took them out a few miles outside of town, stripped them off and left them there. We didn't have too much trouble after that.'

Bill and his fellow soldiers in the 2nd Canadian Armoured Brigade then shipped out to England, landing a year ahead of D-Day. For them, coming to the defence of the 'mother country' was a matter of duty. 'We felt a part of Great Britain. We were brought up that way. Brought up strictly that way, that Britain was our mother country, and that it would just be automatic for us (to serve).'

When he arrived in England, Bill was surprised to find himself more patriotic than some of the locals. 'We were so loyal in comparison to when I got to (England). I didn't feel the same enthusiasm from the people here that we actually had (at home). They probably didn't express it, as we were. At home, when they played "God Save The King" at the end of the movie, everybody stood. Nobody left the cinema. (In England) I was amazed to see people getting up and walking out when the national anthem was being played.'

At least the rules around drinking were more relaxed.

'The pubs were crowded. If you didn't get in quick and get a glass, you didn't get a beer. We also had Canadian Women's Army who were in the pub with us as well. We didn't get on very well with them. They were a real tough lot of women. They had it made. Fifty to one if you like. They never had to buy a drink or anything, and consequently they got drunk, there was so many people buying for them, trying to get their favours. From my own experience . . . that was the sort of trouble we had. Fighting in the pubs over a limited number of women.'

Tommies

The British servicemen who took part in D-Day had lived with the very real threat of invasion of their own country. Around 11,000 of the army's regular soldiers had died fighting the German invaders in Belgium, France and Holland in 1940, with many thousands more taken prisoner. Still more were lost in the Far East. Thousands had died in the battles of North Africa, and other campaigns. While General Bernard Montgomery did recall several veteran formations to take part in the Battle of Normandy, many of the men, whether volunteers or conscripts, were seeing action for the first time. By the end of June, more than 400,000 of them would be ashore in Normandy, including Trevor Edwards of the Royal Welch Fusiliers.

'I was born in a little village . . . called The Ffrwd. It's outside of Wrexham. My mother died with the flu epidemic in 1917 . . . my grandmother brought me up. (My father) was a steel worker. Previous to that he was a collier.'

Trevor left school at fourteen and worked as a grocer for seven years before going into the quarry. He was called up in January 1940, by which time he was working in steel.

'I knew I was going to be called up . . . I could have had a deferment because I was on war work, but at that particular time a friend of mine also had his calling up papers . . . so my father like, he'd been in the last war, he said, "You might as well go now like I had to do, and you've got your friend to go with you as company." So I decided to go. I joined the Royal Welch Fusiliers.'

Trevor's father had never talked much about his own experience of war. 'He didn't mention much about the army, me father. He just said that it's not only the fighting, it was the conditions that you lived under, and things like that. I always remember him saying to me that the conditions of living in the 1914–18 war was worse than actually fighting.

'When I got to (the train station) there was about twenty of us there. Young men, and we all had our cases . . . we were mostly all Wrexham boys. When we got to the camp, we were for about a week without a uniform. Some just had a cap. And we'd be marching up and down. We were conscripts, and the people in charge of us were regular soldiers . . . They seemed to resent us . . . Their attitude was, why didn't we join the army before? They give us a bit of stick on that, like.'

After training, Trevor served in the 8th Battalion, Royal Welch Fusiliers. It was a holding battalion, and provided drafts of men to reinforce other parts of the regiment. In 1944 the unit was based in Fleet, England, which is close to the large British army garrison of Aldershot.

'I liked to drink like, I was one of the lads. There was the RAMC training depot there . . . and also the Canadians were there. There used to be a kind of a feud going between the Royal Welch Fusiliers and the Canadians. We used to wear a black Flash, you see. And it all started over one of the lads getting this Flash ripped off. It was ripped off as a souvenir, and then there was fighting, like. When we were walking home like, they'd waylay us on the road, you see. A couple of Canadians. These lads would come in the billet with a black eye. And we'd waylay them the next day. It was a bit of fun like, really.' In an attempt to stop the fighting, an agreement was reached between the Canadian and Welch COs to alternate the nights that their units would go into town.

Trevor saw his first gunshot casualty before he ever reached France.

'A lad was cleaning his rifle in one hut and he had a round

up the breech. He pulled his trigger and the bullet went straight through the hut and took (another) lad's eye out.'

The soldier who lost the eye was from the same town as Trevor, and worked with him at the steel works after the war. 'We were all like Wrexham lads. Local boys, most of us.'

Major John Howard became one of the best-known British officers who served in the Second World War, but the odds of him ever obtaining a commission were stacked against him. 'I had a very poor childhood . . . I was born in a mews off Tottenham Court Road in the West End (of) London (in 1912) . . . as the eldest of a very poor family. I had to become a breadwinner as soon as possible.' John left school at the age of fourteen, and worked in several offices. His living conditions were hard. 'Let's face it, I lived in slum conditions. I won't go into the details of it now. It's embarrassing.'

At the age of eighteen John lost his job in the 'slump of 1931', and made the decision to join the army. Of course, thousands of other men had the same idea, and the recruiting process was extremely competitive. This was no issue to a man of John's disposition. 'I had ambitions of getting on in the army . . . I wanted a commission, which was very, very difficult from the ranks in those days.'

The men John was serving with were 'very rough and tough. They were very mixed bag, as you would expect, and they were very rough and tough. And in the Shropshires there was a very high proportion of Welshmen from the mining villages. And I freely admit I cried my eyes out for a couple of nights when I was in the back room with these toughs and wondered if, you know, if I, I'd survive.'

John did survive, spending six years in the army before leaving and becoming a police officer. He was recalled to the service following the outbreak of war, and quickly rose through the ranks, becoming the regimental sergeant major of the King's Shropshire Light Infantry. He then achieved his earlier dream of becoming a commissioned officer, and by 1942 he was a major and Officer in Command (OC) of D Company, 2nd Battalion, Oxfordshire and Buckinghamshire Light Infantry, known amongst soldiers as the Ox and Bucks. A year earlier, they had been re-roled as glider infantry, and in 1943 they joined the newly created 6th Airborne Division. 'A lot of Londoners were posted into my company and as a Londoner myself, I was pretty pleased about this.'

John set a high standard for himself and his soldiers.

'We didn't follow the normal pattern of training. We had to do certain things, (like) drill . . . I used to take the company drill instead of the company sergeant major. Perhaps on reflection I think it's probably wrong, but you felt you had the command and the respect of (the men) by doing it. I used to take the whole company out for three or four days . . . at a time on exercises, sleeping rough, things like that, whereas the other companies would follow the normal routine, you know, of drill in the morning, weapon training in the afternoon, all of them normal programmes with very few exercises at night, night training and things like that. And then I'd bring them back and give them the day off.'

John believed that this instilled a strong sense of spirit and camaraderie in D Company. 'There's a sort of effect of, well, *we're different*. And it all helped to build up in D Company a tremendous esprit de corps. We were very good in all the sporting events. More often than not, we ran off with the swimming cup, cross-country cup, boxing, anything that was going. And we probably made more noise than anybody else with that cheering and jeering. God knows what. But it is all part of esprit de corps as far as I was concerned.'

The men of D Company were eager to get to grips with the

Germans. They were warriors, and without an enemy in front of them, they would sometimes go in search of one on English soil.

'A lot of my men got into trouble outside. One of the most serious punishments you could give an airborne chap was a RTU. That's Returned To Unit, and it was a disgrace. They lost their red beret and the honour and everything that went with it of being in the airborne division. And some of the people who got into trouble because of this staleness (ended) up fighting in the town with the guards or the military police or something like that. It was a military police offence.'

John would have to go in front of the CO and plead his case that the man remain in the 6th Airborne Division. 'Many a time I went up to placate my colonel and explain that this chap is one of the best.' John referred to these men as his 'scallywags', born fighters and leaders who could not hold rank when in garrison and training duties because they were constantly in trouble. John believed they were exactly the kind of men that were needed when they crossed the Channel.

'And by God, they didn't half prove it, all the scallywags, when we got to the other side. They were the best. Unfortunately, most of them were killed 'cause of their nature.'

John's D Company were given one of the most critical missions on D-Day; taking and holding two bridges on the eastern flank of the Allied beachhead, from which Allied armour could then break out.

Twenty-two-year-old Royston 'Roy' Vallance served in the 2nd Fife and Forfar Yeomanry, a Territorial Army unit equipped with Sherman tanks. Like many soldiers of his generation, Roy's father had gone to war before him.

'My father was an invalid, having been gassed in the First World War. He died when I was very young . . . He was gassed, and he never really recovered health from that. My mother also died when I was very young.' Roy was raised by foster parents until he was fifteen. 'And then I got a job and looked after myself.'

He was called up and began his military service in March 1942, and enjoyed his time in uniform. 'We used to go down into Newmarket for our leisure. Go to the pubs and that sort of thing. I used to spend quite a lot of time, illicitly, in a wood at the back of where we were camped with a .22 rifle and got the odd pheasant. That was quite good fun. We used to go out and get mushrooms, and supplement the food. All together it was a very happy time.'

William 'Bill' Dunn was fourteen years old when he left school and started work in Silksworth Colliery. When the mine shut at the beginning of the war he moved to Chester, building blast walls around oil-refinery tanks to shield them from German bombing. He continued this work until he was called up in 1942. 'I didn't mind, because actually I thought the army was a lazy life, (compared) to what I'd been used to.'

Bill's father had served in the First World War and gave his son some advice. 'He always said, "Well, you've got to make the best of it when you're in." It was a bit rough at first, but once you got settled into it, it was really enjoyable.'

Bill felt that his background in mining had given him an advantage over men who came from office work. He was enlisted into the King's Own Yorkshire Light Infantry before being transferred to the 70th Battalion of the Essex Regiment.

'While I was at the Essex Regiment I did commando training. Went up to Fort William with the commandos.' The battalion was disbanded in March 1943, and Bill found himself in the Royal Armoured Corps. 'We had to train on all different types of tanks, and I decided that I would be a driver, a mechanic . . . we did quite a lot of training with the tanks there, and then they put me on a Churchill.

'Every man was trained in the tank to do the job of another crewman. If there was a crewman injured or anything like that, another man could drop in and do his job if he were out, say the tank was on its own. Radio operator got hit, any one of the crew could take over the radio. And I had a co-driver sitting alongside me. If I got hit he could take over. So we could do each other's jobs, you know, which was a good thing.'

An important part of Bill's training was learning to recognize different models of enemy tanks, and to know their strengths and weaknesses. 'We were told about the Tiger tank having so much armour in front of it, and where to fire the guns at the Tiger or any other German tank for penetration purposes, or to knock them out.'

While Bill was preparing to go to North Africa with the Royal Armoured Corps, it was decided that a special unit of Royal Engineers would be formed for the invasion of Europe. Bill found himself in his fourth unit in two years.

'There was twenty-six drivers taken out of our lot to go to join the Royal Engineers. And we had to train the Royal Engineers on tanks, and they had to train us on the engineer side of it. And this was how the assault squadrons was formed, and I think it was about eight or ten assault squadrons at that particular period of time, and I was in the Two-Six.'

These assault squadrons of the Royal Engineers were equipped with the modified tanks known as 'Hobart's Funnies'. 'My tank . . . we were trained to carry the fascine.' This was a bundle of heavy-duty rods that could be dropped into a ditch or trench, acting as a bridge for vehicles to cross the obstacle. Other 'Funnies' carried flamethrowers, flails that would set off buried mines, or mortars. They proved incredibly important on D-Day.

Of course, there could be no invasion across the Channel without sailors.

Ray Smith was seventeen years old when he first went to sea. 'I joined a ship at Rosyth and went straight to Iceland. I'd never been to sea on a ship before.'[3]

Aboard the destroyer HMS *Middleton* Ray took part in the infamous Arctic convoys. As well as dangers from U-boats, German surface vessels, and the Luftwaffe, crews had to contend with conditions so extreme that bare flesh would stick to the frozen metal of the ship. The temperatures dropped below −30C, and the seas were so rough that the waves were described as mountainous. In such hostile environments, humour was an important weapon. 'I was old enough to be sent on Russian convoys, but not old enough to draw my rum ration,' Ray joked.

These dangerous missions were vital to supply the Soviet forces that were battling against the Axis on the Eastern Front, and would have a direct impact on the Battle of Normandy – the more German units were engaged in the east, the less could be diverted to compete against the landings in the west. The Arctic convoys paid a heavy price for this success: 3,000 Allied servicemen, 85 merchant vessels, and 16 warships were lost to enemy action alone. 'I think we had more damage done by the sea than enemy gunfire,' said Ray. 'If we could survive that, we could get through anything.'

After being taken off convoy duty, HMS *Middleton* was put on anti-submarine operations in the North Sea. 'We had one or two near misses. We (dropped) loads and loads of depth charges but nothing came up,' Ray said, meaning wreckage or oil from a destroyed U-boat. For a while the *Middleton* was sent to the English Channel to hunt enemy shipping. Then the preparations for D-Day began. 'As D-Day approached we were doing training with various landing craft – we were doing that for quite some time, getting used to what we were doing with the convoys and getting ready to go to France.'

Several British units that would fight in Normandy had already seen action in other theatres, but they would need to be brought up to strength by soldiers who had yet to see combat.

Twenty-one-year-old Berkeley Meredith joined the Staffordshire Yeomanry when the regiment returned from North Africa. 'When war broke out they were a Territorial regiment, and believe it or not they were on an exercise in Syria . . . And their first battle honour was one in Syria. They were fighting the French.' These were the Vichy French who had made peace with Germany, and taken up arms against the Allies. 'From that day on they remained in the desert. They were Desert Rats. 7th Armoured Division. They were in El Alamein and all the previous battles. They were very, very battle-hardened.'

Berkeley saw a difference in the TA regiment compared to the other units he had served with in the army.

'I think there must have been a very different comradeship in a regiment like that . . . a different relationship between the ranks between that and a regular regiment. I'm not saying that discipline was any the less, but I think there was a different spirit because when you think back a lot of these people had known each other in civvy street. They were in maybe different walks of life, but they'd had to live with each other not only in their service commitment, but as civilians. So I think there was a more relaxed atmosphere between the various ranks in a regiment like that than there could ever have been in a regular regiment.'

James 'Jimmy' Wilkinson was one of the battle-hardened soldiers returning to England for D-Day. He had worked in the coal pits before joining the Durham Light Infantry in 1940. At the time he was sixteen years old.

'I'd already passed for the navy at fourteen, but my parents wouldn't let us. I was adamant that I was gonna go into the services. I just thought, everyone else is going, I may as well go as well.' Jimmy's neighbour, an ex-regular soldier, came along to the recruiting station to vouch for him. 'I said that I was nineteen years of age . . . And they accepted that.'

As well as basic and infantry training, Jimmy went through a period of commando training.

'Captain Black, he was an ex-police officer, and he was the jiu-jitsu expert. I was just a laddy, and he got me running up a bank with a naked bayonet, not sheathed. Three times he got me up, running at him, and he was tipping me up, because it's easy. You might not think it is but it's dead easy. It's just a matter of balance, and when you're running you're out of balance. So he got me twice. Threw us. The third time I stopped a yard from him, and I hit him. And he went down. When he come to, he give me such a hiding, and he was laughing all the time. I says to him after he'd given us a hiding like, "You know if we'd been on active service you'd have congratulated me for doing that to an enemy. You expected me to just carry on, and you could just throw me about. That throwing about hurts you know. The reason that I stopped short, and hit you with the butt, was because you weren't expecting it."'

Jimmy and his battalion deployed to the Middle East in 1942. He took part in several actions in the desert, where the conditions were grim. 'You get a dead body and it's covered with maggots. Covered with flies. You'd get a scratch, or you'd get a cut. Two or three days it would be septic, and the maggots would be running in it. One of our medical orderlies, he got just a scratch. His hand was all maggots. You could scrape the maggots out.'

While he was at the front, Jimmy received a 'Dear John' letter from a girl back home.

'It went around the Durhams. What she said, you see. I'd been courting her . . . and she was a bit older than me. She wrote to me, and she said it would be unfair for me to expect her to be there when I come home. Anyway, she says she wasn't going to wait. At that time, a lot of letters hadn't come, so I let anybody read it that wanted to read it.'

Other men didn't take too well to similar news. '(It) didn't take effect (while they were) in the line. When they were abroad it didn't take effect. But we had two lads who killed their wives when they came back. They'd been messing about.'

Jimmy recalled one enemy attack when he was at Gazala. 'The infantry came first . . . and then the tanks followed. The lads were in their trenches, and as soon as the infantry came they had a go at them, and they put a lot down. From what I heard myself, and I still hear it today, the tanks got onto the slit trenches . . . they'd turn the tanks, and ground the people (inside). There's a lot of sounds that people make for different circumstances. Now if you get a person that's injured by a bullet, then if it's severe, he cries, and he's crying for help. It's not piercing. It's just a cry for help. When you get a chap that's burning, now his scream is very severe. When you hear a chap that's being ground into the ground with a tank, you can hear that for miles, and it stays with you. It's piercing. You could hear that quite a lot.'

In another action, Jimmy came across three Axis soldiers in a tank pit. 'I killed them all with a bayonet. And I kept on (stabbing them).' After the battle of El Alamein Jimmy was put in front of a psychiatry board.

'Somebody had reported me I think, for the way I killed them Germans. They were asking various questions. 'They said, in their deliberations, they'd come to the conclusion that I'd be better off in the (Pioneer Corps). I said, "I'm an infantry soldier. If I can't fight with the infantry, in the regiment that I'm with, then I think you should send me to Blighty." And the next day I was back on the line.'

Action in Sicily followed, where Jimmy became separated from his unit. He joined a group of other soldiers and came under fire from massive naval guns mounted inland. 'They killed fifteen of them lads. All but me.' When Jimmy visited the graves after the battle, he saw that one grave had his name on it: he was presumed dead.

At the end of the hard campaign the 9th DLI were visited by General Montgomery, who would command the armies that landed at Normandy. The men weren't pleased to see him. 'We refused to break ranks for him. He's a wily old bird. He knew that he was going to take us home for the invasion of France, so because we wouldn't break ranks he says, "I'm thinking of taking you home to England." He didn't say for the invasion of France like.'

It was not the last time that Jimmy's unit took issue with a visiting figure.

'The King saw us prior to the invasion . . . He came to the 9th first, and we had a new colonel.' This officer, Humphrey Woods, had received several gallantry awards during his wartime service. 'Which meant to us he was a good lad.' The King asked the colonel if all the soldiers were old hands, to which the colonel 'naturally to please', answered, 'Yes, your majesty.' 'The King then asked, "And how long have you been with the battalion, my man?" . . . He was plumb aghast. So, he never got an answer yet, so the King says, "Speak up, man! Speak up! When I ask a question I want an answer, and I want it now!" The (whole) bloody division heard. So we had orders that when the King went out of the field . . . he had twelve MPs in front of him, twelve behind, and he was in a Rolls Royce. So we were supposed to break ranks automatically, run to the side of the field where the road was, and . . . throw the hats up in the air, and let him know that we were pleased to see him.'

This did not happen.

'We didn't break ranks at all. We had to be marched to the side. When the MPs come, up went the hats, and shouts of Hooray to the MPs! and we slouched when (the king) came, and when the MPs behind (came), up went the hats again.'

After that the battalion was given seven days' Confined to Barracks by their colonel, 'but (you) couldn't find five men for (guard duty),' said Jimmy. 'The lads all went out. They weren't happy at all. Everybody went out, and they didn't believe that it was just for the colonel to give us seven days' CB.' Presumably alcohol was enjoyed by those who left the barracks. The next day the colonel addressed the men on parade. 'He says, "If any of you chaps want to ride in my car, all you have to do is ask, but I definitely dislike having my car stolen, and (you) firing revolvers out the window."'

Jimmy explained the reason behind the men's actions. 'It was purely and simply because (the colonel) was a good lad, and the king had pulled him to bits. He had no right to talk to a man of his position in that manner, especially in front of us. I don't think there's anybody closer than the man that you've got to fight with. You go through hell for them. And they go through hell for you.'

The battalion was a tribe, and would fight anyone that threatened it. Even Allies.

'The American air force had had the run of Saffron Walden, and the Americans had bashed some of our lads about. So they came back, blooded . . . and informed the lads that was in the camp. Now everybody that was in the camp went down. Armed. It was in the *News of the World* that the DLI had sacked Saffron Walden. But all it was, if they'd left the lads alone quietly, to have a quiet drink, there would have been no bother. But they caused the bother, and that was it.'

Thirty-one-year-old career soldier Major Herbert John Mogg joined the 9th DLI when they returned to England. 'The commanding officer was Humphrey Wood . . . he was a highly experienced desert commander, having got two DSOs and two MCs, and had been blown up on mines a couple of times. He was slightly deaf in one ear. He was young, he was beloved by his battalion, he was a bachelor, and he couldn't have made me more welcome. Every soldier practically had three campaign stars on his left breast, and quite a lot of them had Military Crosses, DCMs, Military Medals, and I was in quite a disadvantage over all this having not seen a shot fired in anger . . . Apart from that I found I might well have been in a foreign country, because I just couldn't understand the Geordie language.

'I think quite a lot of them were a wee bit bomb happy because they'd been at it from the time we got to the desert, until the time they came out of Italy. They'd been fighting practically the whole time.' This led to some men believing that they had done their bit, and taking the matter of 'leave' into their own hands. 'There was quite a lot of desertion . . . Just before we sailed, an awful lot of them returned.'

The Durhams would take part in several bloody battles in the months to come. For other regiments in the Allied invasion armies, their losses would begin before they ever reached French soil.

Exercise Tiger

In the run up to D-Day, large areas of Britain became training grounds for the Allied soldiers. At Slapton Sands in Devon, land, sea, and air forces combined to practise amphibious landings on a large scale. On 28 April 1944, it was the scene of a great tragedy for the Allied Expeditionary Force.

Leon Schafer was a US naval officer aboard a flat-bottomed Landing Ship, Tank (LST) designed to carry tanks and troops directly onto beaches.

'We were training army units to load the LSTs, and it was on April the 27th, we finished training the army troops and loaded them to take them back to wherever they were going. (There were) twelve LSTs in our group. Six of them were three abreast in front of us, and we made a feint to Cherbourg.'

This feint was intended to provide intelligence on the German coastal defence reaction times. The LSTs were protected by a large screen of naval vessels, and it was hoped that any sortie by German torpedo boats would allow them to be destroyed in advance of D-Day. Like many plans in wartime, it did not survive contact with the enemy.

'German torpedo boats attacked those six (LSTs) in front of us,' said Leon. 'They sank two and badly wrecked one of the LSTs. We lost a tremendous number of men. Army personnel that were aboard the ship. A lot of them were thrown overboard when the torpedoes hit the ship. They were thrown overboard and drowned. That was a Saturday night. We spent all day Sunday picking up bodies, and rescuing those in the water.'

More than 700 men died that night, with some estimates as high as 946. The disaster was kept out of the papers and news-reels, and it was decades before the circumstances around the tragedy were revealed to the public.

The sight of so many dead proved too much for one man of Leon's crew. 'One of our small boat officers went berserk as a result of picking them up. We had to leave him in the hospital in Portsmouth.'

Historians like Peter Caddick-Adams have documented the

often deadly nature of training in preparation for D-Day. He describes incidents of men killed in glider crashes, shot during live-fire exercises, and drowned during practice assaults to name but a few. Such loss of life is a tragic inevitability of realistic training, the result of which may have helped save lives on the battlefield. Still, when we think of the sacrifices made during the war, we should recall that not all of them came at the hands of the enemy.

Interdiction

As soldiers trained in Britain for the coming assault, Allied air-crews began to shape the battlefields to the attackers' advantage.

Air superiority – the ability to control the skies – is vital for a successful amphibious operation. In 1940, it was the resolute defence by the Royal Air Force, coupled with Hitler's disas-trous decision-making, which put an end to any real threat of an invasion of Britain. In 1944, air superiority was a prerequisite for the Allies' invasion plans. Their ships were vulnerable to air attack and they needed to negate the inherent advantages the land defender has against a seaborne invasion. If the Germans could bring their crack panzer divisions to bear on the beach-head, there was a very good chance that the Allies would be driven back into the sea. The Allied air forces would have to slow the enemy's advance, bleed their strength, and keep them under constant attack when they reached the field. To this end, Luft-waffe fighters were hunted in the skies, and airfields in France and Belgium were attacked. To slow German reinforcements, bridges, railways, and rail yards were destroyed. Anti-aircraft positions, gun batteries, and known headquarters were also tar-gets. If it could hinder the Allied invasion, or help the German defence, it was a candidate for attack from the air. That this would inevitably lead to French casualties was cause for concern amongst the Allied leaders but ultimately, as Eisenhower reminded Churchill, it was necessary to increase the chances that the invasion would succeed.

Intelligence gathered by the local population played an important part in planning these pre-invasion missions. André Geloso had been a soldier in 1940, and continued to oppose the Germans as a member of the French Resistance.

'I used to go around the countryside and observe the concentrations of troops and what was going on and so on. There was one point, above Deauville, they were building an underground cave with very powerful guns which were set towards the sea. The man who was in charge of the work there was a Frenchman, and there was a lot of [French] workers there. They used to work all the week, but never worked on Sundays. The (SOE) major said, "When the work is finished. Let us know and we'll get it bombed."'

The Special Operations Executive (SOE) was a secret organization tasked with sabotage and the organization of resistance in occupied countries. When André got word that the construction of the defences was complete, he contacted his British handlers.

'The following Sunday we heard some planes coming . . . There was a terrific bombing there, there was two waves of bombers. There was a lot of casualties of Germans because we saw some ambulances passing all day. No civilians were . . . caught in it.'

André and his sister also helped downed airmen to escape capture, often hiding them in plain sight at a nearby farm.

'There was about twenty-five airmen there, hidden all over the place. Some were working with the farmer. One . . . was a crossing guard. We gave him some civilian clothes. He used to come out and watch the trains, and there were some Germans there . . . It was such a safe place they wouldn't have thought there was anything wrong there.'

The men who crewed the Allied aircraft were overwhelmingly young, with most under twenty-five; anyone in his late twenties was likely to be given the nickname of 'Grandad' or 'Gramps' by his crewmates. The odds for a bomber crew member making it through his tour alive, uninjured, and uncaptured was only around one in four. Of the 120,000 men who flew in the RAF's Bomber Command during the war, more than 55,000 were killed. US bomber crews suffered a near identical casualty rate, with 26,000 KIA in the USAAF 8th Air Force. 16,000 Allied airmen lost their lives during the Normandy campaign.

'You always felt it was never going to happen to you,' said Herbert Kirtland, an RAF wireless operator in the Halifax bombers of No. 4 Group.

'Leave came up about every six weeks, and you'd go away for a week's leave, and come back, and perhaps look out for some buddy in the mess, and say where's so-and-so, and somebody would shrug his shoulders and say, "They bought it two nights ago." You know, you didn't go into it very much. You realized you lost some more pals, and that was it.'

Herbert and the NCOs of his crew shared accommodation with the enlisted men of another aircraft. 'They were a harem scarem bunch, none of them over twenty-one. I woke up one morning about 5 a.m. to find a couple of service policemen with torches going through, collecting their kit. I turned over, and I knew what that meant. Davies wasn't back. And sure enough he'd been shot down.'

'One minute someone was there. The next minute, they weren't there,' said Typhoon pilot Kenneth Trott, who was twenty-one in June 1944. 'I think it was always the feeling that as soon as you took off from this country, that you were over enemy territory, and once you were over enemy territory, well, it would be a nice thought to be coming back again.'

Also flying missions to shape the battlefield for the invasion was Typhoon pilot Ernest 'John' Golley. John also turned twenty-one in June 1944, and had been inspired to join the RAF during the Battle of Britain. 'I used to see the dogfights over Croydon . . . there were a lot of dogfights around. I really wanted to get in (the RAF) like yesterday.'

During the Blitz, John had been on the receiving end of an air-to-ground attack when a train he was on was attacked by a Heinkel bomber. In Normandy it was John who was making attacks on trains and railways. 'I was doing precisely the same thing in northern France. We had eight rockets, four under each wing, and a full salvo was the equivalent of a broadside from a light cruiser. And then we had 20mm (cannon) shells. It was a lethal weapons system, the Typhoon.'

John and his squadron had no illusions about what awaited them in Europe. 'We knew that we were going to give close support to the armies, and that we were going to be on the nasty end of the business. Having a scrap with an aircraft at 15,000 feet was one thing, but flying down the barrel of an 88mm was yet another.'

The German '88' was a formidable weapon in the war. As well as lethal to infantry and tanks, the 88mm gun was a formidable anti-aircraft weapon. Indeed, this was its initial design, and was often its primary role on the battlefield.

Lutz Windisch served in a battery of 88s outside of Rouen. As a child he had been a member of the Hitler Youth, and had once shaken Hitler's hand. 'There's one thing I never forgot. When Hitler came and shaked hands with me, I thought he would look at me, but he shaked hands and looked through me. It really hurt me.'

Lutz was nineteen years old when he arrived in France in the spring of '44. 'I was in charge of the technical aspect of the (88mm) gun. If anything was wrong I was the one that fixed it. We had about eight guns. In the middle was a unit that looked up to the airplanes in order to coordinate the shooting. When the Americans came and bombed the place, and one of the (telephone) cables was broken, you had no communication with the other unit there, which was very difficult, because in order to shoot somebody you have to be guided by an instrument . . . you had to be coordinated.

'I remember one time, I was just maintaining and repairing a gun when I see an aeroplane coming . . . And you wouldn't believe it, I could see the pilot, and the pilot laughed at me. He was flying and I was shooting behind him. He knew exactly what I was doing, but I was much too slow to turn the gun. I could see his face laughing at me.'

Lutz's battery shot down several Allied planes during the war, but they were often on the receiving end of attacks themselves. 'It's horrifying, because you have no protection. We were open, in an open field. You'd be just . . . like a chicken out there.'

The Night Before

The invasion of Normandy was planned for 5 June 1944. In the preceding weeks, tens of thousands of soldiers were moved from their camps around Britain and placed into secure holding areas that resembled prisoner of war camps. Men were briefed on their missions and shown detailed maps and models of the areas that they would be attacking. On 4 June, they were marched to the docks and began loading onto the ships that would carry them to France.

Harry Parley served in the 116th Infantry Regiment, 29th Infantry Division. When he was issued with a new kind of substance for his flamethrower, Harry knew that training was at an end. 'I knew right away that this was it. Of course. You're made fun of . . . constantly saying, "This is it." It became a little humorous saying. Anyhow, I carried the news back that our asses were in a sling now. We knew what we were getting into. It was not much to cry about it. If you had a particularly close buddy, you would talk personal shit, you know, you would exchange stories about your family and your wives. But in the group . . . what kept us going was the constant needling. Constant needling . . . and the foul language sort of always boosted our spirits.

'We were loaded with equipment. There were men loaded with what they called satchel charges. These were a honeycomb of blocks of dynamite. Put it into what they call Z bags that were to be thrown into pillboxes. Each of us had a block of dynamite in our pocket because they said, "If you have to dig a foxhole in a particularly difficult ground, you put this little block down and pull the pin and it will explode the ground. Get you past the roots and the stones."* The assault teams also carried Bangalore torpedoes: tubes of high explosive for clearing barbed-wire obstacles. The flamethrowers and demolition equipment made for dangerous travel companions. '(It) wasn't the safest place to be sitting in a boat,' said Harry.

He and others were put aboard the USS *Thomas Jefferson* at Weymouth, where they waited for the big day.

'There was a lot of gambling went on. Guys wanted to get rid of their money . . . We talked about life and how we expect

* This could be a lethal practice. Captain Llewellyn Thomas Jones, RWF, is remembered on the author's local war memorial. He was killed on 3 July when using explosives to make fighting positions.

to take it if we were wounded. I had a very gentle lieutenant in charge of my platoon. His name was Ferguson. I feel sorry for him because, you know, your platoon lieutenant used to have to look over your mail . . .' This was for reasons of censorship to ensure operational security. 'I realized that he was more involved in each one of these men than we were involved with each other. You know, all their thoughts and all their fears, and it gets you. He must have read my letter home. I don't know what I had written but he asked me what I thought about dying. I told him, "If it comes, it comes. I gotta depend on whatever I've learnt." And he seemed very sad, as if I expected him to take me in his arms. I never saw him again after the event. Maybe they bumped him off on the beach.'

Lieutenant Ferguson did survive D-Day. However, he never recovered from the wounds he received on Omaha Beach, and died from complications in 1954. For his gallant actions that day, he was awarded the Distinguished Service Cross.

Ray Nance was a first lieutenant in the same regiment as Harry, serving in Company A. 'We were loaded on trucks and proceeded to the port of embarkation, which in our case was Weymouth, southern England.' Ray had travelled the road before, during a 'dry run' for practice. Then, it had been empty. Now, it was packed with men and materials destined for Normandy.

Further east along the coast, Bill Dunn and the 26th Assault Squadron, Royal Engineers were in a secure camp at Fort Gomer.

'They had barbed wire and wire fencing right round us. And we weren't allowed out of that camp and weren't allowed to write letters or anything like that. We got bombed a couple of times while we were there . . . bits of shrapnel flying around, because we were all under canvas. I'm saying under canvas. We were under the tank sheets, lying beside the tank.'

At Fort Gomer, the unit was given its specific task for D-Day.

'We did training there because they knew exactly where we were going to land. And we were shown on not maps, but were shown on the ground. And what they did, they built scenes of how it was going to happen, and the culvert. We knew about the culvert we had to drop the fascine in and how far it was off the beach and everything like that, long before I went. So this was drilled into you day after day. You did this training and you're going around Fort Gomer, dropping the fascine into this culvert where it should be, and then retrieving them and doing it all over again. So when it come to the actual day, it's just in your mind, sort of automatic.'

Such levels of rehearsal speak highly to the preparation made for the invasion. Of course, it was one thing to be successful during practice in Fort Gomer and another when enemy shells were flying. Bill and his tank crew would have to run a gauntlet of six to seven hundred yards from the beach to succeed in their D-Day mission.

For the landing, each tank had been waterproofed by its crew. 'We had to go right round all underneath the tanks and seal all the joints. And this compound sealed in, dried into a very hard sealing. We had to put extended exhausts on, and you put extended air louvres on the sides of the tank so that there's no water got into the air louvres or the exhaust. And it, I think it was about four or five foot above the tank . . . and then when you got off to the other side, they had to be blown off. There was a small explosive charge, and it was all coupled to the turret and the tank commander just pressed this button and blew these things off. Blew them off as soon as we got down to the beach.' Despite the preparations, confidence in the unit's survivability was not high. 'We were told not to expect to come back.' These bleak words were not from a nervous man in the ranks, but from Bill's commanding officer.

Also at Fort Gomer were the Winnipeg Rifles.

'The night before we were going to sail the NAAFI ran out of beer. And of course, the Winnipeg Rifles wasn't very happy about it. So they went in and smashed the NAAFI up and poured everything in the middle and set fire to the lot, which wasn't very far from an ammunition dump,' Bill chuckled. 'Of course that caused quite a bit of a havoc. They had to get the fire engines running around and they're trying to get the ammunition and everything out of the ammunition dump just in case. Caused quite a bit of excitement.'

'I forget the number of days that we were there in port,' said Ray Nance. 'But finally the word came on the 4th that we would move out . . . so all ships moved out into the Channel. And somewhere along the way, word came that the thing had been delayed for twenty-four hours. So we returned to the port, same spot, and waited overnight.'

Nobody had told the weather about the importance of the Allied operation, and due to high winds – which would scatter paratroopers, and imperil landing craft with high swells – D-Day was postponed by one day. Many soldiers were never unloaded from their landing ships, and passed this extra day in port.

During this time the men of Company A played cards, and did 'the usual things that troops do when they have leisure time.' This undoubtedly involved talk of sweethearts, when the war would end, prayer, and horseplay. According to Ray, it did not involve talk of what was awaiting them on the beaches of Normandy.

'I think everybody got a good night's sleep and we, the officers, were up around two in the morning and (had) good breakfasts . . . then back to our quarters. And soon came the order to load.'

Before they loaded up onto their different ships, Walter and

Roland Ehlers made plans to meet on Omaha Beach the next day. Then they said goodbye. It was the last time that Walter ever saw his brother, who was one of more than 4,000 Allied troops who gave their life on D-Day.

That battle began in the early hours of 6 June 1944.

CHAPTER TWO

All Americans, Screaming Eagles, and Red Devils

The Airborne Forces on D-Day

'I wondered how I was going to react under fire.
Would I be too scared to carry out orders?
What is it going to be like?'

Tom Porcella, 508th Parachute Infantry Regiment

*All Americans – the US 82nd Airborne
Division on D-Day*

The first soldiers to land in France on D-Day came not by sea, but by air. Two American airborne divisions and one British were dropped in the early hours of 6 June. Their mission was to secure the flanks of the beachheads, destroy gun sites, hold key pieces of terrain that would allow the seaborne forces to move quickly inland, and act as general nuisance in the rear echelons of the German beach defences, delaying any reinforcements.

These airborne soldiers were elite: they had to volunteer to become a paratrooper, and the selection criteria were high. Their commanders wanted men who could think for themselves, and fight by themselves if necessary. This called for high levels of courage, as did the act of jumping out of a perfectly good aircraft.

Tom Porcella, nineteen years old and from Queens, New York, served in the 508th Parachute Infantry Regiment (PIR) in the 82nd Airborne Division. While some parts of the 82nd had already experienced combat, Normandy would be the 508th's baptism of fire. The division was tasked with seizing and holding a number of towns and bridges to the west of the landing beaches, including the key town of Sainte-Mère-Église, which lay six miles inland from Utah Beach, on the road to Cherbourg. In late May Tom's unit was confined to camp in anticipation of the invasion.

'I laid down on the cot and I closed my eyes and I went into deep thought. And . . . I was thinking to myself, "This is it. Just a matter of time now and I will be in combat. I wonder what the hell my folks are doing back home. I wonder if they're thinking about the invasion like we are. I wonder what they would think if they knew at this moment, their son Tom was preparing himself for this big invasion." All sorts of thoughts went through my mind. I was thinking about my girlfriend, and you name it, my brothers, my sisters and all – all the things that you read about in books, well I was thinking about it, when all of a sudden some – some GI hollered, "Hey, it's showtime. Let's go!"'

The paratroopers pulled on their gear and filed to their aircraft, but 'the show' was cancelled before they ever got into the air.

The day of delay left every man with more time to think.

'I wondered how the hell I'd react under fire,' said Tom, 'would I be too scared to carry out the orders? What is it going to be like? . . . Will I be able to kill a man? What am I supposed to do here? You know, all these things. You know, you start to have some of your doubts sometimes. And on and on, and all these thoughts, you know, God, I'm glad when this thing would be over and we'd be on our way.'

On the evening of the 5th of June the men of the 508th were ordered onto the aircraft. This time, there was no coming back.

The invasion was on.

'I could hear the sound of the C47 and engines, they were revving up and they were warming up and they were all on the runway. When we heard, "Let's go, let's go," everybody became quiet, it was a big sound throughout the entire hangar. Then all of a sudden, it was all spontaneous, it was a tremendous roar. Everybody was hollering, "Geronimo, give them hell, let's go, come on!"

'We all started to help each other, buddy up. We helped each other put the equipment on. We all took our time. Everything had to be just right. You couldn't afford to make any mistakes. Some of the guys were already in formation. The other guys were still being helped. Then the sergeant says, "OK, let's go. Let's all fall out. Let's get into line." All you can hear was the officers . . . giving a lot of orders. We marched at a slow pace to our airplane. By this time, it was just starting to get dark and men were silent. You wouldn't believe how silent these guys were.'

The men loaded into the aircraft, which was hard work with so much equipment. The air force crew sergeant, from Kentucky, was doing his best to make conversation, asking the paratroopers about their hometowns.

'We asked the sergeant if it was true that he had the orders to shoot any man who refused to jump. "That's the orders I've been given." He said it so softly that everybody became quiet. I mean . . . a few of the fellows were talking, but when he said that he had the order to shoot anybody that refused to jump, guys got kind of quiet.'

Their faces blackened for camouflage, the paratroopers sat in rows along the fuselage and prepared to take to the skies.

'Our plane began to move . . . We were going on the runway.

That plane was shaking and rattling and rolling. And a few minutes before you knew it, we were airborne.'

Some of the men asked if they could smoke, but were told by the crewman that it wasn't allowed. Whether they listened or not, Tom didn't say. They were in the air for some time before they saw the crewman looking out, and paratroopers craned their necks to see what was happening around them.

'We're being greeted by the anti-aircraft fire from the Germans. I looked out the window, you could see the stuff, the flashes of the burst of the artillery shells. You could see the shells bursting outside the plane and also you could see the machine-gun fire in the distance . . . Looked like the bloody 4th of July. All of a sudden we got the orders, "Stand up and hook 'em." The silence was broken, and we finally jumped up and snapped our hooks onto the wire.'

This wire running along the top of the troop compartment deployed the trooper's parachute when he cleared out of the aircraft. The paratroopers also had a reserve chute that they could pull in case the first failed to function. Once the men were hooked on, they were ordered to sound off for an equipment check, meaning that their gear was in order, and they were ready to jump.

'Being the last man on the ship, I had to (give) the reply first. I shouted, "Seventeen OK!" The next man shouted, "Sixteen OK!" and the countdown continued until it was "One OK!" which is the first man beside the sergeant and a sergeant shouts, "Get in the door!"'

'My heart started pounding and I was saying a prayer to myself. I was so scared that my knees were shaking, and just to relieve the tension, I knew that I had to say something. So I shouted, "What time is it?" Somebody answered me and told me it was about two thirty. Then all of a sudden we heard, "Are you ready?" And all the troopers shouted all at once. "Yeah! Let's go!"'

Next to the aircraft's open door was a red light. When the pilot was over the drop zone he would change the colour and the men would exit. With flak bursting in the air, it must have felt like an age before the light changed to green and the paratroopers began to jump out into a night sky streaked with tracer fire and the flash of explosions.

The men of Tom's stick began to disappear out of the door. He shuffled his way along behind them until he was the only paratrooper left in the aircraft. Without hesitation he jumped into the sky.

'With the roar of the engine in my ears, I was out the door.'

Tom went through his drills and checks and realized that he'd made a good exit, and everything was functioning with the parachute as it should. He now had a couple of seconds in the air before he would hit the dark ground below.

'I looked around and saw . . . the brightness of the tracers flying into the sky, and the sound of machine guns firing seemed to be all around me.'

The ground quickly rushed up to meet him, and Tom bent his knees and prepared for impact. 'I had the shock of my life. I plunged into water.'

Tom had landed on one of Rommel's defences: huge areas of flooded fields designed to deny drop zones to the Allied planners, slow the movement of an invading army, and drown any paratrooper who was unlucky enough to land in them.

'The water was just above my nose. Quickly, I stood on my toes and I was gasping for another breath of air. My heart was beating so rapidly that I thought it would burst. I pleaded, "Oh, God, please don't let me drown in this damn water in the middle of nowhere." Below the water I went and tried to remove the leg straps. They were just too tight and wouldn't un-snap. I needed some more air, so I jumped up and as soon as my head was above water, I began splashing around. I started to pray, standing on my toes with my head barely above water. My heart was beating faster. After a few seconds, I calmed down and decided to cut the straps.'

Tom found the knife in his boot, but after a few attempts to cut the straps he was still trapped: he realized then that he'd been using the blunt edge of the blade. 'Taking another gulp of air I went down again to cut the leg strap. With a few pulls of the knife on each strap I was finally free of the chute.'

Tom had survived his landing, but alone behind enemy lines, he was far from safe.

'My eyes strained to see the landmarks, but I could see nothing in the darkness. I was cold and I began to shiver . . . my teeth were beginning to chatter.

'In the distance, to my left, I could hear the sound of an airplane engine coming in my direction . . . Guns began firing, and I watched the tracers flying into the air. Suddenly, there was a huge burst of orange flames coming from both engines. I could not believe what was happening. I just stood still, seeing and hearing. Suddenly I realized the plane was heading straight for me in a ball of flames.' Tom recalled the sound that the aircraft made as it plunged towards the earth: '(It was) like the scream of a human being about to die. As fast as I could, I moved to the right, trying to get out of its path.'

As Tom tried to wade away the plane crashed and exploded. Only moments later, a silence fell over the countryside.

Tom continued to search for his comrades in the flooded fields. He was almost shot by one of them when he was slow replying to the password. The other paratrooper, Cable, had his gun inches from Tom's face.

'We heard some more commotion and we went towards the noise. And next thing you know, we gave the password again, "Flash", and, and I knew it was safe to give the password because the Germans wouldn't be sloshing around in the stupid water.'

Tom and Cable picked up a couple more paratroopers, including a sergeant, who took charge of their group. 'Daylight was coming upon us very fast . . . and now we could see the outline of trees. We all knew what would happen if we failed to reach the land before daylight.' If they were caught out in the open of the flooded fields, the paratroopers would be easy pickings for snipers and machine-gunners.

'In our haste to reach the high ground, Tommy Lott let go of Cable's rifle and went slightly to our right, and he fell below the water. This time I thought we had lost him for sure. He was coughing very loudly. I rushed over and I grabbed him and kept his head above water. We all told him again and again to stay close. Before you know it, we could see the land very clearly and Sergeant Horn was moving us very fast. He says, "Keep moving, keep moving." Just as we reached the bank, Tommy Lott went under again, but he managed to struggle to his feet again. The four of us collapsed on the bank, completely exhausted.'

As the sun came up the men knew that they needed to be on the move. Even out of the water, they were vulnerable in such a small group. Such bands of paratroopers were roving all over the countryside, searching for their own units, and Tom's group came across another from the 507th.

'They told us we took a hell of a beating on the initial jump . . . and they also said that we lost a lot of our gliders. At this time, the situation looked very discouraging. Everybody seems to be all mixed up, everybody seems to be from different outfits. So we wish them good luck. And we all went our separate ways.'

Tom and his group then came across a glider that had suffered a bad landing. 'We went to see if there were any wounded in sight. To our surprise, there was a medic attending the wounded in there. Except for one, all the glider men had died in that crash. This one particular glider man had his leg crushed and a medic was about to remove it.'

Tom's group continued to grow in numbers. 'While we were proceeding alongside this hedgerow, the column stopped when we received the word that someone heard a vehicle coming down the road towards us . . . Somebody shouted out they believed it was a German motorcyclist. The man in front of me, his name was Canterbury . . . he says, "I'll shoot the son of a bitch." He raised his rifle and he was waiting for the motorcyclist to come down the road. He took careful aim and he waited till the cyclist was about fifty feet away from him and he fired a single shot. The German seemed suspended in mid-air while the motorcycle continued to go on and crashed into the side of the road. The German soldier laid there in the middle of the road, laying on his back, his arms were outstretched. He looked very young. He looked about twenty years of age with blond hair. This was the first dead German I've seen since I parachuted into Normandy.'

They then came across a crossroad, a likely site for an ambush.

'One trooper decided to make his run and be the first one across the road. He reached about the middle of the road . . . A shot was fired and the trooper fell face down. And I'll never forget, his arms were outstretched as if he was reaching for the other side.

'Immediately there was an exchange of machine-gun fire and rifle fire. The hand signal was given to keep going. We were all moving very rapidly. Still, we didn't know where we're going. And we had to leave this trooper there right where he fell right in the middle of the road all alone. It was very sad.'

For the paratroopers, D-Day was a cat and mouse battle

where the enemy could be in any direction, and in any strength. While the 82nd had not secured all their D-Day objectives, in large part due to the scattering of paratroopers during the drop, they formed an effective shield to the west of the beaches, and by their sacrifice, prevented freedom of movement for German reinforcements.

'I know I was scared as hell,' said Tom. While daylight was disappearing, the orders were given to dig in for the night. 'We were told that one man sleeps and the other man stays awake. We were also told not to smoke and keep in close contact with each other during this night. We were going to move at the crack of daylight. Hopefully we should contact regimental headquarters. I remember shivering from the cold night air. My thoughts were, just a GI blanket and a hot cup of coffee, and how the hell did I get into this predicament? My teeth would not stop chattering. And as I continued thinking of England; the mess hall, the food, the hot coffee and a warm stove, it was not possible to sleep at all.'

Screaming Eagles – the US 101st Airborne on D-Day

Formed in 1942 in Louisiana, the 101st Airborne Division received its baptism of fire on D-Day. One of its principal objectives was seizing four causeways that would allow the 4th Infantry Division to push off Utah Beach. The division was also tasked with destroying enemy artillery batteries, and establishing a defensive line to hold against German counter-attacks.

Joseph Lesniewski, aged twenty-three, served in E Company, of the 506th Parachute Infantry Regiment. In later decades, 'Easy Company' was immortalized in the book and television show *Band of Brothers*. Like the men of the 82nd, the 101st had been stood down on 4 June due to the weather conditions over Normandy and the Channel.

'The following morning, early in the morning, they notified us that the weather improved quite a bit, so we're gonna start getting ready. So we started to get ready in the afternoon – getting all the equipment on and all that. We passed a lot of time just sitting around doing nothing, then finally about eight, eight thirty in the evening we started to load up in the planes.'

First Lieutenant Richard 'Dick' Winters was in command of Easy Company's 1st Platoon. He recalled the emotional reaction of British anti-aircraft gunners as they watched the paratroopers walking to their planes. 'That was the first time I'd ever seen any real emotion from a Limey, they actually had tears in their eyes.'[1]

Each paratrooper was heavily laden with his weapon, ammunition, medical kit, rations, life vest, and of course, main parachute and reserve. It made for a hefty load, with estimates ranging from 70lb to 130lb, and they had to be helped up the steps and into the plane.

Robert Williams served in Headquarters Company, 506th, and recalled the moment that they got underway from England. 'About 1030 (PM) the planes all started up, revved up, and took off one at a time.'

More than 1,200 aircraft were carrying the three airborne divisions into Normandy, and the process of gathering in their formations took some time.

'By the time we flew over the Atlantic and came back . . . to the (Cotentin) Peninsula it was about one o'clock in the morning. Everybody was quiet – they were getting pretty bored after having flown around for two and a half hours.'

James Martin of G Company, 506th, remembered anti-motion pills being handed out just before take off, which were issued to prevent airsickness.

'We were supposed to take (them). Nobody knew what they were. I said, "I don't think we should take them." The officers were supposed to sit there and make you take them . . . Some of the guys took them, and they hit the ground and went to sleep and didn't wake up until morning.'

As the air armada approached the drop zones the night sky came alive with the flash of exploding flak, and arcs of tracer fire. It was a surreal moment for many of the paratroopers.

'(You realize) that somebody's down there that's really gonna try to kill you, you know,' said Robert Williams. 'So the pilots ran into a fog bank as we hit the coast of France and they had a really good, tight formation, there was no lights on the plane – tight formation up to that point. But the pilots, in order to avoid this anti-aircraft fire, some of them went up, some went down, some of them went to the left and right because they didn't want to run into each other. So about five minutes later the red light came on and we all stood up and hooked up and by that time the ground fire had increased, tracer bullets were going into the air between the planes, some of the tracer bullets (went) through the planes. As I looked out the open door . . . a plane off to our left must've got a direct hit because it just went up in a ball of fire, there wasn't anything left of the airplane, it disintegrated.'

'You'd see this black puff of smoke, a flash of flame,' said James Martin. 'We saw planes get hit and blow up and go down. But you know what, you never really thought of it. We were all pumped up. We were gonna kill all these damn Germans.'

Joseph Lesniewski was all too ready to get on the ground. 'When we got the green light to jump out, I'll tell you, it was a pleasure to get out of that plane because all the flashes we saw, the flak coming in . . . you could see all that. So I was glad to hit the ground. The chute opened and bam, I'm down. About three seconds after the chute opens I'm on the ground.'

Years later, Robert Williams talked to a C47 pilot from that night. 'We were supposed to jump at about 850 feet, and he told me we'd have been lucky if we jumped over 650 feet, because they had really gone down onto the deck to get outta that anti-aircraft fire.'

Robert was only in the air a few seconds before he hit the ground. '(It was a) moonlit night and partly cloudy. It was a good moon, but the white clouds caused a lot of shadows, and you couldn't really see the ground.' He plunged into water and went under.

'I actually didn't know how deep it was until I stood up. When I stood up my head popped out and it was a great relief to find out it was only three feet deep. But it was pretty tough getting outta that chute. It was a better landing than a lot of my friends had because when they hit the ground some of them got sprained ankles and I think some of our officers had broken legs. So I had a pretty nice landing even if I did get all wet.'

He found out later that many of his comrades did not survive their drop.

'I read that we had thirty-three men drowned because they landed in that water. Some of the planes overshot and went out into the Channel, some of the guys landed out in the Channel (and they) drowned – with all that equipment on, even if you had a life jacket on you, you had to get all your equipment off before you could use a life jacket.'

Robert tried to make his way through the flooded fields to the assembly area at Sainte-Marie-du-Mont, about nine miles south-west of Utah Beach.

'We started off in the dark, trying to find out which was the best way to get outta there. We ran into two more guys but none of these were from my outfit – I think they were from the 82nd. But that made four of us together, and one of them found a hard surface under the water that we figured was a (submerged) road. Then we started getting into shallow water . . . Finally we did come out on dry land and we hadn't gone twenty feet before we run right into a German machine-gun nest. The two guys in the middle were killed, and the one on the left side.'

Robert had a lucky escape: bullets had riddled one of his bulky trouser pockets. 'It didn't hit the hand grenades. It went through the K rations and tore the whole pocket off. The flap on there. It had spun me around, I thought I was hit, I was sure I was hit because of the way it spun me around and I fell down. I thought, "Well I'm on the ground, I'm gonna roll back in that water to get out of that machine-gun fire." They just kept shooting over my head. I got down to where just my nose and my eyes were above water. I stayed there for about fifteen, twenty minutes.

'I put my hand down the side of my pants to see how bad I was hit and I was sure my hand was gonna come out with blood on it and I couldn't believe it. I kept feeling around, feeling around and there wasn't anything there. I didn't try to hook up with the guy on the other side of the road, I just stayed in the water on my side and just started moving away from that machine gun. 'I must've gone a quarter of a mile in that water. It didn't get any better, it still was waist deep. About that time the B-26s came over.'

The American medium bombers dropped their payloads on the coastal defences a few miles away. 'I got to see that, it was quite a show. The sun was coming up. I was looking towards the sun that was coming up in the east and I still can remember today those B-26s with the sun shining on the belly of those airplanes. If I had had a camera that would have made a terrific picture with that sun coming up. It was still down below the horizon but was still showing on the bottom of the airplanes. Of course, there was a lot of noise going on, and the ships were opening up on the beach. The invasion had started.'

Robert was finally able to make his way onto dry ground.

He found a farmhouse where around a dozen paratroopers had gathered. By this time the troops were beginning to come ashore. After getting directions from the French farmers, the band of paratroopers set out.

'We passed a big hole where one of our fighter planes had dropped a bomb on two Germans that had been coming down the road on a motorcycle, and it was a direct hit. The Germans were laying way over there in the field. That was my first experience with what was really going on, besides hearing all the noise and so forth.'

Robert's group made their way successfully to Sainte-Marie-du-Mont, where he was reunited with elements from his own company. 'It was good to get back with some of my own men that I knew. I slept standing up, leaning against a bank. No one wanted to get to sleep because the Germans were in between us, and we were in between them. You never knew when you were going to run into them or when they were going to sneak up on you.'

By the end of D-Day the 101st had secured many objectives, including taking Sainte-Marie-du-Mont and linking up with troops from Utah Beach. There were countless acts of heroism by the paratroopers that day, including those of Richard 'Dick' Winters.

Dick's first jump into combat did not go smoothly. His aircraft went into a dive to avoid the anti-aircraft fire, and Dick estimates that he was travelling at 150 mph and at dangerously low altitude when he got the green light to jump. This made the exit from the aircraft particularly violent, the parachute's canopy opening with such force that it ripped away the knee bags that the paratroopers were using to carry their weapon, ammunition, and other equipment. He landed in enemy territory with nothing but a knife to defend himself.

His objective that night was Causeway Number 2, which led from Utah Beach. After gathering a few men, including some from the 82nd, Dick located their position on the map and set off towards the assembly area. His group continued to grow until it numbered around seventy paratroopers. They ran into a German patrol of four horse-drawn wagons and took out the first two. The others escaped, but a handful of prisoners were taken. When a machine gun opened up on the paratroopers the prisoners tried to rush their captors, but were shot by one of Dick's NCOs, Bill Guarnere, who was twenty-one years old.

'It was as easy as stepping on a bug,' Bill said, before adding that they were different men back then.[2]

That morning Dick regrouped with his parent unit in the small village of Le Grand Chemin. As the senior officer present from Easy Company, he assumed the role as company commander. This position became permanent when it was confirmed that the company commander and executive officer had been killed when their plane went down.

Dick estimated that only about 10 per cent of the company's strength was with him, little more than a dozen men, but there was no time to wait for reinforcements. The causeways leading off Utah Beach were coming under artillery fire, and Dick was ordered to take a makeshift group of some two dozen paratroopers to silence an artillery battery at Brécourt Manor. Dog Company of the 506th had already made one failed attack on the position using a frontal assault.

'That didn't go very far,' said Dick, who went in by himself to reconnoitre the enemy positions before formulating his plan. He recounted the story in an interview given to Rep. John Payne.[3] 'I thought I'd found the trench . . . and I knew from training, take it on from the flank. This is part of your training. It's not something you're dreaming up, and creating on the spur of the moment. This is all part of the training that's kicking in.'

Dick's men were heavily outnumbered – at the very least three to one, and possibly as high as ten – and so he came up with a plan to even the odds as much as possible. 'I hit them on the flank, and that meant that I was taking them on one position at a time. In doing that I could use the few guns that I had to create superior firepower, and then rush one at a time, and that's how it worked out.'

Dick credited his unit's training for forming the strong bonds and cohesion that allowed the paratroopers to be successful that day. There was no need to stop and explain what was needed, the men understood his orders and what each needed to do. 'Everybody is doing his job. You don't do it yourself. It takes everybody doing his job to get the thing done.'

That was true of taking an enemy position, and it would be true for winning the war. From D-Day onwards, Easy Company were in the thick of the fighting.

Red Devils – the British 6th Airborne Division

On the night of 5 June, a small force from 2nd Battalion, Oxfordshire and Buckinghamshire Light Infantry took off for their mission behind enemy lines: their task was to seize two vital bridges on the invasion's eastern flank and hold them until relieved.

'My company was lucky to be selected for what turned out to be a wonderful operation,' said Major John Howard, who led the mission. 'I was briefed six weeks before D-Day . . . under top secret conditions of course, I couldn't even discuss it with my second command or any of my officers. We were a very highly trained unit, as all airborne troops were. And once I was briefed,

of course, we did special training for the capture of bridges . . .
All I could tell them was that we were going to capture bridges
on a big exercise . . . it was a waste of time, really, because everybody throughout the UK knew that the invasion was imminent
at the time.'

John and his men would be transported to the bridges in
wooden Horsa gliders, towed by Halifax bombers.

'Parachuters take a long time to get together and form a platoon and company to attack an objective. Whereas gliders will
land thirty men on the spot, providing the pilots do their job
properly, of course. But I was quite satisfied on that account,
really, in that I knew that for the job we had the very best glider
pilots that the Glider Pilot Regiment could produce.'

The glider pilots who would take John's men into Normandy
had already completed one airborne operation in Sicily. D Company was also reinforced with more soldiers.

'I was given two extra platoons and thirty Royal Engineers.
So that was a hundred and fifty infantry, thirty Royal Engi-
neers, a force of a hundred and eighty. We landed in six gliders.
Approximately thirty men in each glider. Each glider contain-
ing one platoon of around twenty-five infantry and five Royal
Engineers.'

One of these gliders would also be carrying John Vaughan, a
medical officer. He was a recent addition to John Howard's unit,
having made a request for a transfer from the 11th Armoured
Division. In late May Vaughan, along with the other officers of
the 224th Parachute Field Ambulance, had been summoned to a
meeting with Colonel McEwan.

'(The colonel) came to this mess, had a drink with me, and
said, "I want a volunteer for a sort of forlorn hope."' Forlorn
hope was the name given to a band of men who would undertake a highly perilous, often suicidal action in the vanguard of an

army. 'We thought he was exaggerating. There was a nasty silence. Everybody was so scared of this chap, they were more scared of not volunteering and therefore offending him, so we all said we'd like to do it. He said, "Thank you very much, gentlemen," and left the bar.

'About ten days later, I got a message from him, "Come to division headquarters." He said to me, "Vaughan, you wanted some action, you're going to get it now – you're going to be attached to a special force." I was sent down with Colonel Harvey of the 225th Parachute Field Ambulance, taken down in his car to the camp . . . (and) I was introduced to John Howard, of course, and the men. I was eventually marched off with the rest of them to the landing strip and I was in the glider with Sandy Smith. There was a certain amount of singsong going on, lewd military songs, which gradually died out.'

Shortly after midnight, with the Normandy countryside below, the tow rope was cast off and the gliders were suddenly descending.

'You come in in those gliders at about ninety miles an hour on touchdown,' said John Howard. 'It shook the glider tremendously because we were on these skids. Suddenly everything went dark and I felt my head had been knocked rather badly and my own feelings were that, God, I am blind. We've been training and waiting for all this time, and now when the moment comes, I'm going to be bloody useless.'

John was relieved to find out that his 'blindness' had been caused by his helmet tipping forward over his eyes.

'I could hear the glider pilots on my right moaning in their cockpit, which seemed to have been smashed, but I was conscious that everybody in the glider was moving. You could hear the click of the safety belts being undone, and I knew that men were getting out of the glider and people were pushing in front of me to get through the broken door.

'The leading section from the back of the glider was to go up first and put the pillbox out of action by throwing a smoke bomb on the road as they came up from the landing zone and through the smoke with short-fused grenades, throw them through the gun slits of the pillbox and then continue with the rest of the platoon across the bridge.

'I emerged from the glider . . . And I suppose that really was the most exhilarating moment of my life. Because as I stood there, I could see the tower of the bridge about fifty yards from where I was standing.'

The bridge closest to John spanned the Caen Canal. The second crossed the River Orne. They would later become known as Pegasus Bridge, and Horsa Bridge.

'There was no firing at all. In other words, we had complete surprise. We really caught out Jerry with his pants down. But there was no time to wonder about that. I followed the platoon up the track. I saw the smoke bomb explode, the phosphorus bomb. I heard the thud, thud, thud in the pillbox as the grenades exploded and I knew we'd get no more trouble from there. And the leading platoon ran across the bridge.

'Now, I must emphasize that up to this moment, it was all done in complete silence. They were my orders, that we must get troops the other side of the bridge if we had surprise, we had to keep it and nobody was allowed to fire unless they were directly fired at by the enemy.'

Once the first explosions had gone off in the pillbox, surprise had to be followed by violence of action.

'By this time, the leading platoon were halfway across the bridge and they started firing from the hip with their Bren guns, Sten guns and everything else they had. As they came off the other far end of the bridge and the enemy woke up. And it was a tremendous sight to see all the tracer bullets firing in all directions. They seemed to be three different colours red, yellow and white.'

John then heard the crash of more gliders landing. 'I had three platoons down on the ground in exactly the same places where all the briefings had hoped they would be. But by this time, I was suddenly wondering what was happening on the other bridge, which was only a quarter of a mile away. I couldn't see any signs of firing over there. There were no radio messages. And that didn't surprise me because the radios in those days are pretty frail and then crash landing and we didn't expect them to survive.

'No runners had arrived, and I was beginning to consider whether I had to send a platoon or half a platoon over to the river bridge to try and capture that. But then all the luck turned.

'The captain of the Royal Engineers, Captain Jock Neilson, reported to me that there were no explosives under the canal bridge . . . So that was the first good bit of news. And then we picked up to our surprise, our radio message, which said that one of the platoons, Number Six platoon under Dennis Fox, had captured the river bridge almost without firing a shot. The enemy had run away.'

Medical officer John Vaughan arrived in one of the gliders that John Howard had heard crashing.

'I prayed for a parachute . . . (We were) at about five thousand feet, something like that. I saw some flak . . . I'm certain of it, on our starboard side, hit one of the other gliders. We came down and I remember seeing the glider pilots sitting there, smoking cigarettes. It shook me, I thought, "My God, it's going into the sea." We came down from five thousand, I heard the pilots chatting to each other, saying a little more left or a little more right. Anyway, we did the two turns and in we came, and I remember the first landing, because it crashed, and then silence. We bounced off and I remember nothing after that until I woke up and I heard some firing and I also heard some nasty groans. I found myself lying in front of the glider, with my face in some mud. I was lying flat on my face, and my corporals were shaking me saying doctor, doctor, something like that. I remember staggering to my feet. I was standing outside the glider and I got back to the glider, found this chap mixed up in the wreckage, and I couldn't get him out so I gave him a shot of morphine and staggered away from the thing. I can hear those groans now. I walked away in the direction of the bridge, which was only fifty yards away at this stage.

'I found John (Howard) sitting in his slit trench, looking perfectly happy, issuing orders right and left. He said, "What's happened to you, Doc?" and gave me a shot of whisky.

'I said, "John, what is all this about ham and jam?" I was concussed you see.' Ham and Jam was the code word sent over the radio to let command know that the bridges had been seized.

'I then staggered on up the road, which was the wrong thing to do. I found Den, lying on his back in a corner by a cafe, looking up at the stars, looking terribly surprised when I found a bullet hole right in the middle of his neck. I gave him a shot of morphine. By then I'd got some medical orderlies and we carried him back to my trench, my (aid post) that I'd got down in that lane.'

Den Brotheridge had led the charge across the bridge. He died of his wounds and was posthumously awarded a Mention In Dispatches for his actions.

John collected another of the wounded men, who was 'terribly heavy. We staggered with his load down to the RAP, I remember dumping him in our little ditch there. Then I proceed to go back and get the other casualties. We had about twelve casualties, something like that.

'While I was attending to these chaps, I heard a clatter, a vehicle, a car, coming down the road. It was a German staff car and when it approached the bridge, grenades were thrown into it.'

The German casualties were then passed on to John.

'One of the casualties was a small, young chap, couldn't have been older than sixteen years. One leg had been blown right off, and the other leg was hanging off, and I had to remove it with scissors. He didn't survive very long. I spent the rest of the time, in those early, pre-dawn hours, carrying people down. We only had three medical orderlies out of six left, so I was one of the stretcher-bearers. We got the casualties, including the German casualties, down to the RAP.'

It appeared that one of the German wounded was the commander of the bridge's defence. '(He had) a wound in his leg and he was absolutely fanatical. He spoke to me in very good English and he said, "You know you troops are going to be thrown back, my Führer will see to that, you're going to be thrown back into the sea," so on and so forth.' But despite his assuredness of German victory, the man was thoroughly dejected with his own performance. 'He wanted me to shoot him. He thought he'd done a poor job really, his Führer would be very upset with him, and he wanted me to shoot him. So I got out a bit of morphine and shot him in the bottom. After that he was a lot more polite and was thanking me for what I'd done.'

During this time the British soldiers were under constant fire. One of them dropped a yard away from John. 'He was shot in the back and paralysed.'

A decision was made to move the wounded to a more secure location in the village of Bénouville, which sat beside the bridge.

'And this all went on until dawn.'

Around this time there was a massive rumbling sound in the

distance. 'I thought we were being attacked . . . It wasn't. It was the invasion bombardment from the sea.'

Following hotly on the heels of John Howard's men were the paratroopers of the 6th Airborne Division. Piloting one of the aircraft was George Oliver, an Australian flying a Short Stirling bomber for 196 Squadron, RAF.

'When we went out to the aircraft, there were all the airborne soldiers. Black on their faces, leaves in their helmets, grenades, machine guns. They really did look fierce. I remember thinking, "I'm glad they're on our side." An officer said, "Are you the pilot?" Yes. "Have you been over before?" Yes. (He) looked me up and down and said, "Good God man, you look as though you're going to a bloody dance." We were all strangers but we had an instant rapport. He pulled out this five-franc note – the lads from the stick had all signed it.

'My butterflies disappeared once I started the engines up, I was so absorbed with what I had to do. (We had) seventeen on board, with all their equipment, and our bomb bays were full of equipment too. It was very windy and gusty. As we crossed the Channel we could see searchlights, (and) various lights flashing. It was an amazing sight – you could see the dim outlines of all the aircraft around you. How we didn't have any collisions was beyond me . . . Hundreds of aircraft (were about), and there were slipstreams and the aircraft were heavy. (We) had to fly at a defined height so we didn't drop onto aircraft below (us). Not easy, (as) altimeters weren't precision instruments.

'With the load (of paras and equipment), and flying at a slow speed, the aircraft felt sort of wallowy, like a boat in waves. It was quite a tricky business really. We'd been trained for it, we'd got used to it. We did experience a bit of flak. Each squadron lost a Stirling aircraft that night. Several other aircraft were damaged.

The pathfinders received some flak and there were some troops killed.

'Eventually the navigator called out and said, "You should be able to see the lights (of the pathfinders) soon." The bomb aimer, he was in the bomb-aiming compartment. He guided us in much the same as bomb aimers did and gave us the green light when it was time to drop them. I remember shouting good luck but I don't think they heard me.'

One of the men jumping in with the 6th Airborne was Ronald Follett of the 7th Battalion, Parachute Regiment.

'We were going to support the Ox and Bucks gliders who were going to land on Pegasus Bridge. I missed my landing and hit the ground with an awful thump . . . I thought, "That's a great start." My PIAT [anti-tank weapon] had a heck of a smack and was bent . . . (it) was of no use at all. They were very flimsy things.'

Ronald then began to link up with his comrades. 'There were lots of hunting horns being tooted all around . . . I found some 7th Battalion people, including the second in command. We soon gathered together and we all (formed) gradually into more and more companies. It gradually all built, by which time there was a heck of a lot of noise going (on) towards the bridge, where 2 Ox and Bucks were dealing with the Germans.'

7th Battalion quickly reached the village of Bénouville and were soon in action.

'We walked past the mayor's house and round into the cross-roads. That's where we bumped into trouble. They had strong pillboxes and strongpoints there, and we were pinned down into this orchard. 'There was a tank and infantry in positions. A Company tried to send a patrol along the street, and quite a lot of them were cut to pieces by machine-gun fire.'

Harold Cammack had joined the army as a boy soldier of

fifteen. Five years later, as a paratrooper in the 12th Battalion, Parachute Regiment, he was part of a force tasked with seizing and holding the village of Ranville, just to the south-east of Pegasus Bridge. As they crossed the channel in a Stirling bomber, the atmosphere was one of tension and anticipation.

'We didn't speak a lot, which is understandable, I think. Just tried to crack one or two jokes.' The men also replayed in their minds the mission that they had been given, and recalled the maps and models that had shown them the ground on which they'd be landing. 'I had a Bren gun, which is an automatic weapon.'

This Bren gun was carried in a case strapped to the paratrooper's leg. Once he was clear of the aircraft he'd pull a pin which would release the case twenty feet below him. This was to protect the soldier from injury on landing, but it also gave him a valuable 'heads up' as to when he was about to hit the ground. For Harold, this moment came at around 0100 hrs.

'The drop itself was fine. We landed in a cornfield actually.' Harold was only four hundred yards or so from his RV, but high winds carried other men further off the drop zone, with some of them falling into enemy hands.

'About 60 per cent (of the platoon got to the RV) but some of them joined us up within the next couple of hours or so. We had to go about a mile, maybe about a mile and a half, to Ranville, where we were attacking a small village. Once we got there we . . . dug our trenches as quickly as possible . . . because we knew as soon as dawn broke we should be expecting some movement from the enemy, which did occur.'

Hans von Luck commanded the 125th Panzergrenadier Regiment of the 21st Panzer Division. He was in his early thirties, an experienced soldier, and had fought the British in North Africa.

At the time of the landings he was based in a house in Bellengre-ville, about twelve miles from the coast.

'We were sure that the Allies would land somehow, and somewhere. We didn't know where. The main reason was because our intelligence was not good enough. In addition to that, the Allies had 100 per cent air superiority, so we did not send our own (planes) over to England to see what was happening there. We didn't expect the invasion in Normandy, because the distance was long, there was a lot of cliffs, difficult to overcome, but we were training every night to get as familiar with the ground as possible. And Rommel himself visited us several times. He insisted that we would take positions, and dig in. He meant that the invasion could come to Normandy, so we had to be very careful about that.

'The problem was that our division, although very close to the coast, was under direct command under Army Group B. The order was not to move until we would be released. When we realized the landing of paras, and of gliders, we were immediately alarmed, but we couldn't move (due to the restrictions) of this order.'

Such levels of centralized command prohibited swift and immediate action by those at the front. This problem was further compounded by the absence of certain key figures.

'Unfortunately, Rommel wasn't there. He was on his way to see Hitler. And our division commander wasn't there. He was in Paris. We were without command of our division, and without Rommel, who would have acted immediately in spite of this gen-eral order, I think.' Frustrated, Hans did what he could with his regiment. 'We stood in full alert the whole night. But only one company of my second battalion, the fifth company, was out for a night exercise, with dummy ammunition. So unfortunately, some of the paras dropped on . . . a little village. And the company

68

commander was (there), in a cellar, and sent us a message. "Paras are dropping . . ." I think this is right as it is and the company is still out for exercise. So, in spite of this strict order, I gave the order to the other companies to fight this company in.' This counter-attack took 'quite a lot of prisoners.'

Hans believed that, unbeknownst to him and other regimental-level officers, there existed an order that the 21st Panzer should be freed to counter-attack in the event of a landing by paratroopers. If this is correct, that such an order was not communicated to the men who would need to carry it out beggars belief.* 'If we had known this order, with our strength in tanks, and anti-tanks, and infantry, we thought that we could easily get through to the coast,' Hans said. 'Especially because, when paras are landing, there's normally, at first, confusion. I think we could (have got) to the coast, and even to the bridges, and probably take back the bridges. We were absolutely prepared to counter-attack. We were very familiar with the ground. We knew every village. We knew every orchard. (But) we had to stay where we were.'

Ernest Lough was a staff officer in 5th Brigade. He suffered a bad landing due to his aircraft dropping the paratroopers while at a high speed. 'I was in considerable pain, because later my knee came up like a balloon. To get back to the rendezvous at Ranville took a long time . . . and the greatest danger was from our own troops – all of whom were a bit trigger happy. As we converged you could hear the ominous click of rifle bolts and we almost screamed out the passwords . . . this was quite frightening to have all these people coming in and not knowing who's going to shoot

* In 1979 Hans saw the existence of this order mentioned in two letters sent by General Speidel, Rommel's Chief of Staff, to Werner Kortenhaus, who was writing *The Combat History of the 21st Panzer Division*.

at you or not. I think a lot of our chaps must have been shot by our own people. Not a lot, but I think some of our chaps must've been shot by our own people.'

It took Ernest a few hours to cover the couple of miles to Ranville. He hadn't seen any sign of the enemy, but heard plenty of shooting. After reporting to Brigade HQ, he began to make his rounds of the battalions and see how they were faring. He was meeting the CO of the 13th Battalion, Parachute Regiment when a German truck was captured, and its cargo of bread and cheese was liberated by the paratroopers.

'I moved from there down to the bridges, from which we could hear some firing. And I got across the bridges, which was a bit dangerous because they were under fire from the enemy set up in the chateau, which was six hundred yards south of the bridges, and they could cover the two bridges by fire. So one had to be pretty quick in getting over there.

'I went to the dressing station to see how the wounded were being taken care of. We'd had a lot of casualties and the medics were very good. Our parachute ambulances were absolutely first class. Some very high-class surgeons and doctors there. (The wounded) couldn't be evacuated very far . . . we were still surrounded by the enemy and the reinforcements expected from the sea hadn't arrived yet.'

D-Day brought mixed results for the 6th Airborne. The capture of the bridges went as well as could have been dared hoped for. In the late afternoon, when Hans von Luck was finally cleared to move and re-take them, his battalion came under such crippling naval gunfire, artillery, and air attacks that he was forced to dig in on the southern edge of Escoville. But the attack on Merville Battery to the east of Ouistreham went badly from the beginning. Of the 600 men who were supposed to make the attack, only 150 were able to gather after the parachute force was widely scattered. Exemplifying the airborne spirit, this small force pressed on with the attack. They lost half their strength in doing so, but were able to destroy several of the World War One era guns before withdrawing.

The airborne landings on 6 June were fraught with difficulties, but every division fought with tenacity, and built upon the fierce reputation of the paratroopers. They were the first men to fight on French soil that day, but not the last.

CHAPTER THREE

'We'll Start the War from Right Here'

The Battle for the Western Beaches

'These poor buggers on the ground. You can't look
down and see the hand to hand fighting, but by God,
you know it's just a hell on wheels down there. They're
the ones to whom we owe much. They gave their
lives so that we can enjoy the freedoms such as we
know today.'

Harold 'Hal' Shook, P47 pilot who flew
over Omaha Beach

On 5 June, Kenneth Trott's Typhoon squadron was sent on an
interdiction mission in northern France. It was a flight he'd made
many times before, but on this day, Kenneth witnessed something so incredible that no one who saw it would ever forget it.

'The whole of the Channel was literally covered with shipping. Everywhere you looked it was just ship-ship-ship. And
of course, these enormous Mulberry harbours being towed by

tugs.* Flying over the countryside of the south coast, you could see the number of locomotives that were stacked in yards, and so on. Dozens of them.'

That same day, Typhoon pilot John Golley was sent up on a weather reconnaissance mission over Normandy.

'We were to be under strict (radio) silence, and in no way were we to engage anything . . . we flew in at about 8,000 feet. We started to lose height to come back across the Channel . . . as we came down . . . we could see all the shipping assembling for the big show. Hundreds and hundreds of craft. Remarkable. All coming out of little water alleyways, if you like . . . and we knew then, that the show was on.'

Steadfast and Loyal – the landing of the 4th Infantry Division at Utah

Utah Beach was the westernmost of the five Allied beaches, with H-Hour set for 0630. The mission to take it was given to the US Army's 4th Infantry Division who had arrived in Britain in 1944, and had yet to be tested in battle. They had, however, suffered casualties during Exercise Tiger off Slapton Sands, a D-Day rehearsal in Devon.

'Task Force U' was composed of 865 ships that delivered more than 20,000 men to Utah Beach on D-Day. In the early hours, around 4 a.m., landing ships miles offshore began to transfer soldiers into the landing craft that would take them in.

* These were the components of the Mulberry harbours built at Omaha and Sword beaches, rather than the entire harbours, which had been floated across the Channel. There were two in use in Normandy, with one at Arromanches and another at Omaha. The latter suffered severe damage in a storm on 19 June, and was thereafter of no use. The Arromanches Mulberry Harbour was used for six months, until the capture of Antwerp.

An LCA (Landing Craft Assault) was not a pleasant place to be. They rocked and rolled in the heavy swell of the English Channel, until seasick men wanted to get ashore no matter what waited for them. Nostrils filled with the smell of salt water, engine fumes, and vomit.

As dawn crept onto the horizon, eighteen ships of the US Navy let loose their broadsides. Minutes before the landing craft were due to hit the beach, a force of 300 B26 bombers flew over the coast and battered the German defences.

'People don't understand that the visibility was very bad, and we had to fly low,' said Francis Dymnicki, a USAAF radio operator aboard a B26 nicknamed 'Miss Pill'. 'The mission was important so we had to fly under the overcast, and we were flying at maybe about 1,500 feet, which is not very high at all. We normally flew at 12,000 feet.'

The higher the anti-aircraft guns had to fire, the less accurate their aim, but now the bombers had to take the increased risk of being hit.

'We flew over and bombed the guns that were on top of the cliffs. We dropped bombs just before we got to the target and then peeled off, so we were only over enemy territory for two or three minutes. The place was a mess. Planes were all over. There was a lot of guys lost. The navy ships were firing and we could see some of the landings that they were making. We didn't get too much of an observation because it happened so quickly.'

Perhaps, above the noise of the landing craft engines and the slapping of waves against the hull, the soldiers could hear the rumble of bombs as they fell inland. Without doubt they heard the roar of the battleships' broadsides, the massive shells crashing through the air.

Those who chanced to look above the gunwales of the landing craft saw a coastline shrouded in smoke, dust, and flame. In the gloom of dawn they may have seen the flash of enemy cannon, or the twinkle of a machine gun firing, but most of the infantry saw none of this. They were crouched down, shoulder to shoulder, and wet with sea spray. Bullets clanged against the metal of their assault craft, or cracked overhead. Incoming shells threw geysers of water into the air, testing the nerves of every coxswain. For hours the assault craft had struggled closer to shore. Now there was only a final moment for the soldiers to think of wives, of children, and of parents. To make a quick bargain with God, or to replay in the minds the training received, and the mission ahead.

And then, at last, the ramp dropped.

James Nannini was a soldier in the 4th Infantry Division. He had a fear of heights, and didn't enjoy climbing down the cargo net from the troop ship into the assault craft waiting below. 'It was choppy. And of course the guy that was handling the Higgins (boat), he was trying to do a good job to keep it as close to the ship as he could, but it was almost impossible. A number of fellas got their feet crushed in there. I'm sure they had to be amputated, I would think.'

As they were closing in on the shore, James witnessed the massive firepower of the US Navy.

'They were shelling the coast with those big sixteen-inch guns. They made a lot of noise, and when those shells hit the coast it looked like the sun was coming out. I figured, "Hell, when we get in there, there's no one gonna be alive there." Well, that wasn't the case.'

As smoke from the bombardment wreathed the coastline, the first waves of infantry hit the beach.

Harper Coleman, born close to Gettysburg, Pennsylvania, had worked in a furniture factory before he was drafted. Now he was carrying a .30 calibre machine gun into occupied France.

'I was on the first wave, the second row of boats. They put us off waist deep in water. We got on the beach. There was no one there but General Roosevelt, and he was standing there waving, pushing us on through.'

Theodore Roosevelt Jr. was the son of a former president, and the cousin of the sitting one, Franklin Roosevelt. He had requested three times to be given command of the first wave before permission was reluctantly given, and he stayed on the beach to greet and direct every regiment that arrived on Utah that day. He was awarded the Medal of Honor for his actions, but died in his sleep a little more than a month later.

In a stroke of good luck, the first wave had landed about a mile south from where they were supposed to be. Far from heralding disaster, they found this stretch of coast to be both lightly defended and ill prepared. 'All the landmines were marked,' recalled Harper. 'They had a stake beside them. So after we found out what they were you could pretty much avoid them. You could zigzag through them.'

Not every man was successful in this, and Harper saw some dead and wounded men lying where they'd been hit. However, resistance on the beach was weaker than the men had expected, with many of the defenders rendered ineffective by the weight of the bombardment.

'There was artillery (exploding) in the water. There was a big bunker there but luckily it wasn't manned when we were there. It was still empty. It wasn't completed. And that's the only bunker I recall we run into at that time.'

Harper and other troops moved quickly to get off the exposed beach. 'We didn't linger around on the beach at all. There was artillery and small-arms fire I know, because one of the guys behind me got hit. He was right behind me. I didn't know it until years later when I talked to his family in Indiana; he laid on that beach all day. They thought he was one of the dead. And when they found him at night, he was living, and they got him back to England and he survived.'

Inland, Harper saw evidence of the preparations that the Germans had taken to deny the fields to Allied paratroopers. 'We took a left turn up along the causeway until we come to a road. The land behind it was all flooded. We went into that little town of Pouppeville. That's where I saw my first German laying there on the street. If there was villagers there they sure didn't show themselves.'

Though there was some German resistance on the beach, it effectively lasted less than an hour. For some of the soldiers who landed after this time there would be a feeling of anticlimax. For others, it was the greatest relief.

James Nannini's 22nd Infantry Regiment landed at H+76 (i.e. 76 minutes after the hour the operation was due to begin). The dead and wounded of the first wave were still on the beach. 'The first GI that I saw that was dead was floating in the water. The water was red by that time. That first dead GI I saw, that really affected me.'

Combat engineer William Greer also came ashore after the first waves had already cleared off the beach. Having worked in construction before the war, he was interested in checking out a concrete pillbox of the Atlantic Wall. 'Huge thing. It had really been blasted.' William took note of the large amounts of reinforcing steel that had been used in its construction, but he was soon moved along onto a road. Here he saw German bodies that had been run flat by tanks and vehicles. Then, in the town of Sainte-Mère-Église about seven miles further inland, were more enemy dead.

'They'd tried to pick up the dead. The American dead, but there was still just all kinds of dead Germans. Anywhere that they could get behind a fencepost, or anything at all, for shelter, you'd see a dead German. The thing that you can't explain to anyone, and the most demoralizing thing to me, is the scent of war. You have the tore-up earth and vegetation, burnt gunpowder, and all kinds of dead odours. Not just humans, you know. Cows, horses, any kind of livestock that was just all bloated up and stinking bad. You can't make a picture of odour. You have to smell it to know.'

John Witmeyer landed with the 12th Regiment. They pushed straight off the beach and linked up with American airborne forces early that night.

'I spent the first night with a paratrooper,' John said. Both men were jumpy, and could see movement ahead of their foxhole. 'We kept waiting for our throats to get cut, I guess. When daybreak came those moving characters we saw were bushes. They were waving back and forth in the wind.' In the weeks to come, John would see plenty of the real thing.

By the end of 6 June, 23,000 men had gone ashore at Utah Beach. Though the 4th Infantry Division did not achieve all of their D-Day objectives – in part due to landing in the wrong position – they were able to clear the beach in less than an hour. They were also able to push six miles inland, giving a deep beachhead onto which reinforcements could be brought in, and formed up. This rapid deployment was aided by the engineers who made quick work of clearing the beach of mines and obstacles. Upon reflection – and given that the objectives for all D-Day beaches were optimistic at best – it is hard to see the results of the 4th Infantry Division's actions as anything but a great success. The Allied western flank was secure, and men and materials were rolling in. The 4th ID may have landed in the 'wrong' place, but it was about as right as wrong can be. As Brigadier General Roosevelt put it: 'We'll start the war from right here.'

Rangers Lead the Way – the assault on Pointe du Hoc

Between the beaches of Utah and Omaha lay a promontory known as the Pointe du Hoc. Atop of its sheer cliffs, which are a hundred feet in height, the Germans had constructed a series of gun emplacements. Intelligence reported that six 155mm guns were housed in these concrete strongholds. With their sweeping views over the American landing beaches, such guns could wreak havoc amongst the invasion fleet.

The importance of silencing the guns at Pointe du Hoc, and the difficulty of assaulting it posed by the cliffs, meant that the mission to capture and destroy the Pointe must be given to elite troops – in this case the 2nd Battalion of the United States Army Rangers, under the command of Colonel James Earl Rudder.

One of the senior NCOs in Rudder's unit was Leonard 'Bud' Lomell, from Brooklyn. After graduating college, where he had an athletic scholarship, Bud went to work on freight trains. His military service began in 1942, and Bud volunteered for the Rangers. The selection process was arduous and the training after selection was tougher still. As D-Day drew closer there was a lot of close cooperation with British army commandos, who taught the Rangers how to scale cliffs with ropes. Indeed, the close cooperation between Rangers and the British military continued into D-Day itself. Not only did a commando officer, Lt. Col. Tom 'Travis' Trevor, join the assaulting force, but the Rangers were taken into the attack by ships and boats of the Royal Navy.

Bud was First Sergeant of D Company and would be leading from the front. His landing craft launched under the cover of darkness and headed in towards the Pointe. 'Unfortunately they made a mistake and went to the wrong cliffs, which delayed us about forty minutes I think, which is important when you have gameplans such as we had. We landed about 7.10 a.m. on that little ledge, thirty foot wide.' This 'ledge' was the narrow scrap of beach below the cliffs. This mission was said to be the most dangerous mission assigned for D-Day, and that's been repeated by General Omar Bradley.'

The assault force did not go undetected. When the ramp went down, Bud received a flesh wound from a machine-gun bullet. 'I was the first one wounded, but it didn't disable me so that I couldn't go on and do my duty.'

As the LCAs beached on the narrow shore, rocket launchers mounted on their flanks fired ropes onto the cliffs above. After pulling on the ropes to secure the grapples, the Rangers, laden with ammunition and equipment, began scaling the hundred-foot cliffs.

'Had everything gone right the Germans would have been in bed when we did this,' said Bud, 'but because we were late, it gave them enough time to come out and welcome us.'

Out at sea in a 'rocket ship', an LST packed with artillery to bombard the enemy coast, twenty-five-year-old ensign Nicholas Zuras was watching the action ashore through a pair of binoculars. 'As we approached the beach we got the first taste of gunfire for the landing force. I was just standing along with my binoculars, and looking at Pointe du Hoc, which was a tragedy in itself.

'I was seeing these Rangers climbing up metal ladders to the top, and being fired on, and being killed.' These ladders had been acquired from the London Fire Brigade.

The defenders shot at the climbing Rangers, cut ropes, and dropped grenades onto those below. And yet, through feats of sheer bravery and determination, Rangers began to make it onto the cliff top. They were aided by men on the landing craft and the narrow beach, who fired to keep the Germans back from the cliff edges. 'We got up there and fought our way through the Germans to the gun positions,' said Bud. 'D Company, my company, was assigned gun positions four, five and six on the west flank. The rest of the companies landed on the other side.'

Some 200 German soldiers manned positions on the Pointe du Hoc. After pushing back those who were on the cliff top at close quarters, Bud and his men were able to reach their objective of the gun emplacements.

'When we got to the positions where these three guns were supposed to be . . . they weren't there. They were nothing but telephone poles sticking out of these emplacements. And of course, we trained for this mission only from aerial photographs and information that had been given to us. We did not know, as we later found out, that those guns had been removed before D-Day to an alternate position. We could not find any guns on Pointe du Hoc.'

This, of course, did not mean that the 2nd Rangers were out of danger. Nor did it mean that they were about to give up their search for the lethal guns. While D Company set up a roadblock to prepare for a counter-attack, Bud and another NCO went out alone to scout ahead.

'As luck would have it, within the first couple of hundred feet, we came to this hedgerow . . . and I examined on the other side, and there were the guns.' Bud personally destroyed them using thermite grenades. 'By 0830 in the morning, we had destroyed those guns so that they could not be used.'

Bud then returned to the roadblock and re-joined his men. 'We fought there for two days.' On the first day the 2nd Rangers received some reinforcements from the 5th Battalion, who landed at Omaha, but heavy casualties suffered on the beach by the 29th ID meant that it would be two days before the Rangers were relieved by the infantry. During that time they endured artillery fire, sniper fire, and numerous German counter-attacks, all of which caused severe casualties. By the time that the 29th ID arrived, only fifteen of the sixty-five men of Bud's D Company were able to fight. 'Those of us that did survive were just plain lucky.' As a unit, the 2nd Rangers had suffered a 70 per cent casualty rate, but they had achieved their mission, and Pointe du Hoc did not threaten the invasion fleets on either Utah or Omaha. Considering how close the latter landing came to failure, the success of the Rangers' mission cannot be overstated.

Ever Forward – the landing of the 29th Infantry Division on the western sectors of Omaha

Omaha was a six-mile stretch of beach that ran from Port-en-Bessin in the east to the Vire River to the west. The western third of this landing site had a nine-foot-high sea wall, and the entire beach was overlooked by hundred-foot-high cliffs, or 'bluffs'. There were only five 'exits' from Omaha, with the best being a paved road in a ravine that led towards Vierville-sur-Mer. The other exits were a pair of dirt roads, and a pair of dirt paths.

Rommel had ordered formidable defences built in this area, heavily mining the waters and beach, and constructing thirteen strongpoints called Widerstandsnester ('resistance nests'). There was an extensive trench system that connected numerous other fighting positions, and the entire beach was covered by fields of enfilading and plunging fire from the cliffs, turning it into a deadly kill zone. Allied intelligence was aware of the defences, but not of who was manning them: unbeknownst to them, parts of the veteran 352nd Infantry Division were now on the beach. Regardless of who they would face, it was clear to Allied planners that a bombardment of Omaha was necessary.

Twenty-two-year-old Edward Nacey was a navigator aboard a B24 bomber. He began combat missions in April 1944, many of them in support of the coming invasion. His crew's D-Day target was the defences at Omaha.

'We took off about two o'clock in the morning and went through a very elaborate assembly, trying to get into formation. Weather that night was bad, but we finally managed that and flew the prescribed route. Around about the time the sun was coming up we spotted the bomber stream that we were supposed to be joining.' These 'streams' included aircraft flying from multiple bases in England. 'We joined in with them and flew the formation with them. Once we got up to altitude above the weather we were OK. We couldn't see the invasion forces underneath us as we were going across the Channel but we knew they were there, and that was probably the most scary thing about the mission. Our role was to stay with (the pathfinders) and drop our bombs when they did, so the bombs were all in a group in a precise target area. So that's what we did, and we bombed at six thirty in the morning at the H-Hour. The biggest concern to me at the time, and probably to everybody else, was don't make any mistake, and don't drop short on our own forces . . . (The pathfinders) were so concerned about dropping on their own troops that they actually extended the release time a few seconds.'

For bombers travelling at hundreds of miles an hour, a few seconds' delay could mean a few miles' inaccuracy. 'The bombs actually fell about a mile or two behind the beaches. They did a lot of damage but they didn't hit the fortifications as well as everybody would have liked.'

Beneath the armada of aircraft, and some twelve miles to the east of where the 4th Infantry Division were landing with little resistance at Utah, the US 29th Infantry Division were about to hit the western sectors of Omaha Beach. The carnage experienced in the coming hours lived for ever in the hearts and minds of those who fought there. For First Lieutenant Ray

Nance of Company A, 116th Infantry Regiment, the painful memories were all too clear when he gave his account of the landings.

'I don't know whether I can do this,' he told the interviewer. Ray was one of thirty-four men in his unit from the small town of Bedford, Virginia. Tragically, 'The Bedford Boys' would come to symbolize American losses on D-Day.

'It was very rough once you were in the water,' Ray said. 'The British landing craft that carried us in were very light, and they danced around in the water like a feather. There was about two hours of circling in an assembly area, waiting our turn to get in line to proceed to the beaches. And this is when the troops began to get seasick. And due to the low silhouette of these craft, the rough seas sometimes came over the side. We were wet and very uncomfortable and due to the seasickness, it was a very uncomfortable position.'

Ahead of them, the bluffs of Omaha Beach loomed out of the smoke of the naval bombardment. Flashes of light marked the gun positions opening up on the assault force.

'When we approached the beach . . . we came under an intense fire, both mortar and artillery. And as we neared the beach, we came under an intense small arms fire. And at the point the boat touched the sand, our ramp went down. Being an officer, I was the first one to leave the boat. And the beach appeared to me to be entirely empty. It seemed as though no one had been there before us.'

Ray described the beach as an inferno. 'The water seemed to be hot, and smoking more or less, from vapour caused from this hot metal falling in it.'

Despite the incoming fire, Ray had no difficulty in getting his men to move. 'They were very thoroughly trained and had been through this in many dry runs before. Each man knew his job and he proceeded to do it. That is, those who weren't dead already. 'There were seventeen on my boat to start with, and to my knowledge, only five of us came off alive.'

Also coming ashore with the 116th was twenty-four-year-old Harry Parley. 'Boats were getting hit . . . Incoming enemy fire was starting to come out toward us . . . You don't want to pick your head up over the side because things were not too comfortable . . . I could smell the smoke . . . And every once in a while, a guy would look up over the side and say, "Oh shit," and look down again. So I knew it wasn't good news.'

Harry's boat finally came to a stop. 'The ramp went down and your asshole puckered up. You took a deep breath. And you started to pray. I went down the ramp . . . and I went under.' Harry was completely submerged beneath the water, and pulled down by his heavy equipment. 'I couldn't get up. I said goodbye to my mother and my wife. I'm trying to struggle. I know there's no help coming because I can . . . hear the firing. You can hear ricochets on my boat.' Luckily for Harry, the barrel of his flame-thrower was sticking out of the water. 'Somebody grabbed hold of that and pulled me out half-drowned.'

The dead and dying of Company A were littering the beach. It fell on medics like Russell Clark to save who they could. He was nineteen years old.

'I got a good view of the men when the ramp dropped, and they were dropping like flies. They were gunned down. And we knew at that time that we were in for a rough time of it. Some of the men jumped over the side, and I was fortunate enough to jump over the side where the water was only up to my mid-thighs, whereas the men on the other side jumped into water that was over their heads . . . some of them drowned.'

To comply with the rules of war the medics carried no weapons, only medical bags, and their helmets and armbands were marked with a Red Cross on a white background. 'That was a beautiful target for the Germans,' said Russell.

'There was a man right in front of me, and I heard him yell, "I'm hit!" And as I advanced towards the shore he went down, and I grabbed ahold of his collar, and I dragged him up on shallower water. (I) was turning to see if I could help him when I found out he was dead.'

There was no respite from the withering fire. 'There was men on the right, and men on the left of me that were falling. I went back in the water to try and bring some of those men up to shore. And then when I got them up to shore, I worked on them and did my medical work. I could hear the bullets hitting the water. I could hear the bullets hitting all around me.'

Despite the carnage, Russell believed that many men were too busy to be frightened. 'I was frightened going in, I'm not gonna kid ya. Anybody would be frightened when they're going in and knowing that someone's going to be firing bullets at them. But the minute I got into the water, and I started trying to help these wounded men, I wasn't frightened. No. All I had in my mind was trying to help these men. The fright went away.'

It wasn't only the 29th Infantry Division who landed on the western sectors of Omaha Beach. John Raaen was a twenty-two-year-old captain in the 5th Ranger Battalion. On D-Day, his unit had two potential missions. If the 2nd Rangers gave word that they had successfully scaled the cliffs and taken the positions on the Pointe du Hoc, then the 5th would move in behind them; but if no word was received by a given time, they would support the landings of the 29th Infantry Division. When that time came and went, the 5th Rangers headed in towards Omaha.

'Maybe ten minutes after we had made our turn and committed ourselves to the Omaha Dog beaches, we heard the call from the 2nd Ranger Battalion, a radio message, saying, "Praise the

Lord",' John explained. 'This meant that they had been successful in their initial assaults and were asking for us to come in behind them.' Although he and his unit wanted to go to the assistance of their fellow Rangers, they were now committed to their approach. 'There was nothing that we could do but proceed.' John's landing craft finally ground to a halt, and the ramp dropped onto the sand.

'The Germans opened fire with machine guns practically down the throat of the ramps. Anyone who tried to go down the ramp died. I looked back at our LCI and saw that the coxswain was having trouble getting back off the beach. He'd run on so hard that he couldn't pull it off. And just then I saw an artillery shell hit on the fantail and I know he became a casualty as a result of giving us too dry a landing.'

John recalled an unlikely hero at the water's edge: Father Joseph Lacey.

'He had joined us perhaps a week before the invasion. Not much more anyway. And he was little. He was old. He was fat. He was a Roman Catholic priest. We didn't think that he'd last with us. We were all in beautiful physical condition and were expecting a high-speed march across hostile country. But old Father Lacey came out of the boat. And from the reports that everyone told me, he didn't come up to the protection of the seawall. He stayed right down there on the water's edge, pulling men who were dying out of the water so that they could perhaps live a little bit longer, tending the wounded, saying unction, a true hero. A true hero.'

The invasion plan had called for a bombing of the beach to provide craters for the advancing soldiers, but the bombs instead landed miles inland. And so men sought cover where they could, often behind the obstacles that had been placed to impede them.

'They had these great big Xs on the beach, of iron,' said Russell Clark. 'They had barbed wire. They had mines. And they had all kinds of barricades on the beach. Some of the men, what they did was throw themselves on the wire to try and let other men go over them. I was behind one obstacle, and I was taking care of one of the wounded, and I was just crawling over to take care of another wounded man, because he was calling for help, when all of a sudden something hit my helmet and stunned me. I was in la-la land for a minute or two. By the time I got there I found out that he had passed away, but his helmet was lying alongside of him.' Russell took off his conspicuous Red Cross helmet, replaced it with the dead man's, and ripped off his medic's armband. 'I knew that I was a target that the Germans would love to hit.'

Harry Parley had almost died in the water before being helped ashore. 'Now I'm up there – half drowned. Full of water, with eighty pounds of shit on my back, and I'm alone, because the rest of the guys, travelling lighter than I, took off running across to the shelter of the seawall.' Behind the seawall – little more than a few feet high in places because of the build up of sand – were Omaha's steep bluffs, atop of which were pillboxes and gun emplacements. At the base of the cliffs were barbed-wire entanglements, and mines.

'I couldn't run. So I started to walk. And that was my first experience with enemy gunfire. I could see, rather than hear, the bullets going into the sand. Made a little sucking sound like a zip zip zip, zip zip zip, a sucking, you know. I saw other guys falling. There were guys running on the beach already, yelling. Some of them were alive, some were dead, some were torn up. But I could do nothing. I was trying to catch my breath, get rid of the water in my lungs, and I could only walk. I actually walked across that beach.'

Harry explained why he thinks that he survived the machine-gun fire when so many others did not. 'You don't have to pick out particular soldiers (if you're a machine-gunner). You fire as the line moves forward. You lay down your zone of fire and allow the enemy to run into it. The ones that ran ahead of me were running into the zone of fire. And as they ran toward the bluff, or to the seawall, the Germans were lowering the fire to get as many as they could before they hit the seawall. I was left exposed and all alone. I was behind them, I would say easy a hundred, two hundred feet. So there I was, one guy with a flamethrower walking across. They took potshots at me, because I can see it around, but I think the amount of troops ahead of me distracted them. They had better pickings. So actually, the load I carried may very well have saved my ass that day.'

Harry finally made it to the seawall, where the survivors of the first waves were massed together. 'It was one fucking mess. Guys were trying to dig themselves back into England. Wounded and dead and chopped-up guys. Nobody could move. They were terrorized. And, you know . . . they just didn't want to move. They couldn't move. We didn't know where we were. We had no officers. My captain was killed on the beach.'

John Raaen of the 5th Rangers also made it to the base of the bluffs.

'I do remember looking back at the beach and seeing men everywhere, spread across the beach, dead and dying. I remember seeing men in the water hiding behind obstacles. And I remember the DD tanks. These were the floating tanks with those great big pneumatic tires around them. The DD tanks were backing down to the water's edge and providing protection from that terrible small-arms fire we were receiving from the right, driving up across the beach and depositing men at the seawall and then backing down again and bringing up four or five, six more men.

I watched that happen over the period of time that we were on the beach a number of times. And it wasn't just the one tank. There were many of them.'

John witnessed a landing craft struck by an artillery shell, the blast igniting the fuel of a flamethrower man. 'The jelly gasoline was spread from one end of that LCI to the other, and it became a raging inferno in a fraction of a second. It was one of the most awful things that I've ever seen.'

Closer to the water, Ray Nance watched the next wave coming in. 'They had trouble getting through the obstacles. Some of their boats capsized . . . There was a tremendous amount of artillery fire on that wave. The boats were twisting in the surf and the men were all over the place. And it would appear that most of them were killed because I was out front. They did not pass us, those men from that wave.'

Ray was surrounded by the bodies of his comrades. 'When I reached the high-water mark, the bodies floated in and you could see your friends, people you'd served with for years floating face down or face up.

'Our company aid man came along. He treated my wound and also gave me some information about what had happened, what he had seen in his travels up and down the beach. At that time, I was told I was company commander.' The original company commander had been killed. So had many of his men. '(I was) a company commander without men.

'I think I was in shock at the time, more or less, because I'd been wounded. I was wounded just as I came off the boat.' Suffering from wounds to his hand and foot, Ray began to crawl his way up the beach.

In their bunkers, German machine-gunners and snipers sought out anyone who moved, wounded or not. 'From time to time they would come back if they saw anything moving,' said

Ray. 'And it was automatic weapons fire from that pillbox at the mouth of the Vierville draw.' This was the paved road that cut between the cliffs. It was an important exit for the assaulting troops, and heavily defended.

'(The machine-gunner) would elevate and lower and that would cause a beaten path of fire to stitch the sand right towards you.' By changing the elevation of the gun, the machine-gunner could 'strafe' the beach rather than simply fire onto one individual soldier at a time. With so many men on the beach, it was difficult to miss. Under such withering fire, minutes began to feel like an eternity. 'It seemed like hours. But when we got across at the high-water mark, I happened to look at my watch, which wasn't waterproofed, and I was amazed to see that it was still running. It was shortly after 10.00.'

Ray had been on Omaha Beach for less than four hours. In that time his unit had been shot to pieces, with only twenty of A Company making it to the sea wall, and the Vierville draw and its exit from the beach was yet to be cleared.

'I do remember my radio operator calling out from my left saying he'd been hit, and he called to me for help, but I couldn't give him any. That's a pity of the whole thing, because we all had a mission. And that came first. We could not stop for anyone. It wasn't an easy choice.'

Soldiers who had been alive and talking one moment could be lifeless the next. 'A company runner, an orderly, went across the beach alongside of me. We talked to one another. I saw him when he was hit.'

To Ray, the losses seemed unsustainable. 'From where I was, it seemed a failure on this particular beach.'

Too weak to move, many of the wounded drowned as the tide came in. 'I feel that many of them could have been saved . . . had we been on dry land,' said Ray.

Medic Russell Clark was doing his utmost to save them. 'I would imagine I took care of fifteen, twenty, thirty wounded people. The chaos was terrible. The screaming of people that were hit. They were yelling for medics. And I heard a couple of men that were yelling, "I want my mother." A couple of times I was crawling around and I'd come across an arm or a leg that had been blown off.'

He crawled over to many fallen soldiers, not knowing if they were dead or alive. 'In most cases they were dead. But in some cases I helped men with their legs off, or arms.' He applied tourniquets to these wounds to try and stem the bleeding. 'And that's about all I could do for somebody like that. They had to lay there, and wait, until the beach was secure. I'm sure many of them did not make it.'

There was no amount of training that could have prepared Russell for what he saw on Omaha. 'Until you actually had to do the work, you really didn't realize what you were getting into, or what you had to do. When I saw men being hit, and going down all around me, I figured one of these bullets has gotta find me.' Cover was so sparse that at one point he had to shelter behind a fallen soldier. 'I actually pushed him up so I could get down behind him.'

Hundreds of men were down, and the 29th Infantry Division were yet to clear the beach. As time dragged on, and there was no sign of breakout, Ray Nance became worried about the possibility of a German counter-attack that would drive them into the sea.

'I looked to my left and I saw a tank coming down the beach right in the edge of the water. At first I thought it was a German tank.' As the tank got closer, Ray was able to recognize the US markings. '(It was) the prettiest white star you've ever seen. It was ours. I thought that we'd lost the thing, and the Germans were mopping up.'

But the relief was short-lived. 'The tank rolled past my rear. Down to the mouth of the Vierville draw. Headed inland, fired about two rounds, and was knocked out and burned.'

As happened on many of the D-Day beaches, a lot of Omaha's tank support was lost in the water before they ever made it to the beach. Others were knocked out by mines, or the lethal German 88s.

One of the tankers who landed in support of the 29th Infantry Division was William Gast. Willian had enlisted into the US Army straight from school. Now twenty years old, he was a driver in A Company, 743rd Tank Battalion, who began landing on the beach at around 0630.

'You can hear the bullets bouncing off the tank like you're throwing marbles at a car, and you can see tanks sitting beside you that are burning.' There were many horrors that day, but one in particular stuck out to him. 'The saddest part about the whole thing is I may have even driven over some of my own men.'

The losses in William's unit were heavy. 'We had in our company three combat platoons, and there is five tanks to a platoon. Five of us made it out of fifteen.'

Without the promised fire support of dozens of tanks, the navy proved vital. Risking the German coastal guns and mines, several destroyers came within 800 yards of the beach, firing point blank at the enemy positions. Further out to sea, battleships and cruisers hurled their heavy shells at the concrete emplacements.

'Our navy did a wonderful job,' said Ray Nance. 'I wasn't in a position to see it, but they did fire on those beach installations and beach defences, direct fire. Sometimes it would almost raise you from the ground when (the shells) come in over you like that. And in one instance to the right of the Vierville draw, it caused a landslide that covered quite a few wounded that were back under the protection of the cliff. And at the same time, the Germans were putting in their two cents' worth. Mortars. Some 88 over-head fire. That didn't bother us once we got in near the cliff, it fell over to our rear.'

Medic Russell Clark estimated that it took him six hours to make it from the water to the base of the cliff. 'Even when you were down there you had to keep your head down . . . and we had men who got curious I guess, and I'd see them, they'd stick their head up and sure enough a machine-gunner would get 'em.'

Harry Parley was also in the meagre shelter of the seawall. 'I found myself trying to help some of the wounded. I ran out to the beach about thirty feet and dragged a guy that had been shot in the legs. I dragged him to the safety of the bluff. I don't know why I did that because a lot of the guys who did that were getting bumped off. They get shot in the ass or in the back. Anyhow, that was my claim to heroism that day.'

Harry was soon wounded himself. 'Some shrapnel hit me in the cheekbone . . . someone said, "Jesus, you're wounded." I thought I was dying. But actually when I touched the skin, (it was) a tiny piece, about the size of a pinhead.'

When he looked back to the water, Harry witnessed sickening scenes.

'You can see the boats blowing up . . . and the personnel flying in the air and everything. And you thought everything was lost because there were tanks coming off and trucks coming off far out in the water and sinking. Landing Ship Tanks with the big equipment were being hit now. And then you just turned away, you couldn't look. And right out there like you could touch them were these two big battleships. They were firing inland.

'I crawled farther away, then I found other wounded and all that shit.' Harry then came across a gap that had been blown in the barbed-wire entanglements. 'As I came up to the hole, there were still guys hesitating (to go), and I could see why when I went through. You know, when you mark a minefield for safety, they carry rolls of white tape. And you follow the white tape 'cause whoever's gone forward, and wasn't blown up, takes the tape with him. Each strip was about a yard apart . . . there were about four or five guys going up the bluff ahead of me. I could see one guy had been blown apart. And another guy, both legs were off and he had tourniquets around his legs . . . that's the price they paid for being the first guys to come through.'

Harry was about to go further up the hill when someone started shouting at him and the others to come back down: the big guns of the navy were going to fire onto the clifftops.

'I never went back,' said Harry. 'I didn't want to go back down to the beach because I was afraid to get killed. That was a stupid thing to do, and the USS *Arkansas* opened fire. They opened up that bluff like a saucer. D'you ever sit in the front seat, in the front row of a movie, looking up at the screen? That's the way it looked. Never touched me. And these giant shells were blowing the hill apart.'

At the base of the bluffs, John Raaen of the Rangers watched as 'an old sergeant from the amphibious brigade (was) lugging a calibre 30 water-cooled machine gun. He . . . set it up on a tripod that he'd apparently already put in. And then he went back, and with a young lieutenant in a green sweater . . . they carried the water and some boxes of ammunition, and they set up the machine gun very methodically. And then the sergeant got behind it and began to traverse and search the hill to our right front.

'I looked over to the right front and I could see troops trying to fight their way up the bluffs. There was a lot of smoke, a lot of action over there. But clearly someone from the 116th, or A and B of the 2nd (Ranger) Battalion, had begun to get off the beach and to try to get up those bluffs. And the sergeant was firing in support of their advance.

'The lieutenant, absolutely oblivious to what was going on, turned his back toward the fire. At some point or other in these proceedings he yelled down at the troops that were huddled up against the seawall, cowering, frightened, doing nothing, accomplishing nothing, and said, "You guys think you're soldiers?" He did everything he could, trying to organize himself, his own men, trying to organize the troops of the 116th that were up there on the seawall, but to no avail.'

After receiving orders from General Cota, who had landed on the beach, John said that 'D company led the assault up the hill, cleared a number of Germans out of the positions there, and made it possible for the battalion to proceed up the hill. I sat down, perhaps fifty feet above the beach, and looked back at the beach and it was a true holocaust. I could see the two LCIs that had been hit. I noticed as far as the eye could see that ours was the only gap in the wire, and that the 5th Ranger Battalion was the only unit that appeared to be moving off the beach. Now, way down at Vierville, I had seen what appeared to be some US troops attacking up the bluffs. But from this particular vantage point, it was clear that we were the only unit that was moving out from the beaches. There's no doubt about it. We would be followed by reorganized troops from 116th, but at this particular moment, it was the 5th Battalion.'

Harry Parley and others from the 116th made their way to the top of the bluffs. 'We just walked up. There was a path. And we got to the top and we saw all the emplacements, tunnels and dugouts and holes. And they had a couple of enemy troops with their hands on their heads . . . they looked like Mongolians to me. They didn't talk German. And we sat them down with their hands on their heads. They were passed onto the beach.' It is likely that these men were former Soviet soldiers, pressed into service for Germany after they had been taken prisoner on the Eastern Front.

97

Harry now found himself fighting to push inland. It wasn't long until he heard a sound that every infantryman fears: the clanking tracks of an approaching tank.

'The French roads of Normandy have very deep ditches. Some of them were deep, three feet, four feet deep, covered with overgrowth. And I dived into one onto the feet of a sergeant. I would say the sergeant at that time must have been about twenty-eight, twenty-nine. He looked like an old man to me.'

The sergeant belonged to the 1st Infantry Division, which had seen action in North Africa and Sicily. 'They had been through combat, so they were experienced. And he was laying there, you know, with his helmet on his head, his elbow up and his head relaxed.

'I was panicky and I screamed at him, "There's a fucking tank coming! What the hell are we going to do now?" And he looked at me. He said, "Let's stay here. Maybe it'll go away." And the fucking thing went away.'

Harry picked up a discarded M1 rifle. Many soldiers were using weapons collected on the battlefield. Some were of German issue, and this led to tragic consequences. After hearing what sounded like a German machine gun firing, Harry and others shot in its direction. 'When the firefight was over, we found the bodies of our fellow GIs. This went on during most of the day. Strangely enough, I have never read anything about it. There were so many tragedies that day that I guess this was just ignored. But it bothered me.'

After the chaos of the beach and the air landings, soldiers of different units were meshing into their own 'war bands', and their blood was up. 'We had been joined by some . . . British commandos, and our own Rangers and paratroopers,' said Harry. 'They were absolutely crazy. I was witness to a number of what I would call instances of butchery where we did capture a German or two. I was witness to throat-cutting and disembowelment. We were crazy . . . if we were suspicious of a farmhouse or something, we threw the hand grenade. I think we killed French farmers. There was a quick remorse when we saw somebody dead in civilian clothes caused by our firing . . . It was kind of creepy because I consider myself a good soldier. And within a few hours I was involved with . . . madness.'

The battlefield beyond the bluffs was no less chaotic than the beach. 'There was about six of us, about two feet apart, heads down, squatting, sort of a squatting, walking along a hedgerow. And suddenly there was this pop. The sergeant's head was blown apart, through the helmet, left his skull like a saucer. And he fell over into my arms. And this may sound cool, calm, but the first thing we started yelling is, "Let's get the hell out of here, we're on the wrong side of the hedgerow."'

Harry was experiencing a new kind of battlefield: the Normandy bocage. 'We had not been trained for the hedgerow fighting. And I think I've carried that grudge for years. I had terrific training for the assault and self-preservation, but they never told me about the hedgerows.'

Due to the heavy resistance, troops from Omaha had pushed a mile inland at most, and night was finally closing in on 'the Longest Day'.

'We decided to get into the middle of this field so we could see that someone was creeping up on us. And we decided to dig a foxhole.' The hard ground made this impossible, and Harry and a sergeant stood in the darkness, exhausted. 'He said to me after a while, "Fuck it, Parley, let's just sit down here. And if they come for us, we take as many as we can." It's real Errol Flynn shit. Yeah. We sat back to back, waiting for someone to come and get us . . . And that's the way I spent the night.'

The beach behind them was littered with thousands of dead

and wounded men. 'I wish I could have done more,' said Company A medic Russell Clark. 'I wish I could have saved more men. But you're limited as to what you can do, and actually . . . you're limited with the amount of medical supplies that you have. My job was to help the wounded, not to find cover. And that's the job I did. I tried to take care of the men on the beach.'

After the battle, First Lieutenant Ray Nance discovered who they'd faced on Omaha Beach. 'We were told there would be a reinforced platoon defending this beach. Later, we learned there was a whole division, I believe it was the 352nd Infantry Division up on manoeuvres. And unfortunately, they used live ammunition on them manoeuvres for us.'

Ray was asked if the beach was like hell. 'Well, I've never been there . . . but if it's like that, I certainly don't want to go. It was a heart-rending experience to lose these men that we'd trained with. Some of them I'd grown up with from childhood.'

Nineteen of the thirty-four 'Bedford Boys' were killed that day, giving the small town in Virginia the tragic distinction of having the highest number of D-Day deaths per capita.[1]

Ray believed that their sacrifice was worthwhile. 'We were soldiers . . . My only regret was that we didn't complete our mission . . . We were selected on the basis that we were well-trained. In other words, some of the best infantry that we had. And it was a great disappointment to see these men die before we could get into a land battle. It was saddening. It was the most heart-rending experience that I ever had. I hope I never have another one like it.'

Sailors

It wasn't only soldiers who were in peril during the landings at Omaha. Larger ships risked sea mines and air attacks, while smaller vessels ran a gauntlet of artillery and machine-gun fire to land the assaulting troops, or provide them with much needed fire support.

Irvin Klimas was aboard the destroyer USS *Thompson*. Irvin had already experienced operations on the Atlantic convoys, and while docked in Britain a pair of Luftwaffe bombs had fallen on either side of his ship. Now the *Thompson* was firing directly onto the Normandy coastline.

'We appeared off the coast of France about three o'clock in the morning. We could see the flashes from the air force bombing the beach. We took our position off Pointe du Hoc. We were ordered not to fire until five thirty in the morning, which we did. We knocked out whatever targets of opportunity we saw. At six thirty we ceased firing when the invasion fleet was moving into the beach. Obviously we didn't want to hit our own people.

'During the day we hovered off the beach and picked out targets. And at one point in time the Rangers had a little difficulty, and we moved in to help them take some of their wounded off. Later that day there was a Ranger spotting party that we had initially met. They came aboard our ship so that we could meet them and talk to them. This Ranger spotting party was about five miles inland, and they started picking targets for us to knock off. We spent quite a bit of the afternoon on these targets.

'I went topside. I saw an LST unload some trucks. And as they were moving down the beach this German gun battery, which was well hidden, knocked them off one after the other. About mid-afternoon the battleship *Texas* pulled up . . . and they walked up that (bluff) with their 14-inch battery. They must have got the hidden German batteries, because from that point on ships could unload without problems.'

That night the *Thompson* returned to England to reload, and her crew took a well-deserved rest. 'We got our first sleep in about thirty-six hours,' said Irvin.

Nineteen-year-old Hilaire Benbow was a midshipman serving aboard HMS *Prince Charles*, a cross-Channel ferry taken into war service. Hilaire's mission was to command a landing craft carrying soldiers of the 2nd Ranger Battalion.

The *Prince Charles* anchored about ten miles off Omaha Beach, with ten LCAs hoisted on the davits. Two or three of them would be used to transfer the rangers to the Pointe du Hoc. 'On that point there was a gun battery that could threaten the anchorage, and it had to be silenced and stopped. These Rangers, under a Colonel Rudder, were to go and assail the cliffs of this high point and capture the gun position. They had all sorts of ingenious equipment. Grappling irons, and ropes with rockets on. I shook hands with Colonel Rudder and wished him good luck as he went down the scrambling net.

'They were taken in by a colleague of mine, Sub-Lieutenant Paddy Kenyon. And then we set out about an hour or so later. We headed towards the main shore. The idea was that when the assault had been a success we would get a success signal, and follow in and enlarge the force there. But seven o'clock came and we had no signal from them. We waited for a quarter of an hour, still no signal, and so our instruction was to head into Vierville.'

Hilaire recalled the approach. 'It was pretty rough, and I had the Americans bailing out with their steel helmets. They were very seasick. They had all their weapons and their wireless stuff in cellophane, or whatever it was in those days.'

The early assault waves had gone in at low tide, but now the many obstacles on Omaha were obscured by the rising tide.

'We had to get in amongst the obstacles, and the craft on my port side hit one of these poles with a mine on the top. And in the blink of the eye there was all these bodies, like statues in a shop window. They were jet black on the bow of this landing craft.'

Hilaire did not turn back. In fact, throughout the day, he felt a sense of invincibility of sorts. 'It was very similar to an exercise in Scotland,' he said. 'We grounded. It was a sandbar. The troops all went forward, and the craft sort of tilted and filled with water.' The landing craft's petrol engine was soon flooded, and would not restart. Hilaire made the decision to abandon the stricken landing craft. 'We had no arms, we had no food, but it was obvious to me that we were not going to get back to the (*Prince Charles*).

'We stayed in the water up to our necks, and one felt safe. You could see the explosions all around you, but being under the water – it was no protection at all – it gave you a sense of protection.' Hilaire and his crew spent an hour in the sea. 'Everything was noise and smoke. I didn't feel alarmed.'

The young midshipman then decided to move up the beach. He and his crew found shelter at the mouth of the Vierville draw. 'There was still fire coming over. These Americans very kindly gave us bits out of their rations, and that kept us going, because we had nothing.'

There was a moment of alarm when Hilaire looked at the sea and saw that no more waves of reinforcements were coming into their sector at Dog Green. 'I had the feeling that it had failed. That the whole invasion had failed and that I was going to be a prisoner of war. I saw some very badly wounded men. I saw a chap with his chin just off staggering along. He was an officer and he had no chin. We gave our handkerchieves, because of course all the first aid personnel had been killed as well. I did have in my possession a little tin box of morphia injections but I didn't give those up. I felt that I might need those for my own men, but they would have been useful for the men on the beach.'

During a lull in the battle Hilaire crawled back to the water's edge. 'I'd lost my sea boots in the water, and I was in bare feet. I couldn't spend the day on shingle in bare feet. There was literally a wall about two feet high of dead bodies, all along the surfline.

The sea had washed all of their clothing off, and they were naked. Their shirts were off and so on. And the strange thing was, they all had cropped heads, and as the sea came in their hair lay flat, and as the sea receded it all stood up on end.' Hilaire took a pair of boots from one of the dead. 'I used them for gardening for years afterwards.'

When he made a second trip to the surfline to get another pair of boots for one of his men, Hilaire saw that craft were coming in half a mile down the beach. He then spent the afternoon leading his men eastwards to where the ships were coming ashore in the 1st Infantry Division's sectors. During this time they passed an LST that had grounded on the beach, around which the wounded were being gathered. 'That was a shock. All these stretchers were laid out in the shelter of this ship. That brought you up with a shudder.'

The midshipman also witnessed the problem of subsequent waves becoming bottlenecked on the narrow beachhead. 'All these lorries were being landed and they couldn't get off the beach. The fire from the Germans set them alight, and the fire spread from one lorry to the other. The beach was very smoky.'

Hilaire led his men under cover of the smoke to the water's edge. By this time he had also collected naval ratings who had become stranded from other craft. 'I had sixteen of them at least.' He and the men were carried off the beach, transferred to a larger troopship, and returned to Britain that day. From the port, Hilaire was able to call home and let his parents know that he was safe. He also heard a radio broadcast telling the public how well the landings were going. 'I could have smashed that radio. It was so untrue, at least as far as Omaha was concerned.'

In the waters off that beach, Leon Schafer, a twenty-two-year-old from Raleigh, North Carolina, was serving aboard a Landing Ship, Tank.

'The fortifications with 88s were peppering us like mad, but we got our men off. There was no way we could get off our heavy equipment because the beach was not secure. So we milled around the harbour, taking orders to get out of the way of other ships that were sending men in.'

As well as carrying soldiers and equipment into the fight, Leon's ship received those who had been wounded in the battle.

'By virtue of the fact that we carried an army/navy surgical team and forty corpsmen, even before our troops had really been hitting the beach, we were taking aboard casualties. Our doctors were working all over the place. Between the German and American casualties, we had about four hundred casualties aboard ship. They were all on the tank deck in stretchers. The funny part of it is, the Germans and the Americans were exchanging photographs of their families and cigarettes with each other. Just a few hours before they were fighting.'

Although Leon saw acts of shared humanity between enemies, he also saw an ugly side of human nature while close to the beach. 'Some of our troops really had taken about as much punishment as they could. We witnessed some German prisoners coming down and the Americans killed them right there, they shot them.'

Robert 'Bob' Lowry, of New Orleans, was serving aboard LST-538. It wasn't until the afternoon that his ship went into the shore. 'We got most of the gear off. The trucks and the tanks. All of a sudden I saw a bunch of people coming in, and they were wounded, and they put them on the ship. I'll never forget there was a fella, he was down in my living quarters. And he was sitting on the bottom bunk, and he had a patch on his eye, and he asked me if I had a cigarette.'

Bob was sent by an officer to carry a message to the operating room. 'I don't have a stomach for that. They had guys opened up.' The operating room was soon overwhelmed, and surgery spread to other parts of the ship. 'That night, I was sitting in my bunk, and they had a table where you play cards and so on. And they brought a fella in, and they started taking his leg off.'

LST-538 returned to Southampton to unload the wounded and load fresh troops. Their next destination was the British sector. During the night, the crew were called to general quarters.

'You could see boats coming, riding around the water.' These were German E-boats, and a torpedo streaked by the front of Bob's LST. An explosion followed. 'It felt like the ship just came out the water. I had a helmet on. Later on, I took the helmet and I looked at it. It was black almost, from powder. We lost four people. Four people were blown overboard.'

The ship's gun turret had been blown clean off the vessel, and its crew were lost with it. 'And I saw . . .' At this point in the interview, Bob fought back emotion and his voice trailed away.

On D-Day he was eighteen years old.

'No Mission Too Difficult. No Sacrifice Too Great. Duty First!' – the 1st Infantry Division landings on the eastern sectors of Omaha

Irwin Stovroff was the son of a Siberian immigrant. After he graduated from the University of Illinois, Irwin enlisted in the USAAF and became part of a B24 bomber crew.

His first combat mission was on 6 June 1944.

'It was incredible. We got up early and we were told, "Gentlemen, when you prepare your engines, you're going to be part of history, because your first mission is going to be D-Day."'

As they flew towards France, Irwin marvelled at the sight of the armada. 'Going over the Channel you don't see any water, because it was nothing but boats, and boats, and boats. It was an incredible sight.'

After dropping their bombs on the coast and returning home, their aircraft was rearmed, refuelled, and sent up again. 'It was the only time you had to fly two missions in one day,' he said. 'And the beautiful part about it was, by that time, we had P51s. (Friendly fighters) were there on top of us, so we had very little problems on D-Day with going in, dropping our bombs, and leaving. It was really exciting to think that, "Oh my gosh, we're in on it! Right then and there!"' As the bombardier, housed in the front of the aircraft in a glass 'bubble', Irwin had the best view of all the crew. 'You saw everything. It was just an incredible day.'

Eveline Peardon was a young child who had known nothing but the German occupation. She lived with her mother and grandparents, her grandfather the mayor of a village on the eastern side of Omaha Beach.

'What I remember is the early morning of D-Day, because of the noise . . . it was unbelievable.

'I remember at one point, the vibrations of the back and forth shelling, through the windows, it was big windows, tall windows, my mother got up and she said, "I'm going to open the windows to avoid that." I remember the picture of her going to the window, and the window burst into her face. She didn't get hurt or whatever but that picture, it's an image that I can't forget.'

Harold 'Hal' Shook graduated as a USAAF pilot just days after the attack on Pearl Harbor. At twenty-three years old he was given command of his own squadron. Due to the versatility of the P47, he found himself flying numerous types of missions, from fighter sweeps to dive-bombing.

'Our mission on D-Day was to cover Omaha Beach at all costs. There were forty of us from our fighter group. (They said,) "If you lose all of them, and you've kept the Luftwaffe off their back, you've done your job." They said, "If you get into a fight, you stay there until the bloody end. If you run out of fuel, you keep right on fighting when the engine quits. If you run out of ammunition, ram 'em." '

No sooner had Hal's squadron arrived over the beach than one of his pilots was shot down by flak. Hal was given permission to go down to see if he could help him, but this brought him into the sights of hundreds of naval anti-aircraft guns in the invasion fleet, and he soon had to pull up and clear out. 'They were trigger-happy. They didn't want any fighter diving on them, so they were gonna have me for breakfast.'

Hal had the utmost respect for infantrymen. 'These poor buggers on the ground. You can't look down and see the hand-to-hand fighting, but by God, you know it's just a hell on wheels down there. They're the ones to whom we owe much. They gave their lives so that we can enjoy the freedoms such as we know today.'

The 1st Infantry Division came ashore onto the Easy Red and Fox Green sectors of Omaha Beach. Unlike the 29th to their west, the 1st Infantry Division was a seasoned formation: D-Day was their third amphibious assault of the war, having taken part in Operations Torch (North Africa) and Husky (Sicily). Though it was regarded as a battle-tested division, many of the 1st ID's soldiers would be seeing action for the first time. New replacements had taken the places of the men lost in the fighting in Sicily, but the old hands were under no illusions about what awaited them on the beach.

William Smith had wrestled for Ohio State before joining the army, and had been with the 1st Infantry Division since North Africa. As a forward observer for artillery and naval gunfire, Smith would be going ashore before the first wave.

Under cover of darkness, William was taken to shore on a raft. 'I knew then that I was all alone, and that's a little bit scary. But I had a friend. And I said, "OK, God. I know you didn't . . .

put me through North Africa and Sicily . . . and give me one of your precious damn radios, just to get me killed before I can use it." '

It is testament to the D-Day preparations that William knew exactly where he needed to go to get into position. 'I had to find three posts with the wire wrapped around it. That was the only safe gap. If I missed it, I was done.'

In darkness, William found the wires exactly where intelligence said they would be. Then he followed a path through the beach obstacles and onto the soft sand. He knew from the aerial photographs that there was a clump of rock that would provide him some cover during the coming battle. 'I put my feet in first, got my tail under cover, then all this rock that I had scattered, I pulled it around me.'

After evading the mines and boobytraps, William celebrated his successful insertion onto the beach. 'I took the first drag on that pipe that I'd had for about twenty-four hours. I pictured my darling in (her) chair, with a cup of coffee up near her lips. And I said, "Boy, thank you God, I needed that." '

William waited for daylight, and saw that the Germans were oblivious as to what was ahead. 'All the lights came on in concrete blocks. You can see guys in there washing their faces.'

The storm of steel began shortly before dawn. 'The *Arkansas* fired at about 0530, and I thought, "OK, it's showtime," and I flipped on the radio.'

William, who hadn't eaten in twenty hours, called down fire on a blockhouse where Germans were taking their breakfast. 'That was the first target that I took, was that damned guy that was eating. I fired a whole battery of four guns on a battleship at that thing. Then, I took to firing on this one which was raising Cain. That 88 was just chewing up the whole place. They couldn't miss. I was trying to find it, and I could not. And then all of a sudden here comes the snout of that thing out of a hole. That was where they were hiding.'

William called in the 88's position and it was soon knocked out. His actions that day undoubtedly saved many men in the approaching landing craft.

One of those heading into the beach was Bruce LaRose. A soldier in the 1st Infantry Division, this was his third amphibious assault of the war. Having served as a rifleman, he was now part of the regiment's cannon company using 105mm M3 howitzers. 'We left the mothership, it was about 0330, 0350 in the morning.'

LaRose was going ashore on a DUKW, an amphibious truck which was launched from an LST. 'The doors opened. The ramps went down. Down (the DUKW) went. It sunk. I took a nice long step out into the ocean, and stripped everything. This was my third landing, and I knew you don't tie your shoes. Your belt's open. The buttons on your trousers are all loose, very loose, so that it will all come off. Pop your webbing on your cartridge belt, that will release your trousers. That's why everything comes off. I had a tin hat, I don't know what happened to that. I had a prayer book in my pocket and a wristwatch, both waterproofed.

'I'm floating about in the water and a boat with two sailors come by. They pulled me out. I'm breathless. I see the ramp blown off. I don't know how far we had gone, but then the water came in, and it went down.'

Bruce now found himself floating in the Channel for a second time. 'And then a DUKW came by, full of ammunition. That one didn't sink. The waves didn't seem as bad. Maybe that was because we were closer in.'

He was then transferred to a ship carrying anti-aircraft guns. 'It was just guns on the deck. And from that one I was transferred to another boat that took us to a PT (patrol torpedo) boat, but none of these ships can go in. By now we're right up at the beach, but I couldn't go ashore in the PT boat. So they took us over to an LST.'

Bruce climbed a cargo net to get onboard. The LST came into shore and hit a sandbar. 'We ran out the front. Hey, Hallelujah, I'm on Omaha Beach!'

But any relief Bruce had for being ashore was short-lived.

'They shot the hell out of us. You couldn't move. You'd think everybody in the German army was shooting at you. A lot of guys were killed in the water.'

Chuck Thomas was also coming ashore with the 1st Infantry Division. 'As we approached the beach, the coxman on the boat was killed trying to open a ramp from the outside. Then Lieutenant Scott was hit in the arm trying to open it. He finally got it open, and I was last off the boat because I had a pole charge and I was in the corner.

'The boat was bobbing in between obstacles with Teller mines on the ends. I jumped off the ramp in the water about waist deep. But before I knew it, it was over my head. Although I know how to swim, I was scared because there were bullets landing all around in the water. Now you have thirty pounds of T&T to worry about, my helmet slung back on my neck, and I was dragging my rifle by the sling one arm underwater, and I couldn't reach the bottom, so I squeezed my life vest . . . I choked on salt water and coughed.

'Then besides me, a sergeant bobbed up . . . and he can't swim. Swinging his arms. He dropped all his equipment. Scared the hell out of me because all I could do myself was try to reach the bottom with my feet. So I push my pole-charge into him. Told him to hang on, and I left him.

'Finally I felt the bottom, but it was still slow going. In my head it seemed like an hour before I got to the shoreline, but it

111

was probably ten or fifteen minutes. When I finally got ashore there were a lot of wounded and dead, but you couldn't tell who was who. And we had orders when we reached the beach (to) get as far in as we could. Don't stop to help any wounded because the medics would take care of them. And we'd get shot ourself if we waited too long.'

Sergeant Robert Blatnik knew this. He was an experienced soldier fighting his third campaign. 'When we landed, the Germans were in full force. Man, we were slaughtered. Bodies were flying everywhere. One of my soldiers asked me, "Sarge, do we dig in?" I said, "Hell no, if you dig in, you're digging your grave. This place is zeroed in. Our only salvation is to go forward. Once you face the enemy, you got a chance of getting out alive." How in hell we ever made it off that beach I'll never know.'

'(The waterline) was crowded with men being killed and wounded,' recalled Chuck Thomas. 'Some are trying to dig in with their bare hands. There were mortar and artillery shells landing all over the place. I don't know why, I lay out on my side and open my fly to urinate. I was soaking wet anyway. One guy next to me had a (piece of shrapnel) slice through his helmet. (It) went through a pair of socks he had and carried with him inside his helmet. Didn't hit his head, so he was lucky. Now another buddy had a large chunk of his buttocks blown away. So we poured sulfur powder on it and he was laughing. I guess he was numb from shock.' Chuck saw three tanks nearby. 'Two were knocked out. Colonel Taylor was there directing the fire of one tank that was left.'

Bob Miksa, of the 745th Tank Battalion, came ashore at Easy Red. 'I was driving for the platoon leader, Lieutenant Davis. The other fellas were right behind us, following. I couldn't see nothing because the water was splashing, the periscope was clouded over with water. When I was on the shore, then I could see the big cliff in front. All along the shore were the guys that were wounded.

We couldn't move too much because, you know, we had so much debris, and the guys were laying there. All you could do was wait, pray, see what's gonna happen. We had one tank commander that stuck his head out and a sniper got him. That was the first guy of our outfit that got killed.'

Bob recalled the carnage on the beach, and knew what it meant for families back home. 'You could see guys lying there – bodies, half bodies, heads off, arms off. I kept thinking about their mothers that would get a letter from the government saying their son was killed on Omaha Beach. But if you see what he looks like now, you wouldn't be too happy.'

Those who survived the landing now fought to gain a foothold inland.

'My unit then took Colleville-sur-Mer,' said Bruce LaRose. He should have been manning one of the unit's howitzers, but all six had been lost during the landing. 'That meant that we fought as a rifle company with the 1st Battalion.' They cleared the coastal villages before becoming engaged in hedgerow fighting. Bruce described the terrain: 'For a thousand years, farmers have piled the rocks from their fields, and dirt, and trees grow out of it. They were great protection, but they were also protection for the Germans, so we had to get a way to get through these hedgerows. Tanks had a hell of a time there, I think, but a better time than we did.'

Chuck Thomas was also able to make it off the beach. 'I worked my way over to a bombed-out house but with no roof, just walls. For the first time, I found a lot of my buddies. To my surprise, a lot of them didn't even have a rifle, and a lot of them bummed cigarettes off me. I had two and a half cartons and all my equipment. Just beyond the wall in the house there was a ditch with barbed wire and a path going up the hill . . . We finally blew the barbed wire with Bangalore torpedoes, long pipes of TNT put together. When it blew, we started one at a time to go over the collapsed wire under machine-gun fire. When it stopped, one of us would run and jump through the wire. I tripped but managed to crawl through it.

'When we got to the top, I can see the whole beach. What a mess. We only had enough men to make up two squads. So I mean, about twenty-five, maybe thirty guys after we met at the top of the hill. So we divided up and on both sides of the field, along the hedgerows. We had no radio or communications to anyone. As far as I could see, the Germans could have swept us off with brooms if they knew we were there with so few men. My best buddy from Chicago, named David, put on his glasses. He said, "Now I can see them." Ten minutes later he was killed. I felt sick about it.'

The Cost

It wasn't only servicemen who lost their lives on D-Day. Maurice Franklin was part of a British anti-aircraft unit that landed at Omaha, and learned this first hand.

'We managed to advance a bit into this village eventually. I don't even remember the name of this village. I'll tell you something that happened that shook me. When we advanced on top of these cliffs . . . we found about six luxury caravans. Now I don't know, none of us knew what luxury caravans were doing on the front line of a German unit. They were beautiful. Opened the doors of these caravans, they were beautifully equipped, most modern caravans, magnificent. I thought, soldiers couldn't live in a place like this. When we got into this village it was deserted, nobody was there, it was empty, the Germans had left. That's when we discovered what these caravans were for . . . these were mobile brothels which the Germans had brought to the front line. When we went to this well to get water, we found out that when the Germans retreated . . . they cut the throats of these girls and dumped them in the well.'

No two beaches on D-Day differed more in their ferocity and bloodshed than those assigned to the US First Army. While Utah saw the lightest casualties of any landing, with the beachhead secured in a matter of hours, Omaha was a meat-grinder where victory was far from assured. Of all five beaches on the Normandy coast, it was at Omaha where the greatest fears of the Allied planners, personnel, and public were almost realized.

This, of course, does not diminish the actions or sacrifices on Utah. 'Light' casualties of around 200 still means that many men died in their youth. In history, we too often say that 'only' X numbers of casualties died in a given battle, but for the parents who lost a son, or the child who lost a parent, 'only' is 'everything'.

Estimates range from 3,500 to 6,000 casualties on Omaha, with some 800 men killed.

The cost of the battle is a reflection of how close the landing at Omaha came to failure. General Omar Bradley, commander of the US First Army, worried that the 29th Infantry Division had 'suffered an irreversible catastrophe'.[2] But while the unexpected presence of the 352nd Division – with 12,000 men either on, or close to Omaha – almost tipped the balance in Germany's favour, the tenacity and bravery of the assaulting troops, coupled with support of naval gunfire and domination in the skies, triumphed in the end. The 'ifs, buts, and maybes' can be left to historians and armchair generals to discuss. For the troops who took part in the landings at Omaha, the reality was a bloody, but decisive victory. From 6 June, each shipload of men and equipment that landed in Normandy was one more nail in the Nazi coffin. The end was not near for the Americans who survived D-Day – some continued fighting right through to Germany, and many died doing so – but after Omaha, it was at least in sight.

CHAPTER FOUR

To Win or Lose It All

The Battle for the Eastern Beaches

'We were firing. There was a machine-gun post in the
front. Big concrete pillbox. And shells was coming over,
and mortars. Blokes are screaming . . . shouting, "Medics
here! Stretchers, here!" It was just hell to me. I didn't think
I'd come out of this.'

Norman Madden, 1st Armoured Battalion,
Coldstream Guards

With the United States Navy largely engaged in the Pacific campaign against the Japanese, it fell to the Royal and Merchant
navies to provide most of the ships that would be used on D-Day,
with around 80 per cent of the 7,000 vessels involved flying British flags.

Many of the naval crews involved in D-Day were already seasoned sailors. John Carlill, eighteen years old, was a veteran of
enemy action in the Mediterranean, and served as a midshipman
aboard the cruiser *Mauritius*. He recalled one of his final moments
before boarding. 'I had been one of the last ashore before sailing,

and had been surprised, and a bit disturbed, because many of the young Wrens in the Greenock Base had been in tears as I, and others, had handed in the personal records of our ships.' The *Mauritius* then began to make her way south from Scotland for the assembly of the largest seaborne invasion force in history.

Born in Tonypandy, Arthur 'Larry' Fursland was a stoker aboard HMS *Belfast*, a cruiser that had served in several major actions. In March of '44, Arthur was awarded the Distinguished Service Medal for the following action:

> As a L/Stoker on board *Belfast* on December 26 1943 in the Battle of North Cape, the action that sank the *Scharnhorst*, he was at action stations on the port main diesel generator on his own for 12 hours. During the action the cooling water for the engine started to fail and overheat, so he went to the passage above and connected a canvas hose to a fire-main and ran it down to connect it directly to the diesel cooling system; he was later told that his actions had kept a gun turret in action and was awarded the DSM.[1]

Although his duty station was below decks, Arthur was able to watch as the *Belfast* made her way into the English Channel. 'I had free time to watch . . . I never went down below. I enjoyed everything. Once we got round Land's End I never seen such an armada in all my life. All the bays and all the coves, ships of every description coming out. Hundreds of them. Hundreds.'

Minesweeping vessels preceded the task forces, laying out coloured buoys to mark the cleared channels.

'We were cruising between two lines of red and green lights,' said Joe Minogue, a gunner in a Sherman flail tank of the Westminster Dragoons, who was watching from aboard an LCT. 'The whole thing were just a great motorway which somebody had

British paratroopers of the 6th Airborne Division aboard
an aircraft en route to their drop site on D-Day.

Officers and crew of the frigate HMS *Holmes* keep watch from the ship's bridge
as aircraft and gliders carrying the British 6th Airborne Division reinforcements
to Normandy pass overhead on the evening of 6 June.

'We'll start the war from right here.' American troops of the
4th Infantry Division land on Utah Beach on D-Day.

US soldiers protect themselves from artillery fire on Utah Beach.
Young men unused to war found it hard to believe people were trying to kill them.

Naval gunfire supports assault troops landing at Omaha Beach on D-Day.
The first waves faced heavy fire from formidable German defences.

American assault troops of the 3rd Battalion, 16th Infantry Regiment, 1st Infantry Division,
stopping in the shelter of the chalk cliff on Omaha before pushing inland.

Canadian soldiers from the 9th Brigade land with their bicycles at Juno Beach during D-Day.

British troops from the 8th Brigade, 3rd Infantry Division of the British Second Army come ashore on Queen Red sector, Sword Beach, as medics help wounded men on the shoreline.

Having cleared the beach, men from No. 4 Commando, supported by Sherman DD (Duplex Drive) tanks of 'B' Squadron, 13th/18th Royal Hussars, advance towards Ouistreham.

A moment of shared humanity, as a German prisoner poses
with a British soldier in the early days of the invasion.

American soldiers looking for German gunmen lying in ambush in a village around Carentan in June 1944.

Men of the Durham Light Infantry attending to German wounded near Lingèvres, 14 June.

US medics taking an injured man for treatment in the bocage, inland from Utah, in June. Fighting through the hedgerows was slow and attritional.

Hawker Typhoon pilots of No. 181 Squadron RAF leave the briefing tent
at B2/Bazenville for a midday sortie over the Normandy battlefield.

German troops studying maps at a camouflaged
anti-aircraft position in the Normany countryside.

American troops entering Cherbourg, which was liberated in late June.

American soldiers enjoying some 'hot chow' after the liberation of Cherbourg.

devised . . . It was a fantastic sight really to see so many ships of all shapes and sizes heading down the Channel, and all going one way.'

But although the sights were inspiring, the conditions at sea were far from enjoyable, particularly for the men on the flat-bottomed landing ships which rolled around in the swell.

'One felt absolutely dreadful physically. One wasn't being actually sick but you felt fit for absolutely nothing. Most of the journey we spent lying in a tarpaulin stretched around the tank, and just wishing to God that the whole thing would be over, or at least that we could get on dry land. I would say that the success of the actual invasion was simply the fact that the soldiers were so glad to get off the landing craft and to escape the seasickness. They were just ready to go anywhere by that time.'

'Battle ensigns were hoisted,' John Carlill recalled. His cruiser *Mauritius* and other vessels approached the coast through a dense smoke screen intended to keep them from the sights of the coastal guns, but there was another threat on the water: two German torpedo boats came out of the port of Le Havre and attacked John's group. 'One of our escorting destroyers, a Norwegian, was sunk. And other ships, my own included, were near-missed by torpedoes. The attack was successfully repulsed, but it had been an unwelcome curtain-raiser.' The Norwegian vessel was the *Svenner*. She was struck amidships, broke in half, and quickly sank. Thirty-three of her crew were killed, with the others rescued by nearby ships.*

Sailors who were not on duty came on deck to watch the action unfold.

'I came off watch at 0400,' said Arthur Fursland on the *Belfast*.

* The *Svenner*'s anchor was recovered in 2003, and is now a memorial at Sword Beach.

'My vantage point was in the welldeck by the catapult. There was an hour and a half before the main landings. I shall never forget it in all my life . . . All of a sudden all hell broke out.'

As part of Task Force E, which was assigned to the eastern beaches, the *Belfast*'s first target was the German gun battery at La Marefontaine.[2] Arthur watched in awe as hundreds of ships pounded the French coast. 'There couldn't have been a rat alive.'

Gordon Painter was one of twenty-six men inside a six-inch gun turret aboard the *Belfast*. 'We started our bombardment about half-past five that morning. 'It was quite noisy, of course. We were firing broadsides, which means that all the guns were firing together. The whole lot. Twelve six-inch guns. It rocks the ship backwards and forwards. It was some experience.'

Though the men at the ship's guns were an integral part of the operation, they saw little of the invasion taking place.

'The only time we could leave was if nature called, and you had somebody to take over from you. I didn't see a lot that was going on. We had a spotter plane which was attached to us. Who that guy was of course I'll never know. It would have been nice to have met him. He was radioing back to the *Belfast* to tell us exactly where our shells were dropping.'

'We were shelling just past where the troops were landing,' recalled Ray Smith, aboard the *Middleton*. 'We spent a long time bombarding the coast. It was constant, the noise and everything. We had two trips back to port to refuel and rearm, then kept doing the same thing until they were established (on the beaches). (The battle) was frightening really. The continuous noise of those guns was the worst thing really. The noise and the damage being done was awful. We saw a lot of the tanks that were supposed to be amphibious . . . In rough seas they sank almost straight away.'

From the *Belfast*, Ted Cordery watched as landing craft took the infantry towards the shore. 'I was looking over the side thinking, All these poor buggers, how many of those were gonna go back home?'

'After a while there was bodies floating around,' said Arthur Fursland. 'Picket boats was going through the bodies, but they'd stop and take the disc off them.' This would be to identify the men who had died before they ever made it to the beach.

Aboard the *Belfast*, the crew were told the results of their gunnery. 'They put a notice up on the board,' said Arthur. 'We silenced, I don't know, whether it was eight or eleven (emplacements) in twenty-seven minutes.'

The *Mauritius* was also firing onto the coast, and inland. 'Our targets varied from artillery positions, tank and infantry concentrations, down to single machine guns,' said John Carlill. 'In return, my ship was subjected to spasmodic but accurate shelling. The Luftwaffe, potentially the greatest threat, hardly put in an appearance.'

Twenty-year-old Norman Madden, of the 1st Armoured Battalion, Coldstream Guards, watched the action from the deck of an LCT. '(A battleship) was firing these shells over . . . the whole boat used to rock as we passed it. They seemed to be firing over us, and it seemed non-stop in my mind, and I thought, Well, nobody can be alive when we land.'

The massive bombardment was audible for tens of miles, no doubt souring the stomachs of many of the men who would have to stand against the invasion.

Gunter von Waskowsi was a twenty-three-year-old in a Wehrmacht heavy artillery regiment. He had already seen combat on the Eastern Front, and experienced Allied bombing in Germany. In June 1944, his 184th Battery was based in the Fécamp area of France, about fifty miles north-east of the landing beaches. 'In general we had very good relations with the French,' he said. 'They seemed to go along. What else could they do? (Soldiers) stayed with families. I think in general there was quite a good relationship. Later, what you can hear about the underground, I think that was mainly in bigger towns. In little villages it didn't happen there. At least it didn't happen in our place.'

Normandy was a relatively peaceful posting, but that was about to change.

'I was sent up as forward observation officer to the coast, and suddenly I came up to near the coast, and saw this . . . well, one can't describe it, really. To see the bay full of ships. There were hundreds of ships there, some firing. I'd never seen anything like it. It was so unbelievable. And at that time I felt, you can't compete with that.'

Gold Beach

While the armada was impressive, and its bombardment powerful, it would come down to the infantry and other combat arms to drive the Germans back from the beach.

The defences at Gold were manned by elements of the 716th Division and the 1st Battalion, 352nd Division, which was focused around Le Hamel and consisted of better quality troops than those of the 716th. Most occupied houses along the coast, which were vulnerable to heavy artillery from the sea and bombs from the air, but half a mile inland, on the outskirts of Longues-sur-Mer, was an observation post with four 155mm guns protected by thick concrete. In Bayeux, the Kampfgruppe Meyer, a mechanized detachment of the 352nd, had been well drilled in rapid manoeuvres to the beach should the Allies attempt to invade.

'In the dawn the whole thing seemed to come to a standstill, and we were just swaying about off the coast,' Joe Minogue said. 'The fears were mounting. I wouldn't say that we were cowards as such. I think that everybody who was involved in the invasion was afraid. And later one learned to realize that this was what war is about. That it's really two groups of very frightened men facing each other.'

Joe's fear was that he would be drowned before reaching the beach. 'We were more scared of that business of coming down the ramp of the landing craft, and going into water that was so deep that the whole tank would be submerged, and we would just be drowned.'

His LCT hit the beach at 0725, five minutes ahead of schedule. 'We were the fourth tank off the landing craft, and we were all very worried about this business of the water. And I think the driver of the tank was a bit more apprehensive than the rest of us, because he blew part of the waterproofing (a little early), and we all thought. "This is it, we've been hit and this is the end of it!"'

Though Joe's tank had not been hit, several others were already in trouble.

'I saw that the three (tanks) in front of us were not doing too well. The first tank had stopped because its commander had been killed, the second tank had been a bit too close to him and had slewed to the right and had hit a clay patch on the beach . . . and the tank behind him, they had a hit on the petrol tank which set the thing on fire. And we saw the crew busily scrambling out. This didn't do a great deal for our confidence.

'At that moment the tank commander hit me on the head with his microphone, which was his famous signal for me to do the 360-degree traverse to break the sealing around the turret. This gave me really an absolutely fantastic view of the whole thing.

'As the turret came back towards the sea you could see the infantry beginning to come ashore, and it was like something from a kind of cartoon in a way . . . I suppose there must have been a couple of machine guns which were raking across the beach, and you'd see chaps coming off these small landing craft, they'd be waist deep or chest deep in water, and they'd begin to run forward up the beach, and suddenly you'd see the odd figure fall here and there. It wasn't a matter of a whole line of men going down, it seemed as though one in five, or a small group might go down, and a chap would be lying doubled up on the beach, and some people would run past him, another couple of his mates might drag him.'

Joe's tank flailed the ground as it moved, detonating several mines before they made it onto the road at the top of the beach. It was deserted but for a single enemy soldier.

'There was a dead German there, and it was just like something from a film.'

To clear his machine gun of any waterproofing or debris, Joe fired it down the empty road. 'And at that very moment . . . three of our infantrymen burst through a hedge at the side of the road, and suddenly one of them fell as though he'd been hit, and the other two dragged him back.' For the rest of his life, Joe would wonder if it was his bullets that had struck the soldier.

D-Day was Joe's first time in action, as it was for many British soldiers, but General Montgomery had insisted that several veteran formations take part in the landings. For many soldiers of the Devonshire Regiment, 6 June marked their third amphibious operation of the war.

'We'd done Sicily and Italy,' said Cyril Wright, an experienced soldier of that regiment. 'We knew what to expect.'

'Everyone in the battalion was very seasick,' said William Hanna, a sniper in the Hampshires. 'I wasn't so much worried about what the German army were doing, or how strong they were. All I was concerned about was getting my feet on dry land.'

William's assault craft grounded before it ever reached the beach. 'We had to wade ashore.'

As well as his rifle and personal equipment, William was

carrying bombs for the mortar platoon, and the weight of his gear meant that he was up to his neck in water.

'We then come under very heavy fire. We come under artillery fire, mortar fire, and of course we suffered a lot of casualties from small-arms fire. That was the reception for us when we landed.'

Men began to disappear in the surf.

'As soon as we hit the water we then started taking in casualties, which meant that some soldiers, young soldiers who had done a lot of training, long arduous training . . . they actually got killed in the water without firing a shot. They never fired a shot.'

The assault troops had been told to press on no matter the casualties.

'We couldn't attend to people as they were dropping around you. You had to get on, because the idea was to get inland as quick as possible. Your orders were, leave them right where they are. If you can pull them out of the water, OK, do so, but you mustn't hold up the attack.'

Every second that went by seemed to bring more casualties. 'You could see people falling all around. But you had your own problems and you got on with it.'

Cyril Wright saw men disappear beneath the water, never to emerge. While some of them were hit by enemy fire, others were dragged down by their equipment and drowned. 'Where our people had been shelling and bombing before there was all craters (beneath the water), and a lot went down in (them).'

Ronald White, also of the Hampshires, was returning to the country where he had served with the ill-fated British Expeditionary Force in 1940. He landed behind the first wave, coming ashore with the support company at around 0735.

'Snipers, that was the thing we dreaded. They were everywhere. Our CO, he got wounded as he landed. And Major Martin, he come to shore to take over. He stepped ashore, he got shot. Sniper got him. And when I landed, I was speaking to a wireless operator. He just sighed, and fell forward. We had no tank support at all . . . It was so rough they were sinking. They stopped sending them.'

On other sectors of Gold Beach, the armour was having more success.

'We drove off the tank landing craft and up the beach, and all hell let loose,' said Norman Madden. 'I was scared, believe me. I was only nineteen. I seen, in my mind, over a hundred killed and injured of ours. Quite a few tanks was lost.'

The tank crews endeavoured to give as good as they got.

'We were firing. There was a machine-gun post in the front. Big concrete pillbox. And shells was coming over, and mortars. Blokes are screaming . . . shouting, "Medics here! Stretchers, here!" It was just hell to me. I didn't think I'd come out of this.'

Infantry went in to clear the enemy out of their positions at close quarters.

'They brought in the flamethrowers. This was two men, and they opened up with these flamethrowers onto these pillboxes . . . when they got to the pillbox, I was all watching this from the tank, as they passed the pillbox they'd be throwing grenades in.'

Richard Gosling commanded the 431st Battery of the Essex Yeomanry. He came ashore ahead of his self-propelled guns so that he could direct their fire.

'We quite expected a lot of us would be killed, but we were entirely confident (of victory), and we were very well trained. As we got nearer (to the beach) we could see one or two flashes from German guns on the other side. Then we heard something, which, because I had been born and bred in the country, I thought it was a swarm of bees. It wasn't. It was the German machine guns.'

Richard's unit was mostly made up of men from the same towns of Essex, many of them friends from before the war. 'We knew that whatever happened, we were going to have friends with us. And this was absolutely vital, because when we landed, I had to jump ashore, and I held the hand of a man behind me, and I said, "If anything happens to you I'll pull you ashore." And sure enough, as soon as we started to wade, he disappeared from sight, and all I had left was his hand sticking out of the water. And he'd put his foot into a shell hole under the water there, but I pulled him out.'

Richard then set foot on foreign soil. 'This was the first time I'd been out of England. And there I was wading ashore in France to fight the Germans.'

He had only been ashore for a few moments when he was hit by an exploding shell. 'There was a great bang just behind me . . . and suddenly I found my legs were kicked away from me . . . and poor old Nelson Smith, the colonel next to me, his arm was shot through the elbow . . . and I could just hobble.'

Try as he might, Richard had no luck in contacting his unit by radio. 'I couldn't get any messages through at all. We scratched ourselves into the sand dune, and we could hear these Germans firing their machine guns through the rushes over our head.'

A corporal and a few wounded men of the Hampshires lay next to him. '(The corporal) put his head up to look over the sand dunes, to see what was happening on the other side, and as soon as he done that he was shot straight through the chest.'

Richard decided that he needed to see what lay ahead of them and, although wounded, began to crawl up the dunes, holding the revolver that had been given to him by an uncle who had served in the Boer War. When he reached the top of the dunes, Richard found himself looking into the eyes of a German soldier.

'I didn't like the look of him and he didn't like the look of me. I fired my revolver, hopefully in his direction, and I slid back. By that time the rest of the battalion of the Hampshires had come in . . . And you could see some of the Essex Yeomanry behind us. Some of the guns had started to land.'

These self-propelled guns had been landed late, and out of position, but were soon put to work ashore. Earlier that morning, they had been providing fire from the decks of their landing craft.

As the beach was cleared, Richard was taken to an aid station that had been set up in a knocked-out pillbox. 'Breakfast was still on the table.' He also found a letter, presumably written by the French girlfriend of one of the German soldiers. '(It said) I will meet you behind the pillbox at six o'clock in the evening on the 6th of June . . . and it was signed Madeline. And so we all looked out and waited for Madeline to come along, but (she) never did come.'

The 9th Battalion of the Durham Light Infantry landed on Gold as part of the reserve brigade. Having seen war first hand, soldiers like Jimmy Wilkinson didn't hold out much hope for their survival in Normandy.

'I thought most of the first and second waves would go down, like most people did, but never mind. There was nothing you could do about it, that was the thing.'

'We heard a hell of a noise going on the beaches,' said Major John Mogg of the 9th DLI, who landed at 0900. 'It was a scene of really a lot of activity by the beach brigade trying to make holes through the mines. There were flail tanks trying to flail up the mines. There were one or two (Bren) carriers that had been brewed up. There was the odd sort of tank that had been brewed up.'

Richard Phillips was the intelligence sergeant of the 2nd Battalion, South Wales Borderers. Though his regiment wasn't scheduled to land until the afternoon, Richard and three other men from the battalion's intelligence section landed with the assault brigade. This was to allow them to mark the route and forming-up points for the battalion to follow when they came ashore.

'We landed with a company of the Hampshire Regiment, and several tanks. It's all very difficult to (explain) the amount of shelling that was going on at that particular time. There was an awful lot of young fellers in the surf. They'd never got onto the beach. They were still in the sea. There was an awful lot of them.

'We got the jeep through the water quite safely, and then the shelling began to get a bit more furious. I saw a tank which had been blown (onto its side), and I told the jeep driver to go and try and get behind him to give him an amount more shelter.'

Richard realized his mistake when the jeep became stuck in the crater of the mine that had destroyed the tank. His captain ordered two of the men to try to recover it, while he and Richard proceeded inland with the signage that would direct the battalion. Their only weapons were two pistols containing six rounds of ammunition apiece.

'Although it was our first time there, we knew exactly where we had to go. Every house was put down, shown on the relief maps before we left the (staging area in Britain). We put down the signs from the beaches to the rendezvous area, where the battalion arrived at around two o'clock in the afternoon.'

As they moved from the beach inland, Richard saw the effects of Allied air and sea power.

'There was an awful lot of dead Germans. They'd been shot up by aircraft. In one jeep there was four young German officers. They'd been decimated really with the fire from these fighter planes that were coming over. Just prior to that there must have been around about a platoon of infantry, and they had been made the target of the two battle cruisers that were lying broadside on . . . that was a real awful sight really. You could pick up any part of a human body. They'd been blown to bits. And God knows how many French people had died in Le Hamel, because that was shelled and bombed quite heavily.'

Like every beach on D-Day, not everything on Gold had gone to plan.

'I think anybody that has been in any army in the world knows that if anything can go wrong, it usually does,' said Joe Minogue.

'We were promised a lot of artillery support, mortar support, the flail tank,' recalled William Hanna, 'and we also should have had tanks with us. Now, it was obvious very, very quickly that that support wasn't available. Only two supporting boats out of sixteen actually arrived at our beachhead. So it really meant that the Hampshires, we had to fight entirely as an infantry battalion with the infantry weapons that we carried. So we really went into it headfirst. There were 182 casualties out of the battalion in those first few hours. Which is quite a percentage out of 600 people.'

But despite these casualties, the battalion pressed on towards their objectives of Le Hamel East, Asnelles-sur-Mer, Hamel West, and Arromanches.[3]

'We had confidence in ourselves, in our brigade, and our Hampshires. Everybody,' said Ronald White. 'We done it twice, and we couldn't see us failing . . . And we never did. I'm very proud of those lads . . . They were marvellous.'

Joe Minogue's tank was supposed to rendezvous with several others in the village of Le Hamel. 'Only one tank ever got into Le Hamel,' said Joe, 'and he was shot up . . . two of the crew were taken prisoner and the other three hid in a cornfield all day. We finished up eventually with only two tanks which were on the road. Ours, and the one which had been following us.'

Joe's tank became stuck in a bomb crater inland, and the infantry used it for cover. 'They all got their fags out and had a bit of a breather. Eventually another tank came along and gave us a tow out of this hole . . . We finally finished up in a Frenchman's garden. I think he smoked about forty of our fags in about three hours.'

Their own D-Day mission complete, Joe and his crew became spectators of the invasion. 'We had a kind of bird's eye view of this fantastic build-up during the rest of the day, of all the stuff and equipment that was coming ashore.'

25,000 men were landed on Gold Beach on D-Day. Forward units pushed six miles inland, connected with the Canadians from Juno Beach, and reached the heights above Port-en-Bessin. The Caen–Bayeux highway was not cut, nor was there a link up with the Americans from Omaha Beach. British casualties at Gold are estimated at around 1,000, with some 350 men giving their lives.

Decades later, Joe reflected on his experience that day.

'I would hate for anybody to think that there's any kind of heroism about it. We'd got a job to do . . . I don't think any of us were patriotic men in the sense that we would stand rigidly to attention and wave flags, but I think we were proud, in some way, that we'd done it. And that the army we'd been in for so long, and with all sorts of experiences about how they could bungle things, had actually managed this invasion. It had been a fantastic piece of organization, and looking back . . . I can hear it, and I can see it, I can smell it. And I think anybody who was there must have exactly the same impression. It is something that they will always remember. And you read back now into the kind of afterthoughts of the historians, who can piece together all the bits that we didn't know . . . we were aware that we had been very, very lucky indeed. For us, it had been a kind of really glorified exercise, that our fears had fortunately not been realized. But we also realized something else. That we would never, whatever we were called upon to do, be quite as afraid again.'

'We Stand on Guard for Thee' – The Canadian Army's landing at Juno Beach

Michel Grimaux was an eleven-year-old living in Graye-sur-Mer. The small village lay a half mile inland from Juno Beach, where a bloody battle was about to begin.

'We were awoken by a roaring noise which we realized afterwards was the naval bombardment. In the room where I slept was a piano and on the piano were different objects which rattled. And very quickly we realized it was the landings. We left our house and we went into a trench which we had dug in the garden.'

As Michel and his family sought shelter, the men of the First Canadian Army were making their way towards the Normandy coast.

There is a video of the D-Day landings which is impossible to forget. As the doors of a landing craft open and the men file out towards the smoking buildings ahead, a soldier places a reassuring hand on his comrade's shoulder. The words that they shared are lost to us, but the simple gesture speaks loudly. The video was taken at Juno Beach, Nan sector, and caught the action of the North Shore (New Brunswick) Regiment, which had been training in Britain for three years. Twenty-three-year-old Havelyn Chiasson was one of their number, and about to experience battle for the first time in his young life.

'You had no idea that it was gonna be like that. No idea. No idea at all. Later on in the war of course, you realized what war was all about, but until then you didn't.'

The North Shore paid a heavy price for their part in the first wave, which landed at around 0800.

'Some of (the landing craft) hit mines and were blown up. Others hit reefs and got stuck there . . . a lot of (the men) were drowned. We lost a hundred men in our regiment killed or wounded. That was the biggest shock of all. We knew something was going to happen but we had no idea that that many men would be killed or wounded. And then of course the next day it didn't make any difference – it was just that somebody was killed, and you didn't pay much attention to it. You just had to keep on going.'[4]

Allied warships had opened fire on the German defences at 0617. The beach was six miles wide, and defended by the 716th Infantry Division, particularly the 736th Infantry Regiment. The bombardment had failed to destroy all the German gun emplacements in the Nan sector, and one concrete bunker system inflicted heavy casualties on the North Shores until it was finally silenced at 1130.

The Canadian landing at Juno was supported by several British units. Essex-born William 'Bill' Dunn was serving in 26 Assault Squadron, Royal Engineers. 'The waves were so high I think everybody would have fought to get off the landing craft.' Bill's LST ground to a halt on the shore at 0800 and the order was given to disembark. 'We all shout "good luck" to each other. One of these Canadian tanks came off in front of us with the flail and I was following him.

'The atmosphere in the tank was a little bit tense because you're battened down, and I was the only one that could see (through) my little visor that I had in front of me. And my co-driver was sitting behind me and kept asking me what was going on. My main concern when we got off that morning was seeing all the lads in the infantry being shot down and lying on the beach. And I was a bit concerned in case I hit any of them.'

Bill didn't know if the prone soldiers on the beach were dead, wounded, or taking cover.

'You had to pick your way through so you didn't catch any of them. But once I got off the beach and followed the route that I had to do, my mind straight away went to the job. And of course, we drove up the beach. Following this line, following this flail (tank), and the mines was going off as he was hitting them with the flail. But the trouble with the flail, it's all right going along level ground, but as soon as you start to go (up), it misses.'

It wasn't long before the flail tank's track was blown off, rendering it immobile. Bill's tank would have to take the lead.

'I had to push him to one side to carry on to where I had to go. And when I got to where we had to drop the fascine, we couldn't see it.'

'(I) couldn't see the culvert at all. But in my mind, that's where we should be. So I said to our sergeant, to my tank commander I said, "Jim, I can't see the culvert." So he radioed back to Captain Ewert who was on the beach and the orders we got (were to) carry on.' But when Bill drove forward, the front of his tank plunged down into a tank trap and filled with water. The crew had no choice but to bail out before they were drowned.

'Bullets were flying all over the place. I was last man out, and I start to swallow water actually. Because it was all coming in the turret and I was last one out. As my co-driver got out he put his knees in both sides of my head, and as he came out, he dragged me with him . . . Bill Hawkins was standing just outside of the turret, waiting on me coming out, to drag me out. And when we got out, he just hit me once in the stomach. He hadn't time for any niceties or anything like that. It just brought the water up and that was it. Of course, the bullets were still hitting the turret.'

Bill and the rest of the crew were aided to cover by the help of their officer. 'Captain Ewert . . . he'd come up then to see what was happening. And he put his tank between us and the Germans and drove and brought us back to the sand dunes. He went away and left us then. And we just lay down behind the sand dunes, and Jim Ashton started to sing "Kiss Me Again". Because, like a father figure, he was a good lad, he always did this. Tried to settle us all down . . . he always did something like this, he'd always sing or something, just trying to settle you, and he just started to sing when the mortar bombs came and dropped between us.'

The explosions had a devastating effect, immediately killing two of the crew, including Jim Ashton, and injuring the others. 'I was wounded,' said Bill, who had multiple fractures and shrapnel wounds. 'Bill Hawkins was badly wounded. The co-driver, he rolled over to me, and he had a hole in his back that I put me fist in. And he said, "I'll call for help." And he crawled away. I just saw him roll over there after he got about a hundred yards from us. And I was told that's where he died.'

Bill needed to find both cover and medical assistance, but his situation went from bad to worse.

'I rolled down into a minefield. In fact, when I looked up, there's a big board, "Achtung Minen", straight above me head. Cor blimey. So I managed to get onto my feet and I ran about fifty yards.'

He was later told by a doctor that this was impossible given the state of his injuries. 'And I said, "Well, when you're frightened and there's bullets flying around, it makes you do queer things." But I collapsed, my legs just gave away from me and I just collapsed. I didn't know how badly I was wounded then. Then I had two lads come and drag me, and I told them that Bill Hawkins was still up there and (they) asked me about the others. I said . . . "I'm pretty sure the others are dead." They took me further back and lay me beside another sand dune and gave me a cigarette and a drink. I was left there for quite a while, and the first one (who) came on the scene after that was a Canadian medical officer.'

Bill was given an injection of morphine for his pain, then left alone.

'I must have been lying with me eyes shut. Two Canadians came and they start to go through me pockets. And they took my watch, and my whistle, and I had a commando knife stitched to me trouser leg, and they took that. And then I opened me eyes and one of them turned around (and said), "You better leave this bugger, he's alive." '

Bill was finally carried back to the shoreline by two men from his own unit, and was reunited with his friend Bill Hawkins. Fifty feet away from them was a bulldozer with large plates of armour covering its door.

'(A) shell hit the armour plating. (It) must have been hit twice because the one had hit the engine. (Another) hit where the driver was sitting, and it just jammed (the plate against the door). I mean, he wasn't wounded, just jammed him in. He couldn't get out, and the armoured bulldozer was on fire, and nobody could get near it. And that was my worst experience. Because you heard this man screaming. And there's nobody who could do a damn thing for him.'

Bill was then witness to one of the few Luftwaffe sorties against the beaches. 'All of a sudden these fighter-bombers came along . . . putting bombs along the beach . . . but I saw our Spitfires come along and they sorted them out. They shot them down. There was one engine dropped about thirty or forty feet from us.'

Ian Hammerton of the 22nd Dragoons commanded a troop of flail tanks, AVREs, and bulldozers. He watched the action on the beach as his landing craft came to shore on Mike Green sector.[5]

'A flight of rockets went up . . . and I saw a Spitfire flying along the beach, and it suddenly disappeared in a puff of flame and smoke. It must have flown into the flight of rockets. You could see (the rockets) landing on the shore. Not on the beach, but on the land behind the beach, and the fire burning, and a tremendous amount of smoke. There was some infantry already on (the beach), and there was quite a lot of bodies floating about.'

Like many units on D-Day, Ian was dropped out of position, but his tanks soon went to work. 'The two flails flailed up to the seawall and backed away . . . the bridge tank came forward but the commander was killed by a shell which landed on the turret, and it cut the cable and the bridge dropped. So we then had to make use of the existing ramp, a stone ramp, off the beach.'

This ramp had been blocked by a tangle of barbed wire and welded railway tracks, which would need to be cleared by the tank's gun.

'We'd practised this . . . and it meant the commander sighting the gun through the barrel at every joint of the welding, and that's a lengthy business.'

Once the firing was complete, one of Ian's tanks went up the ramp to push away the debris, but in doing so it hit a mine and blew up. The ramp remained blocked. 'I had to attach a tow rope to it and tow it down the ramp, and into the sea.' The ramp was cleared, but Ian and his crew had to abandon their waterlogged tank. 'The most difficult thing of all was climbing out of the water and onto the ramp. There was various bodies floating around, which didn't help either.'

Ian's two remaining flail tanks got up the ramp and started to work their way inshore. The other half of his troop had landed further down the beach, and Ian went to check on them by walking along the top of the seawall. Happy with how they were getting on, he then returned to his crew at the ramp.

'My own crew were sitting on top of the seawall with a machine gun. They had the odd crack at a few snipers, but that soon passed.'

The men, soaking wet, set about preparing some soup to

warm themselves up. It wasn't until the next day that they'd dis-cover that they'd been sitting on top of an anti-tank mine the whole time. Fortunately, the soldiers were too light to set it off.

The Royal Winnipeg Rifles had begun to come ashore at 0749. The unit's war diary noted that the supporting tanks were late in their sector, and the bombardment of the beach had failed to kill a single German.[6]

'There's a lot of little sounds and there's machine-gun fire hitting the top (of the landing craft),' said Jim Parks, who was nineteen on D-Day, having lied about his age to join the army four years earlier. 'You had to keep your head down and you'd hear the pop pop pop on the side of the boat. (Then) there was a big thump: we hit a mine. We were also hit by a 75mm. The feller that was to lower down the ramp, he was pretty well wounded. He dropped us in the water too deep.[7] When trying to swim to shore, I got side-swiped by one of the landing craft coming in. I got pushed into the water and all I could see was stars because I'd swallowed a lot of water. Your foot would touch the bottom and give you a bit of adrenaline and I'd make my way to shore.'[8]

Jim's mission on D-Day was to help to assist the combat engin-eers, but with his mortar carrier sunk in the Channel, he turned his attention to helping others. 'A lot happens in a short period of time. We'd pull the guys out of the water and all that sort of stuff. We had nowhere to go because we'd lost everything anyway. We pulled some of the guys that had been hit in the water out. We were worried that the tanks were going to come in and they wouldn't see the bodies and just run them over, so we pulled as many as we could as far as we could. Once we started doing that, a few of the other guys did too. The main infantry companies had pushed forward already to the next objective.'[9]

Jim then found some cover up the beach. 'I plopped beside Corporal Scaife. I knew this Corporal Scaife, he was from out west in Saskatchewan, and he was mortally wounded, so I took his Sten gun because I'd lost everything.'[10]

Alex Kuppers was another soldier in the Winnipeg Rifles, serving in the anti-tank platoon. 'We landed later than the assault companies as we had vehicles, and had to have exits so that we could get off the beach. The landing craft tank that I was on was quite a mixture. It consisted of self-propelled artillery, two of our regimental anti-tank guns, and an armoured bulldozer.'

That day, Alex saw an instance of bravery that he would remember for the rest of his life. 'A small navy craft mounting a gun to its rear was backed in close to the beach, and duelling with large concrete bunkers with their gun. (The crew) did not have much in the line of protection, but they were still firing when our craft had to circle away as it was not time for us to touch down.'

When their time finally came, Alex's Bren carrier followed an armoured bulldozer ashore. 'When he stopped, I think to lower his blade, the beach group behind us pulled out with their (Bren) carrier to go by. They went about twenty yards then hit a mine. The carrier was upside down with four of them lying on the sand. All got up quite quickly except for the driver, who had been cut in half.'

Later that day, Alex heard stories from the infantrymen who had landed ahead of him.

'Corporal Holmes was the one who silenced the bunker on the extreme left. (He) stood on someone's shoulders to enable him to toss grenades into the (bunker's) ports, as the entrances were under enemy fire. He said that a little later the shooting started up again. The second time he threw in phosphorus grenades that really brought screams and silenced the guns. Another fellow, Corporal Klos, was found dead inside another bunker on the body of a German he had killed with his bare hands. Lance Corporal Kool had taken a burst of machine-gun fire in his stomach but threw himself onto the barbed wire. His men thought he had done so to enable them to cross over him. We heard many stories of great bravery shown by some of the Rifles. But I guess it was the same with all the assaulting regiments. There had to be many stories. There were many Rifles who never made it off the beach, and many more killed, when they were badly mauled two days later on June 8th. Their stories went with them, and so have never been told.'

By mid-morning the Canadians were off the beach. Hard fighting by the Queen's Own Rifles brought the town of Bernières into Canadian hands, and by 1115, Saint-Aubin-sur-Mer was taken by B Company of the North Shore (New Brunswick) Regiment.[11] By 1140, the Canadians who had landed in Mike sector had advanced nearly two miles inland, and by 1600 the reserve infantry brigade had landed.

When the Germans counter-attacked into the two-mile gap between Juno and Sword at 1950 that evening, the lead Canadian troops consolidated their position to protect their flank, accepting that they would not meet their final objectives on D-Day, including taking Carpiquet airport near Caen, about ten miles from the coast.[12] Even so, they had advanced further inland than the British and American armies. The Canadians suffered around 1,000 casualties that day, and the British supporting them a further 243.[13]

Graye-sur-Mer, the home of schoolboy Michel Grimaux, was liberated by the Winnipeg Rifles.

'We had a friend with us,' said Michel, 'a middle-aged lady, and she went out into the street and met soldiers who said you must come out and go to the beach. So we all went to the main road leading to the beach. We saw a dead soldier on the way. By about half-past ten we were in the meadow where there is now a large petrol station and we were kept there for about three hours while the infantry made sure there were no snipers in the village.

'We were very well looked after – we were given something to eat and we saw all the tanks and the soldiers – all this huge queue of people going inland. Then we came back into the village at about half-past three and we went to the church with our priest. He had been taking a confirmation service about twenty miles inland and he wanted to join his parish. So he took his bicycle and rode across the lines and joined us. The church roof had been destroyed because there had been a sniper in the tower, so we all gathered there to look at the damage before we all went back to our houses. We had different companies and sections of the British army making dugouts and trenches in the meadows, in readiness for the night, and we began to give them flowers and wine. We had kept wine from before the war. They were very cautious at first because they had been warned to be careful of spies but very soon, they realized we were just good friends. It was all very exciting.'

Sword Beach

Compared to the other beaches, the German defences at Sword Beach, which was a five-mile stretch of coast, were relatively light. Beach obstacles and bunkers were scattered along the shore, with a second line of defence consisting of machine-gun and mortar positions in the dunes. In the towns just behind the beach, the Germans had laid mines, dug anti-tank ditches, and built concrete walls blocking the streets. Elements of the German 716th Infantry Division, in particular the 736th and 125th Regiments, along with forces of the 21st Panzer Division, were in the vicinity, while the 711th Division was east across the Dives River.

Seventeen-year-old Jaqueline le Bas was staying in a house

between Langrune and Saint-Aubin, and witnessed the landings that day.

'We could see the sea perfectly. We saw it as soon as it got a little daylight. Even though it was really foggy, we could see the shapes perfectly in the sea with fire coming out of the cannons. We saw flames starting in Le Havre. Then the noise, a terrible noise on Le Havre. Then gradually, on the entire coast. We took shelter in the dining room for a bit. Suddenly, the chandelier started swinging, then the windows, all the panes fell and shattered. So we rushed into the garden, in an arbour, beneath an iron table . . . We stayed huddled. My mother, my brother and I, throughout the landing . . . The neighbour's dog was howling, but the birds were flying as if nothing was happening. It seemed like the birds were unaffected. Several times, we were startled due to bombs going off everywhere.'

Peter Fussell had joined the army in 1939 when he was sixteen years old. As a commando in the 1st Special Service Brigade, he expected no quarter should he be taken prisoner. 'No paratroops or commandos were to be taken alive (by the Germans),' Peter recalled. '(According to Hitler) we were hooligans, we were misfits, we were partisans, we were gangsters, because we used to carry the fighting knife, and I must admit they came in very useful in hand-to-hand combat.'

Peter watched from his ship as they closed in on the French coast. 'When we got up on deck we looked across towards the beaches and we could see nothing but ships. Hundreds of aircraft above, going in relays. Strafing, bombing, using cannon fire. We could hear the guns of the battleships and cruisers opening up, and we could see the flashes.'

Serving in 41 (Royal Marine) Commando, 4th Special Service Brigade was twenty-two-year-old Warwick Nield-Siddall.

'We wanted to go. Most of us, anyway, wanted to go. It was

something that had to be done. I don't ever remember talking to anybody who was frightened. They were all eager to get there and get on with it, because we were that fit, and so well trained, and it had been coming for so long. This was it.'

The commandos were incredibly proud of the green berets that they had earned through arduous training and selection, and eschewed their helmets in favour of them. 'We landed without tin hats,' said James Kelly of Liverpool. 'That became the fashion. For us to fight without tin hats, just a green beret.'

The commandos were offered a stiff drink before they went ashore. 'I didn't drink much of the rum . . . The navy were slinging it out like it had gone out of fashion. What they hoped to gain by that I don't know. I was terrified of drinking in case I was drunk, and did the wrong things, and got meself killed.'

Berkeley Meredith, of the Staffordshire Yeomanry, was watching the fleet as it made its way to Sword Beach. 'I remember seeing what must have been a fuel-carrying vessel being hit and going up in just one tremendous sheet of flame, and a black pall of smoke. Nobody could have got out of that.'

George Rayson was coming ashore with the Suffolks, and remembered the banter on the landing craft.

'We had a Londoner there, one of these happy go lucky fellas . . . he said, "Boys, I'm gonna be bookmaker. I'm gonna take bets on the first man to shit himself."' The joke got a good laugh, but there was a tragic ending for the Londoner. 'He was the first bloke to get killed as it so happened.'

'The barrage was absolutely terrific,' said nineteen-year-old James Blinkhorn, of the East Yorkshire Regiment. 'They must have hit the beach with everything they had in England, because there was just a pall of smoke, it must have been a mile high, and the whole beach was obliterated with smoke. One of the landing craft up from us hit a mine coming in. It bounced off and (it) exploded harmlessly. There was a destroyer behind us got a direct hit . . . That went down in two or three minutes.'

James was the first man ashore from his landing craft. 'We had a pretty good landing. I only got wet up to me knees, that was all. There was some pretty wide posts on the beach, and I got behind one of these.'

It was some cover at least, but not enough to cover his whole body. 'I got a nick in the arm. A bullet nick in the arm. We dashed then onto the beach road, then we were attacking different targets along the beach. (The fire was) very intense. Tanks were supposed to land with us and give us supporting cover. They didn't land, so we had to make do with our own Bren-gun carriers. The first (carrier) that went off the beach, he was hit with a flamethrower. And they were just . . . horrible . . . everything was black. Just black.'

The other Bren carriers fared no better. 'The German heavy guns were just blowing them up.' The effects of this heavy combat left James numb. 'You're more or less walking about in a daze . . . It's each man for himself. It was slaughter . . . I think out of our company of a hundred and twenty I think we lost about fifty on the beach. Fifty dead. There were more casualties than that.'

In the face of such losses, composure from the unit's leaders was vital. 'Major King, he was on the beach, and there was an airburst, and it blew the front of his helmet off and the tip of his nose. And he said, "I'm going to keep this bugger for a souvenir." And he put a bit of plaster on his nose, and he said, "Ah, a drop of whisky will cure that." '

Arthur Blizzard was an NCO in the pioneer platoon of the 1st Battalion, Suffolk Regiment. 'I had the flamethrower, and a Bangalore torpedo. That were extra to my Sten gun.' It was a heavy load, but Arthur was a big man, and his battalion had been trained hard to prepare for war. 'We were two men instead of one. We were real fit. I wish I was like it today, I could go through anything.'

His height came in useful when the men were dropped short of the beach. 'I'm six foot three. I'm about a foot under water when I first go in there.'

Arthur helped other men get ashore, then checked his surroundings. Though they were dropped a little short, the landing-craft crew had put them right where they were supposed to be. 'I landed bang on. I was nearly one of the first to get there.'

Some of those who had landed ahead were already dead. 'I got behind a Sherman which had got burned out. Jerry was machine-gunning us (from a house). So we have to lay there and just (fire) back, that's all you can do, and then run like anything as fast as you could to get in.'

Arthur was soon able to get off the beach and found cover ashore. 'Once we got past that first line I got into a ditch. Mar-vellous ditch it was. It took me about a mile into where I wanted (to go).'

Kenneth Powter was also an NCO in the 1st Suffolks. He recalled the perils of the landing craft's final few yards to the beach. 'We threaded our way through these staggered poles with the Teller mines on top, and I remember leaning over the side, because I was in the front of the craft, and seeing such a small dis-tance between this mine and the boat. The rear of the craft caught one of them. Blew the back right out. Killed the seaman. But by this time we were onto the beaches. They lowered the ramp, and we were off.'

Dead and wounded already littered the beach, but Kenneth was able to make a quick exit. 'A flail (tank) had landed just by the side of us and was making an opening through the defences. I scrambled over the wire and made across the marshes to this rendezvous.'

'(Our CO) was killed immediately,' said Gordon Penter, of the 1st Battalion, South Lancashire Regiment. 'I was with B Company, and we landed behind one of the assaulting companies. One of our subalterns, Lieutenant Bell-Walker, immediately went to knock out a strong point. He did this with a charge, but unfortunately he was killed.'

Heavy guns and machine guns raked the beach with their fire. 'We lost our company commander, which was a very great loss. We were taking losses left and right. Shrapnel was all over the place. You were just lucky if you missed it.'

Gordon ran to an exit off the beach where the engineers had cleared a path through the mines. 'You had to get through it very, very quickly as an infantryman, because the tanks were also getting off the beach, and of course they wouldn't stop for anybody, and if you were unfortunate enough to fall, I'm afraid you'd have gone under the tank. In fact some wounded people actually did.'

On the eastern flank of Sword, 177 Free French commandos landed at the town of Ouistreham.

'We came in at 0720 in the morning,' said Leon Gautier. 'We had known for a week exactly where we were going to land, because we were of course familiar with the coastline, but we had been told to keep the information to ourselves.

'One of the Free French landing craft had been hit as we went in and there were some killed and wounded but the remainder transferred to the other craft and made it ashore. The Germans were shelling us and the water was black from the mud and sand thrown up by exploding shells. The ladder lowered and we rushed into the beach (into) the machine-gun fire from the blockhouse directly in front of us.

'We threw a grenade through the port and the German defenders gave up and surrendered very quickly. We swung left and took all the remaining strong points from the rear.'

'The sand seemed to boil under the bullets and explosions,' said French commando René Goujon. 'A Churchill tank of the East Yorkshire Pioneers had landed a few minutes before us and was supposed to breach the enemy's front-line defences. They had taken a direct hit; the turret was in flames and a man – also in flames – was screaming as he clambered out.'[14]

'Number 1 Troop attacking the casino suffered casualties,' said Leon, 'and altogether we lost nine dead and seventy others injured on D-Day.

'The first other French civilians encountered were hiding in the basement of their house about fifty yards behind the block-house. I searched their house for Germans and I told them to stay under cover.'

The locals believed that the landing was a large-scale raid, such as happened at Dieppe. 'But I told them that this time, we were here to stay.'

Positioned next to the Caen canal, Ouistreham marked the easternmost flank of the D-Day beaches. Nos 3, 4, 6 and 45 (Royal Marine) Commandos of the Special Service Brigade came ashore here at Queen Red sector of Sword Beach.

'It wasn't like Dieppe where the Germans were waiting for us on the beaches,' said commando Peter Fussell, who had taken part in that battle. 'There was shelling on the beach, because the guns at Merville, which were supposed to have been put out of action, weren't . . . There were the big guns from Le Havre, right across the other side of the bay . . . We had an awful lot of mortars from the villages behind Ouistreham . . . And quite a lot of sniper fire was coming as well.'

Under this fire, specialist units had been busy with the dangerous work of mine clearance.

'By the time we landed the Royal Naval beach-clearance people had been in front of us, and they had cleared a narrow strip, and they'd taped the strip had been cleared and declared safe, through which flail tanks were going. This was a great support for us, because at least now we had something to hide behind. We cleared the beaches straight after we hit them.'

Enemy pillboxes were being silenced by a nearby Sherman. 'He was engaging them with his tank fire. Very successfully, too.' Under this cover, Peter and the other men moved into a marshy area where they began to come under indirect fire. 'The mortars were picking us off then.'

These were spotting rounds for the enemy to lay onto their target before a full, heavy barrage was fired. Peter's leaders recognized the signs and moved them quickly inland towards their objective, which was the bridges held by 6th Airborne.

Warwick Nield-Siddall, with 4th Special Service Brigade, remembered the noise and chaos of the battle as the commandos landed.

'The shells were incoming and outgoing, aircraft were flying overhead, and rockets from the shore were landing in the water. We didn't get hit but they were bursting all around. We hit the beach and the ramp went down. I had two young boys with me. Two young marines. They were carrying the radio sets, and we landed in about four feet of water. It was up to my chest, and I was considerably taller than these two lads. They were up to their necks. We got on the beach, which was covered in bodies, and tanks, and smoke, and the smell of cordite. Everything was technicolour. Everything was brilliant in colour.'

'We waded ashore,' said Commando James Kelly, who landed with No. 41 (Royal Marine) Commando, 4th Special Service Brigade at Lion-sur-Mer. 'There was a blinding flash, and a terrible bloody smell of cordite.' The flash was an explosion which caused several casualties. 'I remember kneeling by Charlie Hall. He was bleeding. The blood was pumping out of his neck, and right out of his Combined Ops badge that was on his shoulder . . . I'd only just knelt down, and it was only a matter of saying to him, "Come on Charlie, come on," and this voice said, "Get going, you're not supposed to stop! Get going!" So I went.'

James stopped at a Bren carrier that had two dead men inside before moving up to the beach, where he started cutting wire. He was struck by the calm demeanour of the navy's beachmaster, who was organizing the flow of men off the landing craft and off the beach.

'He was just standing there shouting, "Over here! Keep over there!" Like a traffic copper . . . How long he lasted I don't know.'

The beachmaster also stuck in the memory of Warwick Nield-Siddall. 'The most calm man I've ever met in my life came along swinging a cane. "Come on, lads, off the beach now." Shells are landing, and mortars are landing, and snipers are firing, and machine-gun fire, people are falling and being killed and wounded, and this guy's walking through it.'

The beachmaster these two men fondly remembered was Edward Gueritz, who rose to the position after his immediate superior, Commander Rowley Nichols, was wounded by a mortar. The same explosion killed the army liaison officer, Lieutenant-Colonel D.V.H. Board. Edward described his role as to 'provide navigational marks, assist in clearance of obstacles, mark obstructions, provide incoming landing craft with as much guidance as possible and to expedite their unloading of personnel, vehicles or stores and clear them off the beach'.

He noted that there was considerable difficulty in clearing vehicles off the beach as German mines had created bottlenecks. That British troops on Sword had the luxury of so many vehicles landing so quickly meant that they were 'victims of [their] own success'.

Perhaps explaining James and Warwick's accounts of his

bravery, Gueritz said, 'I felt a great sense of relief, I'd been training for this for three years and the one thing I'd been afraid of was that I would not be fit on the day we went across. I was delighted to be ashore, part of this great thing . . . I wasn't conscious of any expectation that I was going to be a casualty.' Relying on his training and his anxiousness to perform his role to the best of his ability gave Edward a 'feeling of invulnerability'.

Coming ashore at Queen Red sector was Lord Lovat, commander of 1st Special Service Brigade. He was also the twenty-fifth chief of the clan Fraser, which goes some way to explaining why he had brought along his piper William 'Bill' Millin.

'When we landed it was under heavy fire,' said Bill, who was twenty-one at the time. 'Lots of people were being killed . . . I started to play the pipes, and Lovat looked around, he heard the pipes, and smiled and walked on.' Bill moved off the beach and came to a spot where a German machine gun was firing directly down a road. 'There was a load of wounded, all lying about . . . about twelve or maybe fourteen of them, all lying at the entrance to this road. So they said, "Where's the medics, Jock? Where's the medics?" I said, "Well they're coming." I didn't know whether they were coming or not. I tried to pull one or two of them away . . . but (the Germans) were still shooting, so I just had to get . . . into a doorway. I heard a clanking, and I looked around, and there's one of the flail tanks with the chains.' The tank commander could not see the men in the road, and despite Bill's attempts to stop him, he drove on and over the wounded men. 'It churned them all up.'

Bill then went back and found Lovat, who told him to resume his piping. 'The whole thing was ridiculous. The bodies lying at the water were going back and forward with the tide, and I started off piping, going a few paces along there, the next thing a hand on my soldier. I looked around, it's this sergeant. "What are you fucking playing at, you mad bastard? Every German in France knows we're here now, you silly bastard!"'

When Bill finished playing, he saw that Lovat and the others had moved off and hurried to catch up. 'The frightening part hadn't started, because everything was happening so quickly and so sudden.' He left behind a bloody scene at the beach. 'Some wounded, some dead, and their heads blown off, and that lot churned up with the tank.'

The final objective of the commandos on D-Day was to link up with the airborne forces holding the two bridges further inland. Peter Fussell found that many German soldiers were quick to surrender to them as they pressed inland. 'They came out only too willing to give themselves up. We saw very little opposition until we reached Hermanville.'

Lord Lovat ordered that this village, about a mile inland, be bypassed and left to the infantry. Peter's unit moved at 'a very quick pace. We were very well laden, we had our rucksacks, nearly sixty to eighty pounds each man was carrying, plus his personal weapon. We weren't fighting all the way, but every now and again we had to take cover because there was the odd sporadic machine gun, and odd sniper, that kept hindering us, annoying us, from time to time.'

The commandos covered some twelve miles in enemy territory in four hours.

'We reached the bridges just after 1200. We were due to reach them at twelve o'clock, and Major John Howard, who came in with the first gliders, met Lovat on the bridge.'

'We heard the sound of pipes,' said John Vaughan, the medical officer who had landed with John Howard's D Company, 'and I distinctly heard this Scottish piper coming up the road and it suddenly stopped, there was a lot of fire going on. I remember walking up towards the bridge at midday, and the commandos were just wandering across this bridge, some on bicycles, a very casual lot.'

'I piped down the road leading to Pegasus Bridge,' said Bill Millin. 'There was a right battle going on . . . even where I was standing I could hear the shrapnel, bullets or whatever, hitting off the side of the bridge. Wounded were being carried . . . into the cafe. It was a real spot.'

John Vaughan recalls seeing some of the commandos hit by enemy fire as they crossed the bridge. 'Within twenty yards of John (Howard's) slit trench, a man straight in front of him rolled down the bank, and I had a look at him. He'd been shot through the head. At that very moment, Lovat appeared across the road and greeted John Howard at the bridge, and the rest of the commandos came across.'

Bill Millin was asked by Lovat to keep playing all the way to the next bridge, despite several men being shot around him. 'I looked around at Lovat. He was walking around as if he was out for a walk on his estate.' At Horsa Bridge, two paras tried telling Bill to go back into cover, but with Lovat's encouragement, Bill piped his way across, playing 'Blue Bonnets Over the Border'. Once on the other side he shook the hands of the astonished – perhaps, befuddled – airborne soldiers.

'There was a lot of bodies that we passed,' said Peter Fussell. 'Poor chaps from the airborne.'

Further to the east, Berkeley Meredith's Sherman tank was pushing into the Normandy countryside. 'We saw some movement in the bocage on our left-hand side, and we guessed it was a platoon of infantry, so we shot at them with machine-gun fire. There seemed to be some movement there but no response. So we edged over to look over the edge, and what we'd done was to hit some poor old French cow, which was in agony. And again, another ludicrous thing in the heat of battle, we felt that we couldn't leave this wretched animal in its agony, so we tried to depress the gun to put it out of its misery, but we were too close to it . . . So I took the breech block out, and we sited this gun down the barrel to put it out of its misery.'

Kenneth Powter assembled with his company beyond the beach. '(Then) we bashed on to our objectives, which was Colleville. On the outskirts, on the high ground just the other side of this village, was this big emplacement known as Hillman. D Company of our battalion had trained to blow the outer defences . . . and they had Bangalore torpedo teams.'

'(My) Bangalore torpedo was reserved for Hillman,' said Arthur Blizzard, of the Suffolks' Pioneer Platoon.

Hillman was a German bunker complex and command post on the northern edge of Périers Ridge, 2.3 miles inland from the beach. It housed the battlegroup headquarters of Colonel Ludwig Krug, commanding 736th Grenadier Regiment and 642nd Ost (East) Battalion, one of two units, composed mostly of former Soviet POWs, attached to 716th Infantry Division. Hillman had a commanding view of the coast with fields of fire extending to six hundred yards in most directions and was made up of two large bunkers, three armoured steel cupolas, housing machine guns in concrete emplacements 3.5 metres thick, seven more machine-gun posts and a network of trenches covering approach routes.

'That's where I got me torpedo ready, and I blew my first good gap through there,' said Arthur. 'Mind you, I nearly got kaput over it, but I got away with it anyway.'

'It took almost the end of the afternoon before Hillman was captured,' said Kenneth Powter. 'That evening I moved down towards . . . the Caen Canal. We were digging in on the forward side of a big field and . . . heard this big noise behind us, and looked up and saw a vast armada of aircraft towing gliders. They landed in this field where we were. The aircraft appeared to be going back, and as these aircraft were going back you saw their bomb bays opening. They made another circuit and as they were coming over they released all these canisters, which we had to jump in our trenches to avoid being hit by.'

After the battle at Hillman, Arthur Blizzard, along with another pioneer named Alec Bailey, were ordered to bury the dead on the cleared position.

'We got the Germans and we buried them as best we could,' Arthur said, recalling how they took the dog tags of each side's dead so that they could be identified. '(We) wrapped them all in handkerchiefs, kept them separate, and then sent them back to the Red Cross. We was all that day shovelling up the dead Germans.'

After this grim work, Arthur and Alec went to look around the defences at Hillman, and found a stash of Normandy apple brandy, known as Calvados.

'After me and him had drank the first bottle, I said, "We feel better now, don't we?"' The men were about to head back to their unit when Arthur saw a steel door and pulled it open: behind it were sixty German servicemen.

'There was a commandant of the area, with his hands above his heads, he give me his dagger, he said, "Kaput." Well he could have kaput us as easy as pie if he'd have wanted, but that's where my luck came in. I lined them all up, marched them down a road to battalion intelligence platoon. Alec said, "Well we done well today boy, two of us, sixty prisoners." I said, "Yeah, mind you, them poor prisoners, they've been through the mill, they're glad that we didn't shoot them."'

In the late afternoon of D-Day, elements of the 21st Panzer Division launched a counter-attack towards the eastern beaches, where they experienced initial success.

'Parts of this attack came through to the coast, because there was gaps between (the British and Canadian divisions),' said

Hans von Luck, a regimental commander in the division who was launching his own counter-attacks against the British airborne forces. 'Some of our units went through, but then they were heavily shot by the navy.'

Gordon Painter was in a gun turret on the *Belfast*, and took part in this bombardment.

'I do remember being told once that we were attacking a German squadron of tanks. These tanks were approaching the soldiers who had landed.' Several direct hits were reported to have been achieved on the enemy armour, but Gordon took no great pride in killing the enemy. 'When one has to fight for one's country, you just have to do a job, and do as you're told. (The Germans) were human beings the same as we were. We were the age where it didn't really sink home to you exactly what it was all about. And we were sad in doing some of the things we had to do. But that's war.'

The *Mauritius* was also involved in the bombardment of the German counter-attack. Midshipman John Carlill remembered the moment. 'All available guns concentrated on repulsing an armoured thrust by the 21st Panzer division from Caen to Sword Beach at Lion-Sur-Mer. The attack was halted in the early evening.'

Gliders from the 6th Airborne's Air Landing Brigade also played their part in breaking the German thrust. Spotting the large number of aircraft overhead, the divisional commander feared that an airdrop was going to cut their lines of support and he ordered the armour to retreat.

John watched the glider landings from the *Mauritius*. 'It was an incredible and awe-inspiring sight, and no one who saw it will ever forget it.'

There were many other unforgettable sights that day. Some not of awe, but of horror.

Ted Cordery was a craneman aboard the *Belfast*. 'With such

an assault there's a considerable amount of casualties, and they were ferried out to the ships for treatment.' As the crane operator, it was Ted's job to lift the wounded on board. 'They were just on a square box, (and I) lifted them inboard. The amount of damage that those men suffered will live with me for ever. I could have cried. Faces blown away, arms off, God knows what.

'They just brought them back with a sheet over them because there would be so much blood. Some of the injuries were horrific, they really were. They were rushed up for treatment, which was too late anyway. Then they came back on the deck. We just put them in sacks and buried them. Just said a little prayer for them. Nothing else you could do with them. Couldn't keep them onboard.

'A normal burial at sea they wrap them up, give the person that's died the ceremony he deserves. But in war you haven't got time for that type of thing. Because you've got other things to do. And there's nothing you can do, they're past help. We just said a little prayer for them and got back to whatever we were doing.'

What Ted saw that day would live with him for ever.

'I've been in air raids at home and seen bodies amongst civilians, (but) never saw anything like that. I think they're the sort of thing they should show these children, instead of these war games where everybody's blowing everything off the face of the earth. Just show them the consequences of this action. That might make them feel better towards their fellow men.'

Jaqueline le Bas and her family had taken shelter from the Allied bombardment, which she recalled as stopping around midday.

'Then we heard footsteps in the street. We saw men passing by, they seemed like shadows. After a while, as several of them were passing by, I went over and spoke to them. There were ten of them on different sidewalks, on both sides of the road. I approached and asked. I realized they were English. They asked me where they were. I was even more scared as I really had the impression that they were landing right at our place and not the entire coast. That reassured me to think that they would land everywhere.

'Someone from the town hall came to ask us to dig graves, my brother and me, as we were still young and there were dead soldiers that needed graves. You know, I'd never seen the dead before.'

Two graves were dug in the churchyard's cemetery. 'We buried two young English . . . It was very moving.'

The British force that landed at Sword took 630 casualties. 29,000 men were brought ashore, and though they secured many objectives, Caen had not been liberated.

The advance on the city had been delayed because of the time that it took to secure strongpoints Daimler, Hillman, Morris, and Rover. The counter-attack of the 21st Panzer also played its part. Rather than receiving its liberation on D-Day as planned, the battle for Caen would rage for weeks to come.

CHAPTER FIVE

Go to It!

Airborne forces and French Resistance from D+1

'It took days until other armoured divisions could get into the battle. But by then the British and the Americans, as we heard, had made very good, firm bases on the coast, and it was hard to throw them away into the sea. And I remember well when Rommel told us, if there's a landing somewhere in France, and we can't get the invaders back into the sea within the first twenty-four hours, that would be the end.'

Hans von Luck, 21st Panzer Division

The 82nd Airborne Division

Tom Porcella had parachuted into Normandy on D-Day. He'd narrowly avoided drowning in the flooded fields, and spent his first night in France shivering with cold, and thinking of his bed back at base.

'Daylight was coming upon us fast. And I knew that we'd soon get the order, we'd soon receive the order to move out.'

D-Day was just the beginning of a long campaign for the

Allied paratroopers, and Tom soon found himself involved in 'a fierce battle.

'This battle raged on for about a half a day, on and off. There was no activity really in the corner of the field where I was at, so I didn't see much of what was going on.'

The paratroopers were then pushed on through several more hedgerows before a sergeant appeared. 'He was asking for volunteers to go back into the field that we just left and see if we could find any wounded, because we never knew what happened to those troopers over there.'

Tom and around a half a dozen other men said that they'd go. 'We enter this field and we saw two troopers laying on the ground. I looked at this one trooper there and he had his head completely blown apart, and was unrecognizable.'

When Tom checked the dead man's dog tags he discovered that it was someone he had known well.

'He was one of the original paratroopers from 3rd Battalion. And it was a terrible shock to me to see what happened to him . . . I hope that he died fast.

'A few feet away from him, there was another trooper laying down . . . He was just butchered meat. There was blood all over the place. One leg was mangled and the other leg was sort of grotesquely underneath his body. So I tried to find out who it was, and I pulled out his dog tag . . . (he was) another H Company man. While I was moving him around a little bit, I heard a groan. I thought for sure he was dead . . . I was glad to see the guy was still alive, but I don't know whether he'd ever make it.'

The wounded man was loaded onto a stretcher, but the paratroopers were so weak from fatigue and hunger that it was a struggle to carry him. They finally got him back to a field that was full of airborne casualties.

'All the troopers were laid in this field, right alongside the hedgerow, as far as I could see. Exactly how many troopers were there, I don't know.'

Tom and the others then went back to look for more wounded.

'I happened to notice in the corner of the field there was a German evidently trying to escape through the hedgerow and some troopers shot him. He never got through the hedgerow. He was half on one side and half on the other.'

They also spotted a wounded enemy soldier.

'Some of the troops come along and shot him while he was trying to bandage himself.'

Their search for their own wounded continued, but the next men that they came across were also German.

'They were lying on their back. There was this one German, he had his both hands together, like he was praying and begging for his life and his eyes were wide open. I just could visualize, by judging by the look on his face, that he was terrified, and I could imagine them . . . begging this trooper not to shoot him. And his expression seemed to be frozen right on his face, and it looked like fear. He looked like he was pleading for his life.

'A few feet away from him, there was another German laying on his back. And he had a different look on his face. He looked like he had a sneer. Who knows? He could have been cursing this trooper out. Maybe he knew the trooper killed the other German . . . and he figured he was going to die, but he had a sneer on his face.'

After this grim discovery came a poignant one.

'They found the remains of a fountain pen. And I recognized it because it was the fountain pen of a Staff Sergeant Williams. I know it was his pen because I was with him on Tennessee Maneuvers when he received it from his girlfriend.'

There was no sign of the sergeant. Tom didn't know if he was taken prisoner, killed, or died of wounds.

'A voice called out to me, "Hey trooper come over here."'

The voice belonged to a wounded paratrooper.

'He wanted to know how badly he was hit. Looking down at him I saw all the flesh was blown away from his right side of his face. He started to cry and he was reaching for his face with a hand that was black with dirt . . . He asked me for a cigarette and a drink of water. I didn't have any cigarettes because I lost everything I had in the water. He said he had some in his pocket. I removed one of the cigarettes, (and) lit it for him.'

The suffering on the battlefield was not confined to soldiers. Later that day, Tom and others came across an inconsolable French woman. Through her tears, she was demanding to know why the Allied soldiers had not come sooner. One of the para-troopers could speak French, and told Tom that the woman's daughters had been taken away by the Germans.

When Tom was finally reunited with the rest of his regiment, he asked about the fate of some of his friends and comrades.

A favourite NCO in the regiment had crashed through the roof when he landed.

'The Germans had been at it and mutilated his body. And they cut . . . they cut his testicles and his penis off and stuffed it in his mouth.'

The loss of their friends brought the men to tears.

'Tears are running down my (face), and the fellers telling these stories, they're crying. Yes, we do cry as paratroopers. We're still human beings. We still feel the pain and anguish. And when your loved ones die, and we loved each other, we shed a few tears.'

During his time in Normandy, Tom was a continual witness to the degradation of morality.

'Somewhere in the distance, there's two soldiers with their hands raised above their heads who were walking towards us to surrender . . . When they were in just about a full view I guess about all of us seen it, we heard two shots rang out, bang, bang. The two Germans fell before they were able to take another step. I remember hearing, "Stop firing, stop firing you damn fools, they wanted to surrender."

'After a short time went by, two more Germans appeared . . . and they was carrying a white flag. So they started to come near our positions, we all had our guns trained on them. And they wasn't too far away from me. And all of a sudden I heard a couple of more shots and the Germans fell. And I assumed that they were shot in the back by their own officer for giving up. Was a hell of a thing to see.'

Surrendering on the battlefield could often be fatal. One day, Tom noticed a group of paratroopers standing in a circle around a foxhole.

'I finally got there and see what was going on. And I looked out into the hole, there was this German, he looked very young. Could've been anywhere between fifteen and seventeen.

'There was all kinds of remarks being made about this German here, we ought to shoot the son of a bitch. We ought to kill him, we ought to do this, we ought to do that. But nobody shot him. First, it takes a lot of nerve to shoot a man in cold blood just like that and especially when you see their eyes and they're pleading not to be shot. And I remember one of the troopers said to me, "Tom, you shoot him." I looked at the trooper, a little bit of disgust. I said, "No, no, no, no, I am not going to shoot him, let's take him prisoner." So some of the guys said, "Nah, let's shoot", this and that. I said, "Nah, nah nah why don't we take a prisoner? Maybe he's got information?"

'That's the only way you can save a guy's life is if you say maybe we can get some information out of him. So they all agreed to that. We yank this German out of the foxhole. And the poor kid, he was scared half to death . . . I often think I saved his life. I hope he appreciates it.'

One incident in particular stuck with Tom about the brutality of war, and men's behaviour in it.

'There was a body in this road, and that's not the first body we've seen. But when I got up there, I passed the body. The head was gone. It was just a torso left. And there was a big hole in their rib cage.

'So what got me all upset was that some of the GIs, as they marched, they were eating K rations, (and) they were throwing the wrappers and the cans inside this body. My decency was stunned. I couldn't believe, even if we were out in war, that we'd have such disrespect for what remains of a human body. I just couldn't believe it. I couldn't believe these guys were doing this. And I didn't understand why. Because the truth was we were with the good guys. We were all kids, we were all kids at the time, and I just don't understand how could they change in such a short time? But today I realize why they may have done it. Some of the fellows that may have done this, they may have lost a lot of good brothers. And I lost a lot of good brothers, but I don't think I could do it, I know I didn't do it. I was wondering, why? Why did they do this?

'It's something I'll never forget.'

Tom had seen terrible things in France, but a moment of kindness would live with him for ever.

'I got word that there was a lady who was cooking pancakes for the paratroopers.

'I entered the house and they found a few more paratroopers in there, eating and lining up, waiting for this lady to cook these crepes. To me, it seemed kind of strange, but here we are in the middle of combat somewhere, and at this strange farmhouse were lining up as if we were back at Camp Mackall.

'I looked around the kitchen and I saw a lady standing there, and her back was towards me. She never turned around. She just kept saying things in French . . . It occurred to me, I don't know that she's ever looked at anybody. She just didn't want us to see her face. As I reached her and she handed me a pancake, she looked at me . . . and you could see the tears in her eyes.

'I can never forget her face, with the tears streaming down. And that look will always remain with me.

'An act of kindness and compassion is something that one never forgets. But certainly, when you consider all of the death and destruction that we have seen in a few days, I truthfully believe that anyone who stood on that line remembers that lady that was passing out these pancakes.'

Some thirty years after the war had ended, Tom returned to Normandy and thanked the farmer.

Wayne Pierce was a glider-borne officer in the 82nd, and came into Normandy on D+1. The night before they left for battle, the men enjoyed a final hot shower.

'One of the men in our unit, Lt. Galey, had a good voice and he sang, "It's a lovely day tomorrow" in the shower that night – made us all feel good. But Galey was one of the first men killed the next day.'

In the early hours of 7 June, the soldiers lined up for a hot breakfast.

'One thing that happened that morning that we were going in to eat our breakfast, there was an officer standing behind the mess – evidently he was there to see we were fed properly and so forth. But as I came by with my mess kit he called out, "Good hunting." (It was) supposed to make me feel good, but it didn't make me feel good. If that had come from anyone but a rear echelon man, I would've been happy with it.' Rear echelon men were the troops who operated behind the front lines. In any war, a kind of friction exists between them and the combat soldiers.

'We went into Normandy at seven o'clock in the morning,' said Wayne. 'I had quite a riot going into Normandy. We were in a British Horsa glider that would hold twenty-nine, thirty men plus a pilot and co-pilot. When we took off, in addition to these twenty-nine men we had in the glider, we had boxes of mines, machine-gun ammunition and the water – everything tied down in the centre of the glider. When we took off we could tell that the tow plane was having a problem pulling us, we were loaded too heavy . . . The glider kept losing altitude . . . we were probably down to three hundred feet. I stood between the pilot and the co-pilot to ask them what was going to happen, but they were doing the best they could, fighting the glider and trying to stay up.'

Wayne ordered his men to toss what they could out of the glider.

'By the time we got that out I could see that the glider was gaining a little altitude . . . By that time, the coast of France was coming into sight. Up until that point, I had no fear of impending combat because I was too concerned about keeping the glider afloat. But we got across the coast of course, the glider was cut loose. We took the top off a tree and landed properly in a field that was as good a landing spot as any you could have picked over there.'

The men had set down a few miles from where they had expected to land.

'(We landed) near Saint-Marie-du-Mont . . . I had practically a platoon of men with me . . . we were organized very rapidly.'

Wayne saw little of the enemy the first day or night, and it was some time before they were ordered into an attack to drive the Germans out of their positions on a causeway.

'We crossed (a) ford and came into the orchard. C Company

166

was on ahead of us . . . tracers were flying through the air – lighting up the area like daylight.

'When they moved back, the rest of us moved around, through the orchard, past the buildings, and past Colonel Timmes and his men.

'I saw Lieutenant Brewster-Johnson in that area, he had been on the attack . . . he slapped me on the back and said, "Pierce, they can't shoot worth crap." But he was killed within an hour after that.

'We crossed two roads and we went down through a wheat field and down towards the church . . . We captured one prisoner and he went right along with us. There was a small orchard, and then we came to a road that was somewhat sunken. There, Colonel Sanford, myself and a couple of runners and maybe a couple other guys, we were all laying in the ditch, and when the platoon went across this road, there the firing picked up and it was like daylight, the tracers that were flying through the air, going both directions.

'Then it quieted down for a bit. Sanford moved up to the road. I was back about twenty yards maybe. He came back to me and he says, "C company is wiped out," and I thought, "How can he know that?", the men are still out there.

'He said we're moving back to the orchard so he went back, telling the other men in the little group we were in there, and they got up and followed him. I looked back, it was getting daylight by that time, I looked back to the wheat field and saw them running through the wheat field, heading back to the orchard. I still didn't think that C Company was wiped out, and I could find the men, so I ran across the orchard to the other side. I knocked my helmet off running under an apple tree and went back and picked that up, expecting to be shot any time.

'There was a German howitzer in that orchard and maybe

another one down the line a little further. I got to the other side and looked through the bushes to see if I could see any of the C Company men. I could see no one, all I could hear was German voices across from me. I sat there for a little while and decided I should better get moving too. So I unloaded my binoculars and my dispatch case, I put them under the bush, I thought I could go back and get them. Then I went back through the wheat field, over the knoll. There I found about eight or ten men from C Company. They told me the (other) men had surrendered.'

Wayne organized the survivors of the group into two squads that could fight their way back to B Company.

'Fighting was sporadic but it was bad. Before we got started we started receiving fire from our rear . . . At that point I gave up, I said, "Men, we're going back to the orchard." So we made a run back into the orchard. There I found Sanford, he was on his radio trying to get regimental headquarters across the river. He finally made contact and got artillery fire directed that would help us. We dug foxholes there and waited.'

The next day the 90th Division began passing through Wayne's unit.

'We felt elated that we had some help.

'I went back over to the same area where I had left my binoculars and dispatch case. They were gone, but I saw the dead piled up that they were picking up from the causeway, and it was a terrible sight.'

Such losses left 'dead men's shoes' to fill, and Wayne was informally given command of C Company. Weeks of fighting on the Cotentin Peninsula lay ahead.

Wayne recalled one of those battles.

'There was a German anti-tank gun, or a small tank, started firing armour-piercing shells at us. An armour-piercing shell would hit a tree and it would roll over and cut a swath right through the tree's brush and everything. It also cut one of my men almost in two. When this happened, one half of the battalion bounded forward and the other half, which is the half I had, stood fast. When we got our chance to move forward, we did. But we found that we were alone. We came to a road and I was trying to make up my mind which way to go next and I looked back and here came my regimental S3 with a radio and I thought, "Oh this is great, here comes a major, he can take command." Major comes up and looks to me and says, "Pierce, you're in command of these troops, what are you going to do?" I said, "We're moving down this road," and we started moving down the road.

'It started getting dark and we're still all alone, we hadn't found Sanford, there was a farmhouse and a group of buildings. I told the men to set up a perimeter . . . around these buildings.

'That night I was checking the defence . . . I couldn't find my First Sergeant. I looked at the house and thought maybe he went in that house. I went up on that porch and tried the door and it was open . . . sure enough there was a man in bed asleep. I shook him and I said, "Get up Sergeant, we're moving out!" and the Frenchman stood up screaming.'

It was a moment of levity amongst many of horror. Under such conditions, Wayne recalled the difficulties he had in getting men to take part in combat.

'In an attack, the first time you finally decide, "That guy's trying to kill me," you get angry, and if you can get everyone in the company angry at the same time (you can press forward with an attack).

'You never get that. You get half a dozen men that are angry, and you get up and go, and another half lay there and wait.'*

---

* Though the tools and tactics of war change, the nature of soldiers appears to be constant. Heraclitus, who lived around 2,500 years before the Battle

This attitude could also be found when it came to difficult but less dangerous duties.

'The man that helped pick up the bodies after the attack was a man who lives out in Montana, and he told me that he had a tough time getting his men to pick up bodies, you know? They needed some help. He found some Cognac or some Calvados, one or the other. He passed it around, and after the men were able to have a few drinks then, he said, they were able to load the bodies. I saw trucks with men's bodies piled about four high . . . just like cord wood.'

Wayne's battalion suffered heavy losses during their time in France.

'By the time we came back from Normandy, I had thirty-seven men out of a hundred and fifty. The lowest company that we had was company G . . . (they) had thirteen men.'

The 101st Airborne

Robert Williams jumped into Normandy with the 506th PIR. On D+1, while on their way to Carentan, the 1st Battalion came into contact with the enemy in 'the little town of Vierville. I think one of our companies had just gone through . . . and they radioed back to say the village was clear, there wasn't any Germans around there. So we come out of the field and started down the main street of Vierville.*

'All of a sudden somebody opened up with a machine gun . . .

---

of Normandy, had a similar opinion to Wayne: 'Out of every one hundred men, ten shouldn't even be there, eighty are just targets, nine are the real fighters, and we are lucky to have them, for they make the battle. Ah, but the one, one is a warrior and he will bring the others back.'

* Not to be confused with Vierville-sur-Mer, which lay on Omaha Beach.

All heck broke loose after that because the Germans had been lined up behind the hedgerow. What they had done was they had moved out of this town, and they infiltrated back in, and I think maybe we surprised them as much as they surprised us, but they had better positions than we did, they had better cover, and they had a machine gun up in the top of the church tower and we were really pinned down.

'One of our guys, the machine-gun squad, went back to the barn, a stone building right across the street from the church, and found a small hole, like a pigeon hole in the wall. He stuck his machine gun through there, he was firing back at the guys in the church steeple. About that time we heard a tank clacking the road.'

The men breathed a sigh of relief when the approaching tank turned out to be American.

'He was trying to decide who we were . . . when he got abreast of the church we kept pointing to the church steeple up there, indicating that that's where the fire was coming from. He pointed that big gun up there and blew a three-foot hole in that church steeple and eliminated that German machine-gun nest.

'The tank . . . turned around and faced the Germans, and he opened up with his .30 calibers. Our whole company, which was about 130 men, and that tank fired at the Germans. The tide was changing in our favor but we were running out of ammunition. I was going up and down trying to get ammunition for the BAR man because he was doing a better job than we were. My platoon leader decided the tank crew oughta use that .50 caliber up on top of the tank instead of using the .30 calibers (that were fired from inside the tank), but they didn't wanna [go] on top of the tank in case they got hit. So he jumped up on top, he was pretty good with the .50 caliber. He opened up with that gun and he was really knocking them off. So finally, the Germans start waving white flags, they wanted to surrender.'

Given what happened next, Robert hesitated to give the officer's name.

'He kept firing and the Germans were waving white flags.

'Most of our guys quit shooting – they weren't too anxious to run down there and capture the Germans because they didn't know whether some of the Germans weren't waving white flags, some of them were still shooting.'

A major ordered the lieutenant to stop shooting, but he was ignored. Germans continued to fall until the major drew his pistol and threatened to shoot the officer if he didn't cease fire.

'If it had been up to (him) we wouldn't have captured any of them, but that's war.'

The German opposition in the area was the 91st Infantry Division, which included a regiment of Fallschirmjäger; Germany's own paratroopers.

'They were very young – sixteen-, seventeen-year-old kids. Of course, they didn't last long, they were wiped out pretty fast. From there we moved into a hill overlooking Carentan and I remember it was in the afternoon, and the Sherman tanks came up on the back of us. From that hill overlooking Carentan they lobbed shells all day.'

Carentan was an important town for both sides. For the Americans, it would allow them to join the forces of Utah and Omaha in one continuous defensive line. If the Germans could stop this it would give them an advantageous position to launch counter-attacks, as well as preventing the Americans from launching their own attack to cut off the Cotentin Peninsula.

'We stayed there all night as a matter of fact,' said Robert. 'I slept in some German's foxhole . . . I remember before I went to sleep, we heard a plane coming over and it was a Messerschmitt . . . I could see that guy. He was looking down at us, and evidently was a reconnaissance plane because he didn't fire a shot.'

This reconnaissance was followed later in the night by an attack.

'He came over and dropped one heck of a bomb. He was trying to hit the tanks in the back of us.'

The paratroopers then moved on to take Carentan.

'It was just daylight as we got there and Colonel Strayer came down and said, "Everyone dig a foxhole, we're digging in." We dug a few inches in the ground and then, "Pack up, we're moving out." It seemed like the army ordeal was digging a foxhole, then packing back up and moving out again – stop and go, stop and go. So we started off down this road, it was a black top road that led north and west of Carentan. We were trying to go into Carentan [but] ran into too much machine-gun fire, so I think the decision was made to go round the back of Carentan. We hadn't gone down that road but two miles until we really ran into a bunch of Germans (from) a panzer division, and they had some Tiger tanks. I remember we had a little light tank, it wasn't a Sherman tank, it was a little light tank. The firing went on all afternoon and that's when my buddy Joe, in my platoon, he caught a bullet right in his chest. It was getting toward dark and we were worried about the Germans and the 88s that were coming over. That little light tank had .30 caliber machine guns on it so they went down to the fields, spraying (fire).

'I remember that before it got dark, he was just shooting at everything – all the hedgerows – and the Germans did slow down a little bit, firing slowed down. It was at that point that I found that somebody handed me a pair of binoculars that they had taken off a German officer.'

Robert was just finding a good spot to observe the enemy when they opened up on him with what he believed was an 88mm.

'One hit on the outside of this hedgerow and the dust and

the trees and the bushes, you couldn't see. I turned around to get outta there, I was in this little ditch alongside the road. I started (towards) the road and a shell came over the top of that hedgerow and hit on the other side. The dust was so thick I couldn't see where I was going.

'I think what happened was, I was using those binoculars, and the Germans thought maybe I was a field artillery spotter or something. They really went after the spotters because if you knock the spotter out, the artillery wasn't much good.'

Robert had escaped with his life, but the close proximity of the two blasts had left him dazed and confused.

'Combat exhaustion they called it, I don't know what they call it now, they've got a name for it. Anyway, you're disorientated, your nerves are shot and so forth. A tag was put on me and I was put in a jeep and I wound up on the beach at Omaha.'

Robert was evacuated to England.

'Captain Sobel was our supply officer at that time. He was reading the reports on me from the hospital and he came over and talked to me, and he didn't think he was gonna let me go (back into combat). I said, "I can do anything, I can drive a truck, I can do anything you want me to do." But he turned me down.

'I was pretty jumpy, I couldn't stand noise, I guess that's what Sobel was worried about. He wasn't a very lenient officer anyway, he was pretty tough.'

Robert did not serve in combat with the 506th again, and saw out his war as a driver for a medical unit.

Other soldiers felt unaffected by combat. At least at the time.

'I hate to say this,' said Joseph Lesniewski of Easy Company, 506th, 'but I thought I was playing a game, because it didn't bother me one bit. With the shooting, or seeing someone get killed, it never hit me.'

Joseph took part in the fighting in Carentan. Later in the

174

month, he and several other men were chosen for a patrol to flush enemy snipers out of a building.

'Dick Winters came up to pick out five of us to go on patrol. It was me, Bill Guarnere, Maxwell Clark, Billy Wagner and Albert Blithe.

'We were walking towards this house and we didn't see the snipers or anything like that. We separated a little more. All of a sudden a shot rang out, and Albert Blithe, he got hit in the back of the neck.'

Joseph was next to him, and stuffed a spare T-shirt he carried into the wound to stem the blood loss.

Albert Blithe survived his injuries. He served in the Korean War, and was still in US military service when he died in 1967. According to his son, Albert was always troubled by what he had seen in the war, and drank himself to death.[1]

After a month of fighting, the 101st were returned to England.

James Martin was serving in the 506th.

'(Our CO) told us before we went in, "Give me three days of hard fighting and you'll be out of it". Well, there was more resistance than we had thought, and we stayed there and nobody complained about it. We were there for thirty-three days.'

During this time the men did things that many would have considered unthinkable before the war.

'We were sitting on dead bodies eating K rations,' said James.

A passing tank's tracks churned up the dead, effectively skinning the face off one German corpse.

'One of the guys picked it up and put it on his head and said, "Look, I'm a Heinie!" and everybody laughed.'

It's hard to imagine what the soldiers' families back home would have thought of this, or other behaviours in Normandy.

'You could buy a woman for two packs of cigarettes. After

about seven days it took a whole carton of cigarettes to get a woman.

'Everybody wasn't happy to see us,' James said of the French. 'There were those who were very happy. But all those young men had gone, and the Germans had been there four years. I always say biology always wins. Quite a few of those young girls had married German soldiers and that caused problems. One evening this German with a French wife and three kids were walking down the street and got in an argument with somebody and our guy got up and shot him. Nobody said a word about it.'

The 6th Airborne Division under attack

After establishing themselves around the bridges spanning the Caen canal and River Horne, the troops of the 6th Airborne came under attacks by the German panzer divisions that had finally been released by higher command, including the 21st Panzer.

'It took days until other armoured divisions could get into the battle,' said Hans von Luck. 'But by then the British and the American, as we heard, had made very good, firm bases on the coast, and it was hard to throw them away into the sea. And I remember well when Rommel told us, if there's a landing somewhere in France, and we can't get the invaders back into the sea within the first twenty-four hours, that would be the end. All the effort would be too late.

'We tried to get into the very small village which the 6th Airborne had occupied. We tried to get in by nearly permanent attacks every day. But meanwhile, the 6th Airborne, and the 51st (Highland) Division, they had laid out very strong minefields.'

The 51st Division had distinguished itself in the desert and Italy, and spent the majority of its Normandy campaign in support of the 6th Airborne, which included the 12th Battalion, Parachute Regiment.

'We were just south of Ranville,' said Harold Cammack. 'That's when we first came under the attack from these panzers, and we as a parachute regiment don't carry heavy armaments. We had light machine guns, anti-personnel mines, PIAT (anti-tank) guns.

'We had what we called sticky bombs. (We had to) run forward and try and stick them onto the tracks of the tanks . . . and hope it's going to knock the tank tracks off.'

The panzer crews soon got wise to this, and would gun the approaching men down from their turret. There was also the danger that the attacking soldier would be caught in the explosion of his own bomb. Altogether, it was an extremely dangerous proposition, and called for great courage.

Harold recalled the moment when he made such an attack.

'We were laid against this wall, a few of us, myself and two chaps . . . We saw the tank coming round the corner, and we couldn't avoid it actually, because he would've spotted us, so we did the only thing we thought we could do.'

Under covering fire from one man, the other two paras ran out at the tank. 'Two of us ran forward and slammed these sticky bombs onto the track.'

The bombs went off as Harold ran clear. When the smoke cleared the track was still intact, but the men had done enough to give the tankers second thoughts, and they backed away out of sight.

Ernest Lough was a staff officer in the 5th Parachute Brigade.

'On the early morning of the 10th of June, the 12th and 13th Para Battalions reported a big build-up of enemy troops in the wooded area south of Bréville. And as a result, the orders were given for the 13th and the 7th Battalions to establish themselves on the edge of the drop zone, because it had been established that the German force was going to head towards the bridges.'

Ernest joined the 7th Battalion for the coming battle.

'That morning emerged this old World War One (style of) attack by the Germans. You wouldn't believe it if I hadn't seen it. (They) came across the ground and everything opened up. The 13th opened fire, and then the 7th opened up with machine guns and mortars.

'(It was) absolute carnage, which sickened me. All these chaps, all these men, mown down in numbers and coming on, still coming on, just like they were apparently in the First World War. Anyway, it all ended because the remnants got into a wood. At the end of the day, there were 400 enemy killed, 100 prisoners and 100 in a wood, which was later cleared by the 7th Battalion.

'(Our own casualties) were minimal because we were all established, waiting for them to come. We didn't suffer many casualties at all.'

The next day Ernest was travelling by jeep when he spotted movement in a hedgerow. He stopped to investigate, and found two wounded Wehrmacht soldiers. Ernest's batman – a servant assigned to an officer – was a German Jew and translated for him.

'I said, "Why didn't you call for help?" and he said, "We'd been told that the British paratroops would kill us. Anyone who was captured would be killed."

'The German Fallschirmjäger allegedly killed prisoners, but we never did.

'We sent for help and gave them a drink of water and a couple of cigarettes and they were evacuated later.'

The dead from the previous day's battles were presenting a problem on the drop zone, and Ernest was given the task of clearing it.

'I had to go and see the civil affairs officer, who was a Canadian officer, and arrange for the dead to be moved. They had to hire French civilians to move all these German dead. I've got a feeling they were paid for it of course, but I'm pretty sure they were elated to be given the task of moving dead Germans. Another problem we had around there was the removal of dead cattle and horses. In the process of the battle a lot of these lovely animals had been killed or maimed, and they laid there getting quite big with all these gasses inside them, and one of the tasks the French had to do also was to take these things away.'

The Germans had suffered a setback at Bréville, but they remained in the area and continued to present a threat.

'Bréville was on the high ground, overlooking the 6th Airborne Division's bridgehead, so we were under complete observation all the time from the enemy up there. The divisional commander was very conscious of this and at one stage he said, "Right, I'm prepared to accept this no longer because the enemy are getting between 3rd Brigade and the Commandos up there." So he decided that he must take Bréville.

'The only reserve he had was the 12th Parachute Battalion, who'd been reduced by casualties and things to about three hundred . . . so he ordered them to do the attack on Bréville that night. He augmented them with a company of the 12th Devons.'

The attack went badly from the very beginning.

'Everything that could have gone wrong with the operation went wrong on that occasion. The first stonk from our own artillery – our own artillery, not the 51st (divisional) artillery – landed on the start line, killing the CO, my friend Johnny Johnson.'

Harold Cammack was one of the 12th Battalion soldiers taking part in the attack.

'We heard the shells coming over, but they fell short, and Colonel Johnson and two or three more officers, and quite a few men (were killed) by our own fire. That does happen in warfare unfortunately.

'It was pretty horrendous actually, Bréville itself. Less than eighty of us came back.'

Harold survived, but not without wounds.

'As a few of us crossed the road to take a different position, these mortar shells, or whatever it was, landed on the road a few yards from us. It blew me practically back over the archway and I got badly wounded in the right leg.

'It killed two of the chaps who was with me. They were killed outright by the same barrage.'

Harold was pulled to safety by a man from another unit, who he believed to be a commando.

'He just put a heavy field dressing around my leg, and then a lot of the wounded were all put together, including German wounded as well. We was there for maybe not quite two days, and when Bréville itself was taken, they moved us down to the beach . . . and they took us back to England.'

'The cost had been very heavy,' said Ernest Lough. 'All twelve para officers, including the CO, and all the warrant officers, had all been killed or wounded.'

Ernest felt 'wonder at the courage of the men who went in, because there were many other factors that I haven't mentioned . . . But they were led by very gallant people, including the sergeant major, who was later killed. That's all there was to it.'

Bréville was captured by the British in the early hours of 13 June. Ernest was wounded in later weeks, but returned to Normandy in July.

When not in battle, the soldiers lived under constant threat of artillery and snipers. They also had to contend with living in primitive conditions, and with little rest.

Walter 'Wally' Parr had landed with John Howard's D Company, 2nd Battalion, Ox & Bucks.

'I mean, when you work out, the night was six hours of darkness, ten to four, everybody stood to at four.'

Standing to is when all soldiers man the defences to prepare for any incoming attack, which were often launched at dawn.

'That six hours (of night) was divided into three. Two hours' patrol, two hours' stag, which is sentry duty, and two hours' sleep. And then at four you start again, and you go right through the next day and you're just going on that two hours' sleep.'

This meagre amount of sleep could be interrupted by artillery or air attack.

'People was just beat out of their brains for lack of sleep.'

This fatigue was not only uncomfortable, but could lead to men making mistakes that would cost lives. It certainly played tricks on their minds.

'Night time on sentry duty. You're looking into a field, now you know there's a bush there, in the middle of that field, and at times that bush moves! You can see it moving!

'The fatigue really got to the blokes.'

Wally and his comrades also faced a natural enemy.

'The mosquitoes nearly put a stop to the battle of Normandy. That's the truth. Somebody said afterwards, if there have been a couple of mosquitoes, malaria carrying mosquitoes in Normandy, it would have brought the entire thing to a halt. The mosquitoes were the biggest, most vicious I've ever, including India, encountered in my life. We were covered in bites everywhere our neck, everything.

'They were the biggest curse in Normandy, they were worse than Germans, the mosquitoes. You ask anybody about the mosquitoes in Normandy, and if they say they don't remember them, then they was never in Normandy.'

The 6th Airborne did not launch any major attacks after Bréville and dug in on the eastern side of the Orne, where they secured the Allied flank. On the other side of the river, the forces that had landed on the beaches continued their push inland, with a continuous stream of troops coming in behind them. Allied numbers in Normandy were growing by the day, but the Germans were bringing up their own reinforcements, and in the weeks that followed D-Day, British and Canadian soldiers would face the best that the German military had to offer: the elite panzer divisions of the Waffen-SS.

CHAPTER SIX

Lodgement

*The British and Canadian Armies from
D+1 to Operation Mitten*

'It really was horrific. From then on, one feared that you
were going into an attack the next day, because according
to the law of average, if you'd escaped so far, it looked that
it might be your turn next.'

Kenneth Powter, 1st Battalion, the Suffolk Regiment

The battle to take the beaches was over, but without a deep and
well-established beachhead from which the incoming divisions
could deploy, the success of Overlord was still in jeopardy. To this
end, 'lodgement' was vital.

Lodgement meant holding a sizeable area of captured enemy
territory. For the Allied commanders in Normandy, this meant
linking up all the Allied armies and holding everything north of
the Arromanches–Falaise line.[1] The time set to accomplish this
was three weeks.

For D-Day, soldiers had trained in such detail that they
knew the position of the enemy defences and rehearsed how to

take them. There could be no such preparation for the coming battles in June. By contrast, the German troops stationed in the area had learned the ground, trained on it, and knew the ways to move; where the strong positions were to defend, and where the weak points were to counter-attack. And while the beach defences tended to be held by poorly trained, often unmotivated soldiers of the static divisions, the German troops the Allies now faced were the best that the Wehrmacht had to offer. They were well trained, well equipped, well motivated, and many had years of combat experience. Although the Allies were ashore, victory was far from certain.

Sea and Air

The work of the Allied navies was not over after D-Day. They ferried in men and supplies, brought a steady stream of wounded and prisoners back to Britain, and provided anti-aircraft cover and fire support for the troops ashore. As well as the danger of sea mines, they faced attack from the air, U and E-boats, and coastal and railway guns.

Arthur 'Larry' Fursland served aboard the cruiser *Belfast*. 'About three or four days after D-Day they had a big gun at Le Havre, twenty mile away. It must have been on a track. It had the range of this area where we were. This one (shell) come right near the ship, but the shell exploded before it struck. The shrapnel went through across where I was. These two marines, they were in the butcher's shop. One lost a leg, I found out afterwards, and the other died.'

A week or so later, Arthur was watching a destroyer passing close by. 'I was smoking a fag on the catapult before I went down on watch. Ten to eight in the morning. This destroyer went by, all the lads on the top deck, V-sign, all like this.' As the men were waving their 'greetings' their destroyer hit a mine. This was most likely HMS *Swift*, which was sunk on 24 June, with fifty-three casualties. The explosion was so powerful that it broke the *Swift* in half.

Robert Fitzgerald, of the 1st Battalion, Canadian Scottish Regiment, was preparing to transfer from a ship onto a landing barge when a German aircraft made a dive-bombing attack.

'I said to the chap (on the barge), "Was that a Stuka that went over?" And he said, "Aye, it were." He said, "I just shook me fist at him, and I said he never got me in Liverpool or London, and he ain't gonna get me yet, and the beggar missed."'

The man's reaction made Robert think that 'with people like that, we're going to win this war.'

Ray Smith, who was aboard the destroyer HMS *Middleton*, said that '(After D-Day) we were patrolling along the coast for German E-boats. We got engaged by quite a few of those. Unfortunately we had one of our seamen killed fighting against (them). They were very fast and armed with either pom-poms or Oerlikon guns. They were pretty active and they were a job to hit because of the speed they were doing, but I think we managed to sink one or two.'

'After the troops were inland about six miles we were no more use,' said Gordon Painter of the *Belfast*. 'Couldn't carry on bombarding or else we'd be killing our own chaps, and so they sent us ashore to do a bit of clearing up on the beaches. The main clearing up had been done . . . We had time and that to walk up onto the front of the beach, and the houses had all been bombed, and shelled. We went into some of the houses that had been absolutely shattered. Blown to bits. I picked up one or two souvenirs. I picked up a couple of German letters. I assume they were written to their French girlfriends.'

Naval firepower had been critical for supporting the troops

who established the beachhead, but now the tactical air forces came into their own.

'We kept on going over to clear these roads, and so it went on, day after day,' said Typhoon pilot John Golley.

Deadly attacks by Allied fighter-bombers became so common German soldiers would describe them as 'Jabo-Tod', death by 'Jabo', which was an abbreviation of the German word for a fighter-bomber, Jagdbomber.[2] The panzer divisions were often on the end of these aerial attacks.

'We were constantly attacked by fighter-bombers,' said Hebert Meier, of the Panzer Lehr. 'I thought at first, because I had assumed that we still had an air force, that these were all German aircraft. They were constantly attacking us.

'(One) evening, we went into a village and we were the last vehicle there with all the camouflage on top. We were still relatively inexperienced. So we had leaves, twigs on top, and of course, on the street we were particularly conspicuous. But dusk came in and then four more Jabos came, but they still saw us, then they turned around.

'Instead of running right and left, we walked straight ahead like into a sort of field and lay down in the little ditches. I still see the shoes of my comrades there in front of me, and then they came, they fired, sort of, 'Brrrrrrr' flew over us and so on. I'd been counting, the first flew over. Then the second one came, and then he fired too. The third fired as well but the fourth only flew away over us. And then we raised our heads and, of course, our vehicle was already engulfed in flames. So there we were, on the evening of the invasion, (and we) had already lost our first vehicle, and we weren't even at the front yet.'

As well as searching for targets of opportunity, the fighter-bombers worked in concert with the ground troops and their embedded fighter controllers.

'We'd patrol the line,' said John Golley, 'and there'd be a light armoured car with an army officer in it, and he'd call us up, and our callsign was Archduke . . . He would identify the target. The army would fire a coloured (smoke) shell onto the target . . . he would give us a grid reference . . . and we would dive straight down on the target.'

John recalled one interaction with the forward air controller.

'Hello, Archduke leader, are you receiving me?'

'Loud and clear, old boy.'

'Are you religious?'

'Not terribly, old chap, why?'

'I've got a church for you this morning.'

Because of their height and commanding views, church steeples were favoured positions of snipers and artillery observers. Normandy's churches had survived for centuries but many were destroyed or damaged during the campaign.

While some air and artillery controllers operated on the ground, others flew in slow-moving aircraft above the battlefield. Roy Crane, who was flying Typhoons, said of the spotter plane crews, 'I had the greatest admiration for (them), because I think they had the most dangerous job in the war. They did lose a lot of people, but they did provide us with very valuable information.'

As well as the danger of small-arms fire from the ground, pilots had to contend with anti-aircraft artillery, known as 'flak' to the airmen.

'These black puffs would sort of appear,' said Typhoon pilot Kenneth Trott. 'And I'll say this much for the Germans, they always got the height right. And you could hear it above an aircraft engine, so you can imagine how close that used to be sometimes. You knew they'd got their height so you either pulled up high or you went down low.

'My wing commander took us out on a trip one evening after

D-Day. We were going on an armed reconnaissance south of Caen. It was in the evening, and dusk was approaching . . . Suddenly this flak started up. And I mean, you've been to a firework display, you know what a firework display's like. That's what it was like. And I thought, Oh good grief, he's not taken us into that lot?' The wing was ordered to make a 180-degree turn, but their commander paid a price for being at the head of the formation. 'When we formed up again, he'd been shot down.'

The fighter and fighter-bomber pilots were also in danger between their missions, as they were based in Normandy as soon as airfields could be established. This drastically increased the number of missions that they could undertake in a day, but also brought them in the range of German guns, as well as making them a tempting target for the Luftwaffe, who knew that it was far easier to destroy planes on the ground than in the air.

The Luftwaffe's Normandy missions were almost always night-time affairs. This was to avoid the constant waves of fighters that roamed the skies in daylight, and with so many men and so much materiel packed into the tight beachhead, there was a high probability that their bombs and cannons would find a mark. The night-time sorties also robbed Allied soldiers of what little sleep they had.

John Golley recalled a daylight attack on his aerodrome by three low-flying aircraft, causing damage and resulting in casualties. A member of John's ground crew was wounded in the throat and saved by a doctor who placed a glass tube into his windpipe. 'I remember having to hold the thing together,' said John. 'He was pumping out blood, and I didn't like blood, being a bit of a sensitive character, so when the doctor put my hands on his windpipe to hold the glass in position, I looked the other way, and I looked the other way until we got him to hospital.'

He considered the pilots to be very brave – they would have known that there was a good chance that they were flying their final mission. Considering the Luftwaffe squadrons were already low on pilots and aircraft, the daylight raid on John's airfield would have been a calculated risk: their loss was deemed worthwhile if they could destroy the Typhoons that were causing so much destruction on the German panzer divisions. The war for air superiority had already been lost, but there was still a chance that the Wehrmacht could win the ground war.

The Push from Gold

Snipers like William Hanna came into their own in the weeks following D-Day. Although he was armed with a telescopic sight for his standard Lee Enfield .303 calibre rifle and capable of hitting targets at ranges of 600 yards or more, it was rare that this kind of sniping occurred in Normandy. One reason was the terrain: high hedgerows, copses and woods, and sunken roads limited range of sight. Intact church towers were increasingly rare. While the German snipers were able to wait for an advancing enemy leaving cover, the British snipers used their skills honed under the tutelage of men like Lord Lovat to stalk into no man's land, where they could lie in position for days, gathering intelligence on troop numbers, routines, fighting positions, enemy weaponry, and even the individual habits of the soldiers. As the Wehrmacht had a mixture of battle-hardened and fresh troops, identifying the less experienced could prove particularly useful for night raids, when small groups of British soldiers would snatch a prisoner from the enemy lines. Night raids were a staple of the British, who had honed the practice during the First World War. Usually led by an officer, and taking a few picked men, the raids could be anything from stealthy reconnaissance, to a prisoner snatch, to sowing general mayhem and confusion by lobbing grenades and shouting orders to give the impression of a wider attack. These raids were believed to be important for strengthening the fighting spirit of a regiment, and though they could be incredibly dangerous, unit war diaries are filled with entries describing such tasks.

'We were selective with our targets,' said William. 'We weren't so much interested in the ordinary infantry soldier.'

William had been taught to identify German soldiers by their rank and insignia. His priorities were officers, senior NCOs and specialists such as mortar fire controllers.

'If you just had the head exposed, you aimed at the head. Or if you had a full body exposure you'd go for somewhere near the heart. There was no shoot to wound.'

William recalled some of his successful shoots.

'It was a German O-Group. I was in no man's land, and there was a German officer, and they had a map out and they were viewing the countryside and doing their reconnaissance.' The snipers hit their mark and the other men scattered. 'Sometimes it was difficult to see how effective your shooting was because you obviously couldn't go up and have a look at the body. You couldn't confirm it. You were quite sure in your mind you got a hit. You could see the guy going to the ground, but how can you say you killed him? He may have crapped himself. He may have gone to ground and taken cover . . . And people do survive the most horrific wounds.'

Given that their targets were often not engaged directly in battle, the role of sniper required a strong degree of detachment, but this did not equate to heartlessness; merely a willingness to do what needed to be done.

This certainly rang true for William. He and his comrades had compassion towards the ordinary German soldier, and he recalled one incident that greatly shocked them all.

'We were in a location just in front of a wood, and in the

wood there was a German position. Suddenly we saw a crowd of Germans, I'm not quite sure how many, they were coming out of the wood with their hands up, and their weapons down, and they were obviously ready to surrender. And they were making their way towards our position to surrender. And suddenly we heard firing, and we saw these Germans with their hands up going to ground. And we thought, None of our chaps are shooting prisoners? There's nobody firing around our location. We then discovered it was the Germans shooting their own troops. The SS was in that location as well, and they shot their own troops because they were surrendering.' This boiled the blood of the British soldiers. 'Their reaction, when they saw that happening, they said, "Christ, the bastards are shooting their own men!" And our blokes were concerned about the Germans, the ones that wanted to surrender were being shot up.'

Not long after, the Hampshires took the wood where the SS had fired from. 'And when they took the position, they didn't take any prisoners. They give the SS what for. That's typical British soldier, though,' William said. 'Typical British soldier.'

This sentiment was echoed by Ronald White, also of the Hampshires. 'The actual German serviceman, we didn't mind. We captured them. He was like us, he was doing his job. It was the SS and the Gestapo people we had no time for, whatsoever. We had no quarter with them.'

Ronald served as an NCO in an anti-tank platoon, and recalled the peril from German snipers in the Normandy bocage. 'They were everywhere. Up in trees. Tied up in trees. In houses. We used to dread (snipers) more than anything else. You never knew where they were. How far away they were.'

German artillery was also deadly with its accuracy. 'Every time we moved on a little lane, fire came down immediately. They heard the tanks or cars start up, (and) fire came down.'

191

The German defenders had spent their time before the invasion well, recording targets so that fire could be brought down onto positions that the Allies would use as they moved forwards. Ronald recalled discovering one of their forward observation positions.

'As we advanced in this orchard we found a huge tower built of wood.' At the top of the tower was a painting of the terrain with the ranges measured for woods, roads, and other points. From this vantage position, a German forward observation officer could bring down artillery quickly and accurately on any sight or sound of a British advance.

The solution was to avoid all likely routes and approaches. Rather than using roads, the Hampshires began blowing holes through the thick hedgerows. 'We advanced across country, and that surprised them. He had all the ranges for the roads, but not the fields in between, and that started the comeback for us. Instead of using roads we went straight across country at them.'

As though snipers and artillery weren't enough for the British infantry to deal with, there was also the presence of the panzers. In the close confines of the Normandy terrain, the enemy tanks would be almost on top of the soldiers before they saw them.

'You imagine a hundred metres away was hedgerows and trees. You couldn't see a thing. You would just hear them, and until they'd come close to the hedgerow, then you'd see the top of the turret of this tank. Which we had a go at that, we did. I think our platoon got about six (of them). (My gun) got two.'

One day, Ronald and his gun team faced one of the greatest fears of Allied soldiers: a Tiger tank.

'I was on a roadway, right in the open. Nowhere else I could go, and he was coming straight towards us.' It was then that Ronald saw a beautiful sight: American armour. 'The Sherman tanks come up in the field alongside us, and (the Tiger) retreated and went back, which I'm glad he did, because we couldn't have shot it. The armour in front was so thick, you could never penetrate a Tiger tank. Not from the front. 'I said my prayers that day.'

Twenty-two-year-old John Donnelly was a gunner in 1st Royal Tank Regiment, and had already served in the desert. On 13 June his tank went into action at Villers-Bocage. This battle was part of Operation Perch, an advance to the south-east of Caen. On 12 June, the German line had broken between Caen and Saint-Lô as the US 1st Infantry Division advanced against the point where the positions of the 352nd Infantry Division met those of the Panzer Lehr. This left an eight-mile gap in the German line between La Belle Épine in the north and Caumont in the south. Montgomery hoped to exploit this gap and sent the 7th Armoured Division through to encircle Caen.

The next day 7th Armoured pushed south-west to Villers-Bocage, a junction town through which they had to pass to seize the important heights at Point 213, which dominated the surrounding area.

The lead vehicles reached the town by 0830. By 0900 they had passed through it having faced only minor resistance, and took Point 213 with their lead tanks. While waiting for the rest of the division to arrive, the vanguard halted. They were strung out in a column, and an inviting target for counter-attack by the 101st SS Heavy Panzer Battalion.

'They were massacred,' said John. 'Apparently this German officer had shot the first one, shot the last one, and then he went down and shot the whole blinking lot, and they got practically wiped out.'

The 'German officer' was probably panzer ace Michael Wittmann, who brought his force of Tiger tanks to the counter-attack, moving between Villers-Bocage and Hill 213. Four of the

Tigers were knocked out but the British lost fifty-three armoured vehicles.*

John Donnelly scored his own tank-kill at Villers-Bocage.

'The Germans started an attack. Our troop was left on a little hillock. It was our first engagement with a Tiger tank . . . It came right across an open field to make for a clump of trees. I fired on it, and I was disgusted. You just seen your blinking AP shells ricocheting off it, no penetration at all. It went into this wood . . . but this silly man came out again. Reversed out, this German, so we hit him really hard and his crew bailed out. It didnae go fire but we must have damaged it because it wouldnae move.' John was promoted following the action, and his tank commander was awarded the Military Cross.

Lacking reinforcements, the British withdrew from Villers-Bocage on 14 June. After initially being liberated with little damage, the town would now be pummelled by a force of more than 300 RAF bombers, as well as fighter-bombers.

'Whole wings were going, all through the day, firing rockets,' said Typhoon pilot Roy Crane. 'I personally went four times in one day, and each time fired eight rockets into Villers-Bocage. And yet, I go there now, fifty odd years after, and never once has a French person said to me, you killed a lot of our people as well. They only give us so much thanks for the support we gave.'

On the same day that the British withdrew from Villers-Bocage, the 9th Battalion, Durham Light Infantry were ordered into an attack at Lingèvres. Major John Mogg said, 'I heard afterwards that when (Colonel Woods) had the order, he said, "Brigadier, you know if we do this we will have a tremendous number of casualties. We ought to do this attack at night, and

* Wittmann and his crew were killed in an ambush by Canadian and British tanks on 8 August.

we ought to have much more time for reconnaissance." And the brigadier said, "I know that, but I have been told that this is a desperately important battle. We've got to get this village, we've got to go so the breakout can continue from the beachhead. And if we don't do it now we may well find that the opposition is stiffening up all the time, so we've got to do it." '

The 9th advanced with the 6th DLI on their left. All four companies of the 9th were 'up' on the attack, with two on each flank.

'We were supported by tanks of 4th/7th Dragoon Guards, who were utterly magnificent . . . They were out to the flank and shooting us in. As we crossed the start line all hell broke loose from our own side, Typhoons, and the artillery barrage, and the tanks all shooting up the enemy positions in the wood. You could see the ground literally dance in front of you, and trees were coming down, and I thought to myself, Good Lord, nobody could ever live in that thing. We went through the corn . . . we marched about halfway across the corn, with still this barrage going on, but suddenly you saw the odd Geordie dropping in the corn.'

John received a message from the CO over the radio. 'He said, "We are running into terrible trouble here on the left. All the A Company officers are casualties. I am trying to get on with B Company." '

On the right flank, C Company became involved in hand-to-hand fighting. 'We got into the woods, and we discovered afterwards that during the bombardment, the Germans had got their machine guns on fixed lines, and they had a string attachment to the machine gun so that they could lie on the bottom of their foxholes and then just pull the trigger, and the machine gun shot in enfilade fire right across this corn.

'By the time that we got into the woods C Company had lost quite a few chaps. I passed D Company through and we got into the village, again supported by these marvellous 4th/7th tanks, who took every risk and were with us all the way.'

The village was a 'scene of utter destruction. The church was in ruins. Buildings had collapsed. And there was very heavy shelling coming from the far side of the village.'

It was during this time that John received tragic news about his beloved CO. 'I had a message to say that Humphrey Woods had been killed. It filled me with utter despair to start with, then I realized I must do something about it.'

John, now in command of the battalion, pulled together the commanders of the supporting units and his own officers to hold an orders group. Soon after, the enemy launched an attack to recapture the village.

'The first counter-attack of enemy tanks came in. Luckily no infantry.' John had sited his anti-tank guns on the road, which proved a mistake. 'All the German tanks had to do was shoot straight down the road and they destroyed our anti-tank guns. And we lost the only three anti-tank guns that we had there. They were destroyed and most of the crew were shot up too. Luckily, the 4th/7th Dragoons had placed their tanks in enfilade, and as the Panther tanks came down the road, they brewed up four of these straight away, which was the most extraordinary sight.'

John remembered a phrase from his training – 'dominate the battlefield' – and issued more orders in the wake of the counter-attack.

'We'd seen these German tanks ahead of us, milling about on the other side . . . So I thought, Well we better take a patrol out, and see where these tanks are. And stupidly, I went with Sergeant Jordan and Roy Griffiths from D Company, and two other soldiers. We crept along the bank . . . using the best of cover . . . until we poked our nose over . . . and there was the first Tiger tank we'd seen, and another Panther tank.'

John ordered the PIAT man to fire on the Tiger.

'And the Geordie looked at me in horror. In fact it was Roy Griffiths. And he said, "I've never fired one of these bloody things before." And that really is a lesson, because he had carried that thing the whole way from England, across the Channel, and the first time he wanted to use it he'd never even fired it. So there's a lesson there for somebody, that you must not have any leaks in your training.' John had fired several PIATs himself and took over.

His shot was a success. 'We brewed up the first tank, and I can see now the German officer rushing out of it, and two other chaps getting out of the driving seat. So we thought it was time for us to go, and I've never run quite so fast in my life.'

John believes that this was the first recorded instance of a Tiger tank being destroyed by a PIAT. His men repulsed a second counter–attack that afternoon, and at around 1730 a message came from Brigade HQ that the battalion's position would be taken over by another unit. 'I can't tell you how relieved we were.'

Once they were pulled out of the line, the extent of the 9th DLI's casualties became horribly clear. 'The full number of casualties were twenty-two officers, and two hundred and twenty-two soldiers.' This was from a strength of some 590 men. 'People will say, was it worth it? The only thing I can say is that we obeyed our orders, we captured the village, and therefore it was a major strategic and tactical advantage to the division, and it enabled the other battalions to pour through the gap, and so you'll have to make up your own mind whether it was worth it or it wasn't worth it. I just felt terrible that all those young Durham soldiers, and when you go and look at the cemeteries there you look, and you are amazed at the ages of some of them. Eighteens, nineteens, twenties. And the worst thing, in a way, was having two battalions aside each other on this attack – because 6 Battalion had quite a lot of casualties as well – all of them came from more or less the same area, such as Newcastle, Gateshead, Sunderland, all those parts of the world. A lot of them were splendid miners, and mining families from mining villages, and to have all those casualties at once, the morale of those people in the Durham area, and the Northumberland area, was obviously very, very low at having so many casualties and relatives in one battalion. I tried to write to every officer's next of kin, and the officers wrote to every soldier's next of kin, and that took quite a lot of time.'

John received a DSO for his actions that day. He remained in the army until 1976 and retired with the rank of general.

George Elliott also served in the Durhams. An NCO in the 10th Battalion, he had joined the army in 1932. In 1940, as a member of the British Expeditionary Force, George was one of the men evacuated from Dunkirk. Now he had returned to France.

'We moved from the beach through Bayeux . . . We saw the notices of the 51st and the 50th Divisions, and we passed through them . . . When we went through these lads they looked very tired . . . we could see on the higher ground where tanks had been knocked out . . . the odd one here, the odd one there.

'We dug in and I got the lads the meal . . . but before I was able to make tea I saw a farm house, and I went up to the farm and asked if I could have some water from his well, and he refused point blank. And I was offering to pay him, in the Occupation money, and I offered to pay him the money for the water, and he refused point blank . . . So I took a couple of 36 grenades out of me pouches, and I said if I couldn't have water, he couldn't have water. And when he saw the grenades, he let me have the water. I paid him for it, but I had to threaten him with grenades in his well. I said, "Back to France again. Typical."'

George then spotted a booby-trapped hay cart and reported it to the engineers. The next morning, the 10th DLI went into action.

'There was an artillery barrage, and we were told that if there was any difficulties with the enemy, we only had to ring up for the air force and the air force would come in, and this was joy to me after being at Dunkirk, just to ring up and say, "We want an aeroplane." And on top of that, at various times, there was just aircraft circling. Waiting. Typhoons, they were just waiting for instruction.'

The attack was also supported by the warships off the coast.

'When we went in we were the left flank company, and my platoon was the reserve platoon for the company.' The platoons' sections also operated in this 'two up, one back' formation. 'We were being fired on but not as severe as the right-hand companies . . . They were receiving bit of a hammering and I saw quite a number of people fall.'

It didn't take long for George's company to reach the village of Saint-Pierre.

'There was a tank, which had been hit. I don't know if it was one of ours or one of the Germans'. The turret was on the ground with half the body of a crew in it, and the other half was still in the tank.'

George's platoon pushed on until they reached an orchard. At this point they had taken one casualty, a badly wounded private soldier. 'The stretcher-bearers behind us took him away.' More casualties followed when a machine gun opened up on the platoon. 'Two men went down . . . they were both dying, but we couldn't stop to look after them, we just shouted for stretcher-bearers.' The two mortally wounded men were close friends.

'We went forward again for about another three or four hundred yards.'

The men had now entered the bocage country: small pastures surrounded by thick hedgerows and woods, and sunken roads. 'There was a lot of woods . . . we went forward to the edge of

199

a field . . . and we were told to stop. That was the end of the advance.'

The company was then pulled back to the orchard, and immediately set about digging in. In the woods ahead of them were two dead snipers. 'They were hanging from trees.'

Later that day two prisoners came into the position. Having just lost friends to enemy fire, the men in the company did not take kindly to their presence. 'They got very ugly, if you like. They wanted to see their boots off.'

George, the sergeant major, and officers had to point their weapons at their own men to stop them from killing the prisoners. 'The lads couldn't understand why, you see, and we explained to them. We might get information from them which would save (our men's) lives . . . and these youngsters, they were so worked up at being in action, and they realized that we were doing the correct thing.'

That night, George was ordered to go out and find the two men who had been mortally wounded.

'Any dead we were to bury them there and then, and if there was any wounded, to bring them in. I went to the forward part of the bocage where I knew we'd left Private Prest and Lance Corporal Ward, but when we got there both Prest and Ward, their bodies had vanished. But there was also the bodies of some other DLI lying there who had been killed the same day. I think there was three. But they weren't from my platoon, and I didn't recognize them.'

George's party was then discovered by the enemy. 'The Germans opened up. A barrage came up, so I told the lads to get back under cover.'

Whilst this fire went on, George took the dead soldiers' dog tags and emptied their pockets of anything that would be of use to the Germans. 'I saw there was some weapons slits . . . so I took the bodies, wrapped them in a ground sheet, and buried them where they were.'

George did all this while still under fire. When he returned to the platoon, he was told that they'd be going into action again the next morning.

'We went over the same ground that we'd already taken . . . luckily we had no casualties.' They were then once again told to withdraw, this time to the village. 'To me this is crackers.'

After this action, George was asked to provide a Bren group to support another platoon. 'They were all killed,' he said. George was himself wounded as he moved between positions.

'I felt me arm go numb . . . and when I looked I'd received a bullet through the front of the arm. I was back in England the next day.'

The two men who would never return home were nineteen-year-old Kenneth Prest, the son of Percy and Florence and the husband of Anne, and twenty-one-year-old Thomas Ward, who had been named after his father. Thomas also left behind his mother Mary, and his wife Doris. Their young lives cut short, the two soldiers were buried in Normandy soil.

The Push from Juno

Siegfried 'Hans' Siegel commanded 8th Panzer Company of the 12th SS Panzer Division Hitlerjugend, which was known for its fanatical devotion to the Führer.

'On the night from 5th to 6th, we were alarmed at four o'clock in the morning, and had to go ready to fight. We stayed nearly eighteen kilometres south-east of Caen. We started moving north, but after twenty kilometres, (we) had the order to stop . . . We were held in this area for the next twelve hours, and started during the night to the left side (of Caen), because our headquarter didn't know if it was the real invasion, or a diversionary operation.

'In the earlier morning the following day, I arrived with a few of my tanks, perhaps five, at Caen. When I arrived I was ordered by a regiment commander to take a motorcycle and to go in the direction of the coast to look out for Allied forces. After I have gone about one kilometre, perhaps, I was shot at. I stopped and waited, and later, my tanks arrived at my position.'

Hans then led those tanks in an attack on the Allied lines, but despite inflicting heavy casualties they were unable to push them back all the way to the beaches. Had they been sent forward on D-Day itself, things might have been different. 'An early and energetic use of our forces might have changed things,' he said.

One of the men opposing the 12th SS Panzer Division was Jim Parks, of the Winnipeg Rifles. They had taken Putot-en-Bessin by around noon on 7 June, meeting only slight resistance, but on 8 June the Winnipeg Rifles were attacked by elements of the 12th SS Panzer Division, supported by German snipers. In the heavy, attritional fighting Putot was lost then taken again after a counter-attack by the brigade reserve. Casualties on both sides were high. Describing the fighting, Jim said,' That was pretty hectic for a couple of days, getting overrun like that. We didn't know where the heck they were, they would pop up, you'd fire and they'd be gone, they'd fire and you'd be gone.

'We ended up with a hundred and fifty-six casualties on the beach – that's killed and wounded. Over three or four days, another eighty or ninety wounded or killed.' After that Jim remembered things being a bit quieter. He was in a ditch at the village of Brouay when his brother Jack, who was in the same platoon, told him his schoolfriend Izzy Friedman was also in the ditch nearby. The next time Jim saw Izzy was 8 July. 'A shell hit his trench. I'd seen him the day before and he was killed . . . the next day. This happened quite often.'[3]

Jim had many close calls with death. 'I remember this one time I was looking for cover, and I got caught out in the open. (I) ran, got my foot on a window sill, I ducked and the shell landed behind me, and blew me through the window. Next thing I remember I was sitting at the regimental aid post with a cup of tea in my hand . . . thinking, How the hell did I get here?'

Philip Branson, a British officer, saw the result of the actions that Jim had fought in when clearing the outskirts of a village. On the edge of some woods, he noticed the deathly silence and looked round for German activity. 'We came across a pile of bodies. Literally a pile of bodies. They were Canadians of the Winnipeg Rifles, and they were piled high . . . there must have been thirty men there.' All their boots were missing. There was a strong feeling of camaraderie between the British and Canadian soldiers, and the sight stayed with Philip for the rest of his life. 'When one sees German dead, one is fairly dispassionate. When one sees your own dead . . .' his voice broke, 'it gets to you a little more.'

Robert Fitzgerald was an infantryman in the 1st Battalion, Canadian Scottish Regiment. 'Four or five of my friends, they were captured. And they found them, and they were shot through the head.' Such atrocities hardened the men towards their enemy, with the killing of Allied POWs often attributed to the 12th SS Panzer Division. 'So we said right, we don't take any prisoners. And we never did.'

Trooper Dodds, of the 6th Canadian Armoured Regiment (1st Hussars), recounted one brutal battle on 11 June. This hasty operation intended for the 6th Armoured Regiment (1st Hussars) and The Queen's Own Rifles of Canada to attack through Norrey-en-Bessin in order to seize the high ground to the south of Cheux.

They aimed to do this via a right flanking manoeuvre through the village of Le Mesnil-Patry. The attack was slowed by heavy mortar and machine-gun fire, followed by a counter-attack by German panzers and anti-tank guns that left many of the Canadians killed, wounded, or missing in action. To try and clarify what had happened to the missing men, Dodds and other survivors were asked to write accounts of their experiences that day, providing an immediacy to his words which is often lost in recollections given decades later. He described his tank – a Sherman 4A2 diesel with armour plating on the some of the ammunition racks – and how the attack was unexpectedly brought forward a day by high command.

> This left no time for briefing the crew and only a little time for the officers to get in the picture. I was under the impression it would be a quiet HE [High Explosive] shoot with the Artillery . . .[4]

This was not to be the case.

They moved off, some infantry of the Queen's Own Rifles riding to battle on the back of their tanks.

> I saw a knocked-out tank across a road as we approached a town, Capt Harrison gave orders to speed up the attack. I could hear Jerry machine guns going. From the wireless messages, no one could locate it. Our own tank fired HE and co-ax [co-axial machine-gun] at some haystacks and other points – hedges etc . . .

The unit's war diary stated: ' "B" and "C" Sqns seemed to run into heavy enemy Inf concentrations and were expending their ammunition with devastating effect on the Germans.'[5]

The Canadian tanks continued their heavy fire as they moved into an orchard where the German infantry were concentrated.

This promising attack soon turned ghastly for the Canadians.

We got a message on the (radio) saying someone reported enemy tanks in their sector . . .

From the war diary: 'Suddenly both "B" and "C" Sqns reported anti-tank guns and tanks were firing on them . . . It was evident that the enemy were beginning to outflank us.'[6]

German Panthers and Panzer IVs, along with heavy mortar fire, began to inflict severe casualties on the advancing Canadians.

Dodds continued:

Captain Harrison was hit, he bled all down the side of his head but did not appear to be badly wounded, for at the time his head was practically inside the turret. I felt for a field dressing in my front pocket and Sergeant Johnstone, the gunner, said, 'Speed up, Huckell, follow the tank in front until I order differently.'

It wasn't long until Dodds' tank fell victim to German gunnery.

He saw Captain Harrison and Sergeant Johnstone bail out and then Dodds made his own escape. It was a perilous moment, as both tanks and infantry would have their aim on stricken tanks. Killing escaping crews was done by both sides to prevent them from being re-equipped, and joining later battles.

I went out the turret top with all the speed I could, dropped to the ground, and ran about twenty yards into some bushes.

I did not see or hear any more of Huckell until he was found dead beside the tank several days later. From the brush heaps I peered through a hedge only to see a German about fifty yards away. He had a rifle and looked ready for anything. I ducked back into the brush, moved a few feet and lay down, three shots went over me . . . Looking in the other direction, I saw two of our fellows beside one of our tanks, which was burning.

I ran the fifteen yards to them and crouched beside them; one was Timps who had come out of the escape hatch and an officer whom I did not know. He was wounded in the left shoulder apparently by one or two bullets; but appeared able to crawl. About fifty yards down the road was another of our tanks, also burning. All three of us crawled down to it. At the other tank parked close to the hedge were Tprs Loucks, Silverburg and Hancock, of Capt Smuck's crew. Hancock appeared to be O.K., Loucks was burned about the neck, head and hands and appeared to be dazed. Silverburg's clothes were still burning but we quickly extinguished the fire. Two or three Germans appeared in the field about 100 yds or so away, on the edge of an old orchard. About 40 or 50 yds down the road was another of our tanks still burning. We all began crawling down the road towards it.

Sergeant Hancock went running down the road and was found dead a few days later. Loucks and Silverburg also disappeared.

As the Officer and I moved under the tank we could hear Germans coming out of the field through the hedge and on to the tank, all shouting and gibbering. I looked back up the road and saw a Jerry beside the tank we had left . . .

The tank we were under was burning. Some Germans were on top of the tank. I threw a grenade from the front of the tank so as to land it in the hedge alongside the tank. The shouting stopped for a moment and then resumed. Then the Officer lay on his back at the rear of the tank. Pulling the pin from his grenade cost him a great deal of pain and effort with his wounded shoulder, but he got it out and threw the grenade . . .

As a German approached, the officer took out his gun while Dodds prepared to run for it. The unit diary details the officer's likely fate. 'The last report we had of Captain R.H. Harrison he had bailed out of his disabled tank and was throwing hand grenades into the enemy slit trenches. Not one of "B" Sqn Officers returned to the Unit, all of them fighting to the very last. Only three NCOs returned.'[7]

Dodds' own hair-raising flight continued. He slipped by Germans, ducked their bullets, passed destroyed vehicles, and saw three startled civilians who did not return his wave. Finally he found some burned-out Shermans on the road, with three more tanks defending them.

They all three traversed their turrets but I waved my paybook and handkerchief as I approached. I came close to one and spoke to the crew commander – he would not expose himself at all, just showing the top of his head – who directed me to some Canadians in a field nearby, I walked over through a belt of anti-tank mines and into an orchard where there was a group of 3 Div anti-tank people. They fed me some duck dinner.

Trooper Dodds survived that day, and the war. Many of his

regiment did not. It was a day filled with courageous acts, and one particular act of valour was recorded in the unit war diary.

Sjt Simmons collected his crew together after his tank had been hit and was returning to the rear when he noticed a panther was about to use its small arms on them. He told the men to scatter and he himself ran towards the panther so as to draw their fire. He was not seen again.[8]

The unit war diary claimed that fourteen Panther tanks were knocked out during the action, and that one of the unit's gunners, Trooper Chapman, accounted for three of them: he had knocked out five only two days before. Other sources put the German losses at four tanks.

June 11th was the bloodiest day in regimental history for the 6th CAR, with the loss of thirty-seven tanks, and eighty men either killed or missing. Later, the reason for the hasty order to attack was revealed: the advancing German tanks had been part of a divisional assault by 12th SS Panzer Hitlerjugend. Though they failed to secure their objectives, the actions of 6th CAR that day ensured that the 7th Canadian Infantry Brigade was not cut off.

The following day, Patrick 'Bill' Lewis landed as part of the 2nd Canadian Armoured Brigade. Working inside the tanks in summer left the men filthy with grime and sweat, and one day, some of the tankers went for a swim in a river while Bill stood guard.

'I walked around a corner . . . and I looked there and these guys (were) washing in the pond. I was just going to start speaking, and suddenly I see there's a German standing there with a gun the same as me. We looked at one another. He ran, and I ran.'

Roly Armitage was seventeen years old when he volunteered for the Canadian Army. 'I saw a line of guys, asked what they were doing, and they said they were joining the army. So I joined them. It was a very impromptu thing. That afternoon I was in the army.'[9]

His unit, the 3rd Medium Regiment, Canadian Royal Artillery, came ashore on D+10.

'The beach was just packed with German prisoners, and they went out on the boat and went back to England. They were waving at us, saying have a good day.'

As a range-finder, Roly worked in the command post where he helped to plot the batteries' fire missions. 'We'd get the message from the (forward observation officer: FOO). I'd figure out the line and range and then every four hours we got (weather) reports – direction of wind, barometer reading, whatever, and then we'd adjust. When we got on the target, we had eight guns. (The FOO would) call for fire and we'd send in about forty shells. (If) the time of flight was about twenty seconds, we'd set the fuse for nineteen so they'd blow shrapnel in the air. I always felt bad about that.'

Many of Roly's missions involved firing at German artillery. This long-range, high-explosive duel was known as counter-battery fire. He recalled a day when he was in one such action.

'We already had plotted the shots on German guns. (My officer) went out (to take a back bearing on his compass) and another shell came in. When it landed he . . .' Roly's voice trailed: his officer had been badly hit. 'My Sergeant and I both went out. We shouldn't have been out there either. Every officer had morphine on them, and we knew that, so another man, I don't know who it was, reached in and pulled out (the officer's) stuff and went to put in the needle, but he said, "No, put it in this arm, it hurts!" and he just dropped dead, bled out, too many holes in him.

'Two days later we were still in the same position and the Germans had us pinned down pretty good, so our unit was told to dig a trench, which we didn't always have to do. I dug my slit trench, and I was in it one night and the next day it was raining. I remember seeing a bit of tarp down the road and went to get it. I ran back and there were two guys in my hole, I jumped on top, and a shell landed thirty feet away. I was blown out the trench.'

The blast permanently damaged Roly's hearing. 'I got a concussion and bled out the eyes and ears and stuff. After a while I was OK. They wanted to send me back to England, but I didn't wanna go. I was in the forward aid post for about two weeks I guess. Anyway, I went back to the regiment, back on the job.'

Back on the job meant months of hard fighting ahead. Once again, the Canadians were proving themselves to be some of the toughest and most reliable soldiers in a world war.

The Push from Sword

Alfred 'John' Court, was a veteran of the North Africa campaign, and landed on D+1 with the 3rd Royal Tank Regiment.

'It sounds silly to say that one could get very bored very easily. You knew you were going to go into action, and I suppose basically you were looking forward to moving.'

Infantry nearby had knocked out a Panther tank, and asked the British tankers if they'd be interested in seeing it. 'We went along with this infantry officer, and he took us all round through the back alleyways, and showed us this Panther. It came as a severe shock when we saw the size of this Panther. When you realize the size of the gun, and the thickness of the armour, I wish I hadn't seen it, because you suddenly realize what you're up against.'

Stretcher-bearer Cecil Warren saw the aftermath of knocked-out British tanks first hand.

'We had to leave our half-track and go alongside the railway with our stretcher, and this here officer (from the knocked-out tank) was a brave bloke, you could see. We got there and the tank was on fire, and of course, we were a target, but Jerry never fired on us.'

Two wounded men were placed on stretchers.

'I know both their names, because I'll be quite honest, I say a prayer for the one who died every day.'

Cecil recalled another instance involving a British tank regiment.

'This tank came back . . . and (the tanker) told us of his exploits. Three Germans went towards his tank (trying to surrender), and he didn't let them surrender. He wiped them out. He says, "A week before D-Day, I had a letter from my parents saying my brother had been killed, and I'll kill every (German) that I set eyes on." To us that sounded bad, but they done it to our blokes. Which was wrong, on both sides.'

'They were good soldiers,' infantryman James Blinkhorn said of the Germans. 'Very good soldiers. Especially the Hitler Youth. They were the worst of the lot. Youngsters about fifteen, sixteen. I suppose it was drilled into them, right from a young age. You'd be right on top of them and they'd still keep firing till the last second. They wouldn't give up until you actually put them down.'

'They were very stubborn,' recalled Ramsey Bader, a driver in the 147th (Essex Yeomanry) Field Regiment, Royal Artillery. 'Very stubborn fighters. Very well trained and determined to not give ground . . . We found the SS were the worst, and the most cruel in the sense (that), even when taken prisoner, they would put their hands up and still have grenades in their hands. This is the sort of do or die people they were. Very arrogant, even when taken prisoner.'

The SS would even boobytrap dead and wounded British soldiers.

'This made us realize all the more the type of person we were fighting. Some of our troops who had come from the desert in support of us, who joined 8th Armoured Brigade, were not used to this . . . and found they had to find another way of looking at their enemy.'

Such acts hardened the attitude of the British soldiers. 'We learnt to hate the enemy . . . we learnt very quickly to know what to expect from them.'

Ramsey and the Essex Yeomanry were often supporting the infantry. He recalled one day when the Green Howards sent out a patrol. 'I remember thirty-two young lads going up the line, and only five coming back.'

Godfrey Welch was a gunner in a Sherman tank of the Royal Scots Greys. Normandy was his first experience of war.

'The first time we got hit, us two new boys didn't know what it was all about, but the veterans knew, "Oh that's a mortar," but for us we didn't know what it was.'

Godfrey learnt that getting hit was a matter of when, not if. 'It's inevitable.'

The enemy were often well concealed, and Godfrey had fired hundreds of rounds at houses and villages before he finally saw an enemy tank in the open.

'I can tell you my first (tank kill), which is always your best one.' In the cover of a wood, Godfrey's tank had been watching for enemy movement. 'Out from the right-hand side was a German firing out towards the left at something. So when we moved up and got him on the binoculars, it's only a Panther! Now, right, excitement, excitement! My first German target!

'All your training goes out of the window at that time. Panthers, face on, have got a (slanted) front plate, which is virtually impenetrable from a distance with a 75 (mm gun). All it does is ricochet off. This is all part of your training. You've forgot that, you've seen your first good target! So the officer gave the orders, AP action, blah blah blah. Fire!

'Oh I hit him beautifully, right on the front. With the AP shells you've got a tracer on the back, so you can watch the flight of the shell. We watched the flight of the shell. Next thing we know the shell's going up in the air. (The Panther) pulls back, but you could see his gun turning to our woods, so we back off. Next thing we know there's an 88 zooms through the woods, knocking off branches and boughs.'

Godfrey couldn't believe it when later in the day the Panther came back out of the woods. 'And he's turned sideways on to us, going along the edge of the woods.' He took aim and fired.

'Only this time it's gone in the side of him . . . anyway, another one for luck under the hull, and of course he brewed. That's the first one. Oh, you felt so happy about it, but it came so unexpectedly.'

It was the first of Godfrey's three and a half tank kills in the war.

Although northern Normandy was not known as good tank country because of the dense terrain, the panzers' thick armour and heavy weapons made them a nightmarish opponent for the infantry.

Gordon Penter had landed on D-Day with the 1st Battalion, South Lancashire Regiment. In the early hours of 23 June his unit went into action in the area of Chateau de la Londe, Le Landel, where they had an initial success and drove the Germans back. They then began to dig in on the position.

'There was quiet. An ominous quiet. We thought, Well, they'll send tanks up now. It got near four o'clock . . . there was a bombardment. We'd only had chance to scrape a little trench . . . We were taking tremendous casualties . . . And then we heard the ominous sound of tank engines.'

The men of the South Lancs on the position had no armoured support of their own. That they stood to receive the attack speaks volumes about their courage.

'The first thing I knew one of them reared up over this hedge, a monster that turned out to be a Panther . . . and (it) actually fell on one of our sections. Crushed them into the ground . . . There was nothing we could do against it. We were crawling away from it, and unfortunately another tank had come over the other side.

'Their panzer grenadiers followed. Their infantry, in other words . . . we just stood up and met them. There was nothing else we could do . . . You felt you'd gone, any road, so you just faced them, you know. After a short skirmish, there was tremendous casualties . . . I felt a terrible smack in the side of my face . . . it was just like a hammer hitting me on the face.'

Gordon, choking on his own blood and shattered teeth, landed on his platoon commander, who was turning black in the face as he died. Gordon was saved by a lance corporal who ran over and used his fingers to scoop the debris out of his mouth.

'The next thing I knew there was a German officer over me.'

The battalion war diary that day recorded: 'Enemy tanks (approx 6) supported by inf broke into B Coy (positions), causing heavy casualties.'[10] It listed two men killed, thirty-four wounded, and seventy-three missing: many of the missing were dead, and now behind German lines. Others were taken prisoner. The wounded, including Gordon, were evacuated to a German hospital in Rennes.

For infantrymen like Kenneth Powter in the 1st Battalion, Suffolk Regiment, their entrenching tool was often more valuable than their rifle. 'You were just digging. Each time we moved to a different spot, one had to dig. And after a few shelling incidents, the chaps didn't need telling. But prior to that, people were reluctant to dig.'

One evening, as he lay exhausted at the bottom of a newly dug slit trench, Kenneth was awoken by a loud bang. 'A shell had landed on the next trench to me, which was platoon headquarters, and killed the platoon commander, a chap named Hassler, and wounded one or two more. We moved back into the wood, where we suffered several more casualties.'

At 0400 on 28 June, as part of Operation Mitten, the Suffolks began their attack on the Château de la Londe. Their aim was to regain the ground that had been lost when the Germans had counter-attacked the South Lancs; the action in which Gordon Penter had been wounded and captured. 'As we moved up, there was some open ground, we were shelled intensely,' Kenneth recalled. 'We moved up to this hedgerow, which was the start line. The weather was very hot, and I remember that none of us had any appetite for this food. I think we anticipated what was going to happen.'

Just before dawn an intense bombardment took place.

'We moved forward, and it was very dark then, but as we moved forward the shell fire almost lit up all the area in front of us.' Men were falling all around from enemy fire, but the Suffolks were able to drive the German defenders away from the chateau and surrounding area. 'From there we were counter-attacked by a tank. It transpired that we were being shelled from the flank . . . We took over some of the German trenches. I remember two MK IV tanks coming up, and our PIAT man knocked one out, which immediately caught on fire. Two crew came out of the escape hatch. They were shot by our Bren-gunner in my section. Then a MK IV came up the hedgerow and started to throw grenades, but when the PIAT opened up he withdrew quickly. We secured that position, and we were there for several days.'

The attack was extremely costly for the Suffolks.

'We had a hundred and sixty casualties in that morning . . .

(It) was terrible, really. It really was horrific. From then on, one feared (hearing) that you were going into an attack the next day, because according to the law of average, if you'd escaped so far, it looked that it might be your turn next.'

Arthur Blizzard, of the Suffolks' Pioneer Platoon, was also present at Château de la Londe.

'It was terrible. You didn't know what was what. You didn't know who you was fighting. You could have been fighting your own chaps. God, that was terrible. Terrible. We dug in on the corner of the field, and in the middle of the field was all horses and cows laying on top of the field, all blown up. Hot summer. God, well it's a wonder we didn't catch all the diseases in the world.'

The CO ordered Arthur and the pioneers to bury the dead animals. 'I blew big holes in the ground and rolled them in. It was the only way, you see. Rolled all these poor old animals in and filled the dirt. At least that relieved the smell.'

The Suffolks' dead were also buried.

'I gathered our dead up with Alec. I think there was about forty-six or fifty. So we said, "What about these poor old Germans? Are we going to put them in (the grave)?" We found a tank dugout and we put them in there and filled it in. It took some time but we done it.'

After this was done, Arthur wanted to create a memorial for his fallen comrades.

'I wanted to do a cross, and I knew I wanted a little brush. And I thought, Where would you get a brush? And I could see these eight little tiny cottages, and I thought, I'm going to creep up there and see if I can get in there if Jerry ain't in there. There's bound to be a kiddy's paint brush. And I did get in a house, and I did find a paint brush. I got the paint brush and got out the door and Jerry's just coming around the corner to the last house at the other end. God, dear, I (don't) think a paint brush has ever travelled so fast.'

Arthur was able to escape the Germans, who were in the village to set a new line of defence. 'I made it, a wooden cross. I put it up in memory of all these poor boys.'

Liberté

Schoolboy Michel Grimaux and his family lived close to Juno Beach, and had taken shelter in a dugout in the garden during D-Day. 'The weeks afterwards were a thrilling period, and quite extraordinary, because this is only a small village, and all of a sudden it became a big city, with military police at all the crossroads, directing the traffic coming ashore.

'It was also a period of great strain because the German planes came every night to bomb the beaches and the bridgehead, and we were not able to get much sleep – we were living on our nerves more or less.'

Jaqueline le Bas lived close to Sword Beach. 'On Thursday, around noon, we noticed English officers coming . . . They wanted to take a look around the house for the officers (accommodation).

'So that was a relief. It meant a lot to me and immediately lifted my spirits, because we were so scared you know? The front line was really close, you know? And let me assure you, forty-eight hours after the landing you see, that was an extraordinary feeling, it really lifted my spirits.'

During the coming weeks Jaqueline remembered, 'We kept seeing trucks full of wounded passing by nonstop . . . It was terrible.'

She also saw German prisoners being taken to the beach, destined for POW camps in England, and further afield. 'They were in a terrible state . . . some were injured . . . I was a bit saddened by the attitude of some people who were throwing stones at them.'

Thomas Peace was an officer in the 5th Wiltshires. He landed as part of an advanced party and was charged with finding accommodation for the men.

'The CO and I settled in the outhouse of a farm. We were in the outhouse, sleeping in the straw, the farmer and his wife, and their family, they stayed in the farm house. There was never any idea that we would go in and purloin their accommodation for ourselves, we just slept outside.

'There were two little girls. One was I suppose about ten or eleven, the other about six or seven, and obviously they'd been used to playing with the German soldiers, and they were quite intrigued to find English soldiers there. The little girl was a bit of a horror, she played everybody up. The eldest was rather sweet, in fact, I taught them to sing "Who's afraid of the big bad wolf" in English, and they taught me to sing it in French.'

Thomas helped on the farm by rounding up the cows for milking. He remembered his three or four days there as 'an idyllic existence'.

Ramsey Bader had a different experience with the locals: at least at first. 'We found the French were not always too friendly in the sense they were never sure, probably from the experience of Dunkirk, whether we were going to be pushed back into the sea again. Once we got further in they seemed to be very glad to see us.'

'We didn't like them very much,' said Richard Gosling, who was also in the Essex Yeomanry. 'And a lot of them, of course, didn't like us very much. They'd had Germans occupying them for five years, something like that. They'd married their daughters, they helped them on the farms. The Germans behaved very well with the French farmers in Normandy.'

Every field, every farm, every house, and every church that was fought over in Normandy was the centre of someone's life, community, and livelihood. Unsurprisingly, French reactions to the Allies varied, from joy at liberation to anger at the destruction of livestock and loss of human life.

'When we got to know the farming people, we were surprised at their attitude,' said Bill Lewis, a Canadian soldier. 'They were telling us that we were screwing everything up, but the Germans had allowed them to farm their land, no problem, they got pretty good pay for it and all the rest of it. Which shook us up a bit.'

Some of the Allied troops began taking food from the fields. 'That didn't go down well with the French farmer. Next thing we started getting shot at by the French farmers. We were looking over our shoulder from then on.'

'Shortly after we landed a couple of our NCOs got picked off by a sniper,' said John Court, 'and if my memory serves me right they traced this sniper to the upper window of a farmhouse not far from us. And it turned out it was a young woman, who evidently had become very friendly with a German officer who had been killed. And I think they dispatched her a little quickly.'

Whether civilians were glad to see the Allies or not, they were all in danger of being caught in the crossfire between armies.

John Donnelly had been losing a lot of men in the hedgerow country to German Panzerfaust and Panzerschreck (bazookas). To counter this, his crew fired at any movement that they thought might be an ambush. One day, this method had tragic results. 'There was an old farmer and his daughter, and the other daughter had her head riddled with bullets.'

Michael Bendix, an officer in the Coldstream Guards, also witnessed the price paid by the French civilians. 'In one village we had been attacking, there was some civilians there. (I remember) seeing a Guardsman with a little girl, with one leg blown off.'

While attempts were made to limit civilian casualties at times, there was no such protection given to the livestock and livelihoods of farming families.

'Every time you fired an artillery barrage anywhere, normally it was cattle country,' said Richard Gosling. 'Marvellous cattle all over the place. And they were just killed like flies by English shells, and that's why the French didn't like us very much either.'

Many veterans of the campaign recalled this terrible sight and smell.

'The one thing about Normandy which was so nasty was the smell of rotting cows and horses,' said Michael Bendix. 'I don't think you ever forget that. It was horrible.'

The young Guards officer was moved by the plight of the animals. 'I remember on one occasion . . . we were near a cowshed, and the cows hadn't been milked for a long time. So we thought the best thing to do was to strip them by hand straight onto the floor. And that was almost the most dangerous thing I think one could possibly have done, they were in such pain. And the old farmer must have heard about this and he came to thank us.'

William Hanna also found himself attending to livestock. 'All the farmers had left the farms whilst the battle was going on, and they left their cows standing around in the fields. And obviously, in that part of the world, there's a lot of dairy milking cows, and those cows were in tremendous pain, and I could see it, having had a farming upbringing.

'Many of them were injured. Shrapnel in their udders, shrapnel in their bodies and that sort of thing from the shelling, and this struck me as worse even than seeing me own soldiers injured, because the cows couldn't do anything about it. So I got into hot water on more than one occasion. I was to be found milking the cows straight onto the ground in order to relieve them of their pain, despite the fact that there were shots being fired around, but to me that was my first priority . . . I had to do something about it.'

John Donnelly recalled one moment of kindness from a French farmer. 'This little Frenchman came running across the farm with a bottle in his hand, and two wee glasses, and he come jumping up on the turret. He says, Calvados. Well I'd never heard of Calvados in my life, I didn't know what Calvados was.'

The farmer told them that he'd been keeping the bottle for when the Allies came back to France.

John Buchanan, of the Fife and Forfar Yeomanry, had a similar experience with a Norman farmer. 'He gave us a wee tot of this Calvados . . . and if it's possible to be 200% proof it must have been 200%. It went right down to your toes and came stomping back again. And we got some of these bottles of Calvados. We drank a lot if we could get it. French people were always good at giving you bottles of wine. We had this bin which held surplus shells. When we used them up we filled it with bottles of wine and Calvados which had been given to us by the French people. We had a wine cellar (in the bottom of our tank). We drank it like lemonade.'

The British weren't the only ones handicapped by the local brew. Gerhard Franzky of the 10th SS Panzer Division also sampled the Norman speciality.

'We found a big barrel of Calvados. It was buried by the farmer I suppose. We syphoned it out, as much as we could. And as a result everybody got drunk. The orders came to move. Officers came and raised holy hell. Made us empty every canister where we had Calvados in it. Then we had to line up and move out, and drive out. It was a mess. Everybody was drunk.'

Not long after D-Day, in liberated villages and towns, women accused of sleeping with Germans had their heads shaved as punishment, and were subjected to a wide range of shaming and abuse. Richard Leatherbarrow, an army cameraman, filmed this ritual humiliation and believed that the work of combat camera teams and journalists helped to put a stop to this kind of act.

'I felt it was an example of, in a small way, of what film or photographic coverage can achieve, or does provide evidence of, so that the public react in one way or another when they ultimately see the stuff on the screen. And in this head shaving, this was a case in point. The punishment may not have been too brutal . . . but at the same time, what nobody liked . . . what people could not accept, rightly, was the fact that this was an example taking place in a part of liberated France, which was nothing more, in brief words, than mob law. And it had to be stopped. And I think I'm right in saying that what was seen on the screen achieved the ending of this procedure all that much faster by it having been seen.'

John Donnelly also witnessed this treatment of 'collaborators'. 'I thought it was rather cruel . . . you can't live with people for three or four years without getting some sort of relationship with them, you know?'

Jaqueline le Bas and her family were developing their own friendships with the newly arrived Allied soldiers.

'I remember quite a few Royal Engineers coming to our home. We spent the evenings until two or three o'clock when the German planes stopped coming, having dinner with delicious army food – chocolate and tinned biscuits and eggs from the farm. We made delicious cakes which we ate with our new friends, and we were merry for the evening. We had slide shows by candlelight because we had no electricity and then we slept from four until eight and the next day began. This kind of existence went on for more than a month until Caen was liberated.'

The fight for the liberation of that city would include the largest British tank battle of the war, and Allied bombings that some have since termed a war crime. Meanwhile, to the west of the British and Canadian forces, the Americans faced their own bloody struggle, and death in the hedgerows.

CHAPTER SEVEN

Death in the Hedgerows

*The US Army from D+1 to the positioning
for the breakout*

'First I had to change from a civilian to a soldier, and
they did that in training, and then I had to change from
a soldier to a killer, which is what you're there for in
the first place.'

John Witmeyer, 4th Infantry Division

Bocage country

As the Americans began to push inland towards the objectives of
Saint-Lô and Cherbourg, they found the going in the claustro-
phobic Normandy countryside to be every bit as slow and costly
as the British.

Bob Miksa was a driver in the 745th Tank Battalion. After
reaching Caumont a couple of days after D-Day, where they were
rested and resupplied, the 745th began to move south towards
Saint-Lô.

'If we advanced twenty or thirty yards a day that was a good day because you'd advance to the next hedgerow. Most of the infantry, they followed behind the tank, you know? They're the ones who suffered the casualties. Most of the time we were up against light armed fire. Didn't bother us like it did the infantry. They were exposed.'

The raised earthen banks of the bocage posed a deadly problem for the tanks.

'If you wanted to get over (a hedgerow) you had to get up, and go down. A lot of the time on tanks, the weakest spot is on the bottom, the belly, and if you were up in the air, a good 20mm cannon would penetrate.'

This problem was eventually solved by welding railroad posts onto the front of the tank in a V-shape, like a bulldozer. 'Then we'd just come up to the hedgerow and ram it. Sometimes it would be a German machine-gunner in there and we'd just bury them.'

William Gast landed at Omaha with the 743rd Tank Battalion, and supported the infantry in the hedgerow fighting.

'At first the infantry really hated us because the infantry could go along and they could sneak up, and they could do things like that.' The tanks' clanking tracks and roaring engines were not so discreet. 'It gave everybody's position away, so they didn't like it.'

John Rogers, a young officer, landed on D+8 and went straight into action with the 67th Armored Regiment. 'Everything worked and the radio communication was wonderful,' John said of his Sherman tank. 'They were very capable and very dependable.'

Being in combat for the first time was a hair-raising experience, where ambushes lay around every corner, and behind every hedgerow.

'We didn't know what to expect. I know I didn't. You get through that hedgerow and they've got somebody down there with an anti-tank gun, or with a tank sitting down there, firing down, and the first tank through gets hit.'

John's tanks were soon fitted with the 'bulldozer' blades. 'We didn't lose too many after we did that, but up until then we were losing tanks pretty regular.'

'We could fight with a Panther,' said Bob Miksa, 'but the Tiger, we were outmatched. I mean they were so heavy armored, even our cannon couldn't penetrate them. We had to shoot for their tracks – disable them. They had a big 88 on there.

'They couldn't maneuver too good with them because they were so heavy. They couldn't go over the smaller roads or anything. The only way we could beat them was two or three tanks just circle them, you know? We were faster, we could maneuver where they couldn't – they had to stay in the same spot. As far as direct fire, you couldn't beat the German Tiger.'

Often moving ahead of Sherman tanks like Bob's were reconnaissance units using armoured cars. These vehicles carried far less armour and weaponry than the Shermans, and relied on speed and stealth to survive.

Donald Evans was serving in the recon element of the 66th Armored Regiment, and had already seen combat in Sicily. He landed on D+3. 'We couldn't wait to kill some Germans,' he said, but the feeling was apparently mutual.

'As soon as it got dark, the German Luftwaffe were overhead and they were dropping some flares. There's nothing that scares the GI on the ground I don't think like those flares. They drop 'em, and they're on a little parachute, and they're burning and they're sparking and they light up the area lighter than noon. It's really eerie.'

The Luftwaffe would then follow up with anti-personnel bombs, but Donald made it through his first night in France alive. The next day they were sent forward to reconnoitre the German lines.

'We were going through this field. We were walking, and I came upon this sign. And it said "Achtung, Minen".'

Luckily for Donald, the Germans had forgotten to remove the sign from the minefield before withdrawing. They were able to safely avoid it and press on.

'We saw this church with a steeple still on it. And I see Germans digging in the churchyard.'

Donald radioed that information back and shells began to land on the Germans, scattering them and driving them away from the church. It was a moment of elation for Donald, but the shoe was often on the other foot. 'The next day we're dug in on the side of a hill and the Germans are shelling us. It's like tit for tat.'

The beachheads of Utah and Omaha had yet to link up, and Donald's regiment was sent to support the 101st Airborne at Carentan.

'The hedgerows were just full of Krauts, man. They had tied themselves up in the trees, and stuff like that.' Donald saw dead Germans fall from the branches. Some were left hanging from their ropes.

Radioman Wallace Jeffrey was following the frontlines. 'One German, he was tied up in the tree, and I don't know how many times that guy had gotten shot. Everybody that went by him, I think, shot him for (good) luck.'

Donald Evans respected the tenacity of these German defenders. 'They were fighters, man.' And such soldiers took a heavy toll on the American troops. 'We had lost a lot of men. A lot of guys got shot with snipers and stuff like that.'

During one action, one of Donald's crew spotted a Tiger tank close by. Before he knew what was happening, his crew had bailed out of their armoured car and sought cover.

'Once it got dark the Germans could take care of us at their leisure. I called Regiment, and they said no help until after daylight in the morning. Boy, that was sad news for everybody.' Someone then gave an order to make a break for it. The crews mounted up into their armoured cars and made best speed to escape. 'Everybody's on their own, man. It was kind of a mess.' But despite the danger, Donald's car commander ordered them to halt when he spotted a wounded soldier. 'There was a guy from the 101st lying on the hedgerow, there. He said, "I'm gonna die, just let me here." We knew he was gonna die, but if we got him out, he'd die with us.'

One of the infantrymen fighting in Normandy was Walter Ehlers, who had miraculously come through D-Day on Omaha with every member of his squad alive. After the battle on the beach, the experienced soldiers of the 1st Infantry Division began fighting in the bocage. Walter's regiment received support in these battles from the tanks of the 745th.

'They were a lot of help,' Walter said of Bob Miksa's outfit.

During the day the Americans advanced hedgerow by hedgerow. At night they dug in and awaited German counter-attacks and patrols.

'Most of the night it would be still,' said Cosmo Uttero, a soldier in the 29th Infantry Division. 'There'd be no fighting at night. There was hardly any movement at night. Every night there was a password that came out from headquarters. It consisted of one word (as a challenge), and one word as an answer. It could be a foolish thing like "baseball", and "Yankees". It could be a food. It could be a place. It could be a car. It could be anything.'

Movement at night was limited, and digging in for protection against shelling and air attack was vital. 'In training, they made sure you dug a foxhole. In combat, no one had to tell you. If you didn't, and you had artillery come in, you got killed, so no one had to tell you.'

The soldiers in a squad would take turns on guard duty, their eyes on stalks, and their ears attuned for the slightest noise. 'You stood awake. If something happened, or you heard something, you alert down to the next hole. You had to know the password and you had to know the answer. You didn't wait a second (to fire) if you didn't get the answer that you wanted.'

Some nights were easier to see movement than others. 'About half of the month is light at night time. And the other half of the month is dark so you can't see your hand in front of you.'

Under cover of darkness, a German patrol infiltrated the lines of Walter Ehlers's unit.

'When they ran into our position they got fired upon when they came in, but they kept running right on through it. We couldn't fire on them when they got inside because we'd have been firing on one another. So the company commander wanted somebody to take a patrol and follow them, and I got the job.' This was easier said than done. 'We couldn't see our hand in front of us. You're kind of scared stiff.'

Walter didn't find the Germans that night, but he did come across a briefcase that had been dropped. He returned it to his unit, and inside were maps of the second and third lines of defence for the German withdrawal: invaluable information for the Allies.

Walter saw those defences himself on 9 June. His unit was advancing when they came under machine-gun fire. 'I didn't want to get caught out in the field so I rushed my men to the hedge-row in front of me. Then, because I was the experienced one in combat – I could smell the Germans before I could see them – I just went down the hedgerow . . . the sound of the machine gun was down in the corner there. I went up on the bank and I heard some rattling, and I came face to face with four Germans on patrol. All of them had their guns pointed at me. They were pretty close together. I didn't have any choice. I had to make a real fast decision. Either I shot them, or they're gonna shoot me.'

Walter took down all four Germans. He then told his men to fix bayonets before pushing further along the hedgerow. 'I came upon a machine-gun nest and I ran out there and knocked the guy out.' But the German soldier was still alive. Walter's men told him to stab him. 'And I said, "Stab him? I've still got bullets in my gun." I shot him. I didn't want to stab anybody with my bayonet if I didn't have to.'

He continued to press the attack and came across an enemy mortar position. 'When they saw me come up there their eyes got big. And I asked them to halt, and they wouldn't do it.' When the rest of his squad arrived the Germans panicked and ran. 'We had to shoot them all.'

Walter had now cleared two enemy positions, but the defenders had positions in depth, including another machine-gun nest. He advanced and took it out, and the battle was then broken off. At least for that day.

'The next day we had a similar situation come up again.' As his squad advanced towards a hedgerow they began taking fire from two directions. His company commander told him to withdraw, but Walter saw that as a death sentence: 'They'd probably shoot us all in the back.'

Instead he went on the offensive, going up onto a piece of high ground that was no more than an earth mound. From there he suppressed the enemy positions, and was joined by a BAR man (carrying a Browning automatic rifle). 'We kept them pinned down, and our squad got back to the hedgerow behind us.'

It was then time for Walter and the BAR man to withdraw. As they moved, Walter spotted a three-man German crew setting up another machine gun on its tripod. He began to return fire, but was hit. The bullet glanced off his ribs, left a hole in his back, and hit a picture of his mother that he carried in his pack.

The BAR man was also hit. Despite his own injuries, and whilst under constant fire, Walter went to the aid of his wounded comrade and carried him back to cover. 'I turned him over to the medics, and then I went back and got his rifle.'

After the wounded man had been loaded onto the ambulance, Walter told the company commander that he needed a medic to take a look at the wound in his back. 'He says, "My God, you should be dead. You've been shot clean through."'

'It was kind of a miracle,' Walter said. 'I refused to be med-evaced. I went on to lead my squad. We finally got a break, and the next action we went into was the Saint-Lô breakthrough.'

Like Walter, Arthur Blatnik fought ashore at Omaha with the 1st Infantry Division. 'The next morning we were off the beach, and we were heading across the fields. All of a sudden one guy dropped. Boom, another guy dropped.' The shots had come from a tree ahead of them. Blatnik and others returned fire. A body fell down. 'It was a Japanese female lieutenant,' said Arthur.

It is possible that he was mistaken about the sniper's nationality. Female snipers were used by the Red Army and in some cases captured Soviet troops were offered service with the Wehrmacht rather than internment, or worse. Many of these captured troops were Asiatic. Chinese, Mongolians, Thais, and Indonesians were reported to have been fighting in the 'Ost Battalions'. However, it is not beyond the realm of possibility that the sniper had indeed served with the Japanese army. There is a recorded case of Korean prisoners taken in Normandy. The claim is that they had been conscripted into the Japanese army, captured by the Soviets, then captured by the Germans, and finally captured by American troops. If this story is true, and considering how dangerous the point of surrender can be, then these men were incredibly lucky to come through the war alive.

The American forces in Normandy were up against an enemy who often laid in wait and slaughtered the Allied troops as they advanced. One day, infantryman Richard Ford was able to turn the tables, setting his own ambush overlooking a stash of enemy ammunition hidden in a hedgerow. It was a common practice for the defenders to hide these caches across the battlefield, and now Richard only had to wait for the Germans to come to collect it.

'I thought, I'm gonna let them get right up to me so we nail them all. And we did. I only saw two of them turn their bikes and take off. We nailed the rest of them. At the time I thought it was a little exhilarating, and I thought, Well, that pays for all that crap you made us go through on that landing.'

Twenty-two-year-old Earl Tweed was an officer in the 29th Infantry Division, and recalled the peril of enemy artillery in the bocage.

'The Germans were firing at us with artillery pieces, and they were doing a pretty good job of it.' One of Earl's platoon leaders, Lieutenant Moorhouse, began to direct the American batteries onto the German positions. 'Moorhouse, he got to watching, and he was on the right flank, and he adjusted our artillery pieces, and their rhythm of their firing. In the meantime, the Germans had spotted where he could be, and they just started unloading there.' Lieutenant Moorhouse received a mortal injury from the fire. 'His head was practically blown off. It took him several hours to die.'

Assigned to 'Old Hickory', the 30th Infantry Division, Frank Denius was a forward observer in Battery C of the 230th Field Artillery Battalion. He came ashore on Omaha at D+1 and went straight into action.

'My objective as an artillery observer was protecting our infantry and preparing for the attack, and that's what we did our best to do.' Though this was the unit's first time in combat, Frank picked things up quickly on the battlefield. 'It didn't take you long to learn a lot from actual experience.'

He was moved by the reception that the soldiers received in Normandy.

'As we moved through those towns in Northern France, I can't tell you how gleeful they were to be liberated.

'Perhaps vicariously I did enjoy the celebrations, the French people and all the flowers and yelling and screaming and hollering and everything, the kids, and all of that. It probably was more appreciated by troops who weren't combat oriented, so to speak, because the French people gave us a royal reception.'

'Combat oriented' troops like Frank had little time to stop and enjoy the celebrations. 'I think I went about two months without a bath or shower or even a break to brush my teeth.

'If we could accomplish maybe three hedgerows' distance in one day, that was a pretty successful day. It was intense fighting every day, and we suffered a lot of casualties.'

Frank recalled one particular action. At the time he was only nineteen years old.

'We were engaged in a very difficult battle to get through to an objective that would permit us to then prepare for the Saint-Lô breakthrough. I was with the 2nd Battalion of the 120th Regiment, and the officer that was leader of my party, and myself, and my radio sergeant, we were unable to see where the crossfire, and some German artillery, were located in front of us. The only way that we could determine exactly where the German machine-gun and dug-in tank fire was coming from, which was holding up our infantry and really causing a lot of casualties, and caused us to pause, the only way to successfully find that was to crawl out in advance of the infantry unit behind a hedgerow. And that was between the German front lines and the American front lines.'

This meant moving on their bellies as fire flew inches above their heads.

'As we were crawling out to that area a machine gun fired and killed (my officer) instantly. He was about two feet ahead of me.'

With his officer killed, it came down to Frank to call in the artillery.

'I had to fire several rounds and direct that artillery fire, and then zero in finally on the area where I was thinking the German tanks and machine guns were. And to do that I had to expose myself, and I did so. I was successful in knocking out that area. Maybe it's luck. Maybe it's short experience. But anyway, I was successful in knocking that area out. And then my radio sergeant and I crawled back to the infantry front lines.'

Frank's bravery and accomplishment did not go unnoticed.

'The company commander of the infantry said, "You did it," and gave the orders for everyone to advance. I did not know it at the time, in fact it was probably a couple of weeks after that, or even longer, when I was back at my unit, that my battery commander said, "You have orders to report to Corps Headquarters," and that's when I was presented the Silver Star.

'I was not the only one. There was about five of us, and here we are, in a historic French villa where command headquarters were. It was awesome. But I didn't think of it at that time. It was a dramatic moment that you think back at, but at the time it was certainly an honour.'*

Honour and gallantry were present on the battlefield, but so too were acts that some would judge as criminal. Harry Parley came ashore with the 116th Regiment on D-Day, and after the slaughter on Omaha Beach he witnessed German prisoners killed by Allied troops. It was not the last time.

---

* This was the first of four Silver Stars that Frank was awarded in the war.

'My particular regiment was sent a specific order by General Eisenhower . . . and he specified that if he heard of any more killing of prisoners, there would be court martials up and down the ranks . . . because we were killing our prisoners and there was no way to get intelligence.'

Harry explained why such things happened on the battlefield.

'When you take a prisoner, you're usually told, "Walk him back."' This often meant through the enemy's artillery bombardment that was falling behind the front line. 'And so you didn't want to do it. And the result was, you're walking quietly through the woods up to headquarters, everybody started to fire. And then you'd bump the guy off and go back and say he tried to escape.

'If they so much as blinked, we'd kill them. This is very sad to tell you, but nevertheless, it's true. Now, on the other hand, let me tell you why we killed prisoners. Occasions usually arose where there was a brief firefight and a GI would get lost or wounded. And because of the quick movement of the battle, he was left behind. And then . . . he was captured. And we, after many occasions when the Germans had withdrawn, found GI corpses on the trees . . . burnt alive. And that's when all capture of enemies ceased.'

From such prolonged exposure to the horrors of war, many soldiers became totally desensitized. 'There was absolutely no emotion when you're battling during the day. You're running, mostly running, and you become numb, only acting on the reflexes for self-preservation. And there is absolutely no emotion except that. No emotion. And so when you see this grey uniform in front of you, whether he's helpless or not, there is this tendency just to get him out of the way, because you've got to keep moving. So it's a split-second decision. The enemy does not really know whether he's going to live. And you don't know whether he's going to live. You're standing there. His hands are on his head. And you're about to shoot. And some GI says, "Let's get moving." And you just wave him back. And so he stayed alive just by that split second. But there's no emotion, you're not disappointed that you let him live. You really don't care. I mean, it has become apparent to me that, in those conditions, the value of human life is almost insignificant. You do things not thinking, just instinctively. You think about it later, push it out of your mind, and you go on.'

It should be noted that an estimated 200,000 German troops were taken prisoner during the Normandy campaign. The killing of prisoners was a reality of the war, but it was not the norm. Death, on the other hand, was ever-present.

'Sometimes toward evening, everything was quiet. I used to feel, actually, that there's a quiet come over everybody. We would just stare at one another and then out forward across the fields where you're gonna go tomorrow, and you could smell the death of the day. You could smell it. You felt it. You felt all the death that had happened that day.'

Harry would sometimes encounter British soldiers. 'The British troops were absolutely crazy. Absolutely crazy. We had to go through a British position. You can always tell, because that's true about the fucking tea. Every time I stopped, they were making a little fire with tea. And we were walking down this road and in the middle of this road, there's a British GI digging a foxhole in the middle of the road. My guy said, "What the fuck you doing? Why are you digging around?" . . . He said, "Well, that's the only way you can get a tank."'

Harry worked out what the 'crazy Brit' was talking about.

'He had that magnetic mine. His job was to stay in (the hole), so when the Germans counter-attacked with the tank, he would just flip it (onto the tank) and dig himself further down into the trench, wait for it to go on, and explode. Americans wouldn't do that. You know, the British had a different mind. They had been fucked over by the Germans . . . and they were, they were crazed.'

But amongst the crazed behaviour and horror, there were often beautiful moments of humanity. During one battle, Harry saw a hatch fly open on an American tank. The crewman climbed out and ran over to one of the men in Harry's unit and threw his arms around him. As bullets flew and death surrounded them, the two men embraced and cried with happiness. They were brothers.

Behind the front line, and in the skies

Only around a fifth of US troops in World War Two served in roles directly intended for combat. Keeping these soldiers on the front line necessitated a huge number of service personnel, from the truck drivers who brought supplies to the graves registration men who buried the dead. Atop of this logistical leviathan were military branches like engineers, medical corps and intelligence.

Born a Jew in Germany, Guy Stern had seen the brutality of Hitler's regime first hand. In 1942, while he was in America, all correspondence from his family had ceased. Guy was now one of the 22,000 'Ritchie Boys' – mostly Jewish immigrants from Germany – who were trained in Camp Ritchie, Maryland as intelligence officers, analysts, and interrogators in the US Army between July 1942 and September 1945. According to David Frey, more than 60 per cent of actionable intelligence gathered on the battlefield came from the Ritchie Boys.[1]

'I'm tremendously squeamish,' said Guy. 'So I thought when I see those detritus of battle on the shore I will pass out . . . but I got ashore, and there was some unpretty sights. It didn't bother me from that moment on.'

Guy's role in the army was interrogating prisoners of war. 'We were assigned to 1st Army Headquarters. Ours was essentially interrogating for strategic, in contrast to tactical information. However, as we landed, it was all tactical. Ten minutes after landing I was confronted by a German artillery soldier, pretty battle scarred, and I started out asking him a question, and he recited the Geneva Convention to me. I thought, My God, I'm going to be a failure here. And then one of those incidents happened. A shell came over. So we both hit the ground, and after the shell had hit, I was up. And he wasn't. And he must have thought I was a hero, because he knew damn well as an artillery soldier, that when one shell was fired, a second one was likely to follow. And he stayed down, and I was up. He must have thought I was one of those devil may care kind of soldiers. I wasn't!' Guy ordered the German soldier to his feet, and the man obeyed. 'And from that moment on I had him.'

Gowan Duffy was an American artilleryman. He landed at Omaha on D+1 where he saw the work being done by the engineers to keep the flow of men and supplies moving.

'The entire beach was covered with all sorts of debris. On the water's edge you had blown up and sunken Higgins boats. On the beach you had every imaginable type of equipment, and the men that had been killed and wounded. Just prior to our landing, the combat engineers had gone along the beach area and they were digging up mines, creating a path for us to drive through along this beach. And as they went down they laid out two ribbons. If you went either right or left you were in a minefield. As soon as the engineers were picking up the mines, graves registration was coming right behind them, picking up the bodies out of this path, cause they didn't want you running over these bodies, naturally.'

One particular truck caught Gowan's attention. 'The back flap was open. All I could see in this truck was the bottom of shoes sticking out . . . they were lying top to bottom.'

Gowan and his unit drove off the beach, dragging their

guns behind them. Several 'off ramps' had been created by the engineers and their bulldozers. His unit then turned onto a permanent road, but they hadn't gone far before they were told to pull to the side.

'Right after we pulled off this road we come under sniper fire. To this day I don't know what possessed those men to open fire on us because the nearest Germans were more than two miles away. I guess they probably had the mindset that they were gonna die, and before they died they wanted to take a few of us with 'em. As soon as the first shot was fired we grabbed our rifles, crossed the road into brush on the other side and flushed the snipers out.'

After they'd dealt with the threat, Gowan watched as more traffic left the beach and headed towards the front line, but his unit received no orders to get moving. As night fell they were still on the bluff, still expecting to be moved so they hadn't dug any slit trenches, their ears assaulted by the naval bombardment of German positions inland. 'You had this high crescendo of noise. Didn't let up, all day, all night. But when night time come it got worse. It got heavier.'

During daylight hours it was almost certain death for German aircraft to appear over the beach, but when darkness came, they made their presence known. 'The German air force was still flying, going up and down bombing and strafing.'

The danger of the Luftwaffe's presence extended beyond their own weapons.

'At the time we were more concerned with our own troops, because when this increase in aeroplanes come along, every ship sitting out in the Channel that had a gun on it opened fire. And here we are on the top of that bluff, and the German air force running up and down there, strafing and bombing, and all of those ships out there, every one of them opened fire on those planes flying overhead.'

Gowan and his comrades were about to learn the lesson that Londoners had learnt during the Blitz: exploding anti-aircraft shells could be as deadly to those below as above.

'That shrapnel started coming down. And it was coming down like rain. I, like everybody else, dove under the truck, and as I dove under the truck I felt something hit me on the helmet.' Gowan found a piece of shrapnel about an inch square. His guess was that it had bounced off the truck before hitting him 'because it didn't even put a dent in my helmet. Nice little souvenir. I picked it up and put it in my pocket and brought it home with me.'

The Luftwaffe were doing what they could to contest the landings, but their losses were massive.

Walter Krupinksi was one of the war's highest-scoring fighter aces, credited with 197 aerial victories. In June 1944 he was commanding the Luftwaffe's II Group.

'When D-Day started, I went with my group to France. We were fully equipped with forty aircraft and forty pilots, most of them youngsters.' When Walter returned to Germany one month later, he was accompanied by only a single plane. 'All the other pilots were gone.'

One of Walter's opponents in the air was Harold 'Hal' Shook, who commanded a squadron of American P47s. Hal had lost a pilot on D-Day, and another went down on D+1. His unit had been flying fighter sweeps on these days, but as there was little sign of the Luftwaffe, his squadron was then assigned to dive-bombing and strafing.

'Most of my stuff, even before D-Day, was going out knocking out airfields, knocking out railyards, knocking out bridges. Once the troops were on the ground, half the time, maybe a third of the time, we were operating with (them). The rest of the time, interdiction.'

Once the Allies were ashore, German commanders had begun to release their reserve divisions.

'The German Wehrmacht felt like they could get any place within Western Europe, to wherever the invasion took place. They thought they could get there in three days. But because of what we were doing, it took 'em seventeen.'

Hal recalled one mission when they caught a large number of tanks being transported to the front. 'I go knock out a big railyard, fairly deep in France . . . I could see at least one train, all loaded. We just blew the you-know-what out of that rail station. And on the way home, I felt like I might have another (go), so I sent twelve birds home to refuel and I kept my four to work over the tanks. At that point (in the war) the tanks felt they were invulnerable, but by gosh they learnt on that day they're not. We thought we knocked out a couple of tanks, armoured personnel carrier, and a staff car.'

Hal then led the other three planes for home, flying at 300 mph along the 'deck' of the French countryside. They were hopping over the hedgerows when Hal saw a 'big gun' pointed right at him. One of Hal's pilots took out the anti-aircraft weapon, but not before it fired. 'I was still going close to three hundred, and that bird just flipped. Just flipped right (down towards) the ground.'

Through a remarkable feat of piloting Hal was able to slow his P47 and recover out of the roll. He thanked a higher power for saving his life. 'Christ was with me in that cockpit. And my mother was there. My guardian angel.'

Hal was fortunate to survive that day, and the war.

'The loss rate of air-to-ground instead of air-to-air is four to one. Most of the guys we lost were younger pilots. I wasn't that old, but I had a lot of fighter time, and that experience makes a big difference.'

Not all of the pilots were able to cope with the stress of this combat flying. 'One of my guys, we went in and knocked out a railyard. And then on the way back, one of the guys got shot down in enemy territory. And then we heard that the 3rd Armored went out and brought him back in.'

When Hal went to collect the downed pilot he saw a change in him. 'A guy can start getting flak-happy,' he said, meaning that they become incredibly fearful of anti-aircraft fire. To keep an eye on him, Hal made the pilot his wingman on the next mission. As was often the case, they came in for heavy fire from the ground.

'Once you get on the (bombing) run you just stay there. You don't worry about the flak. You worry about your target. 'When we got back on the ground, the youngster said, "Hey, Major, did you see all that flak?" ' The young man was convinced that all the flak had been aimed directly at him, and that somehow the Germans knew he was the man who had been shot down the day before.

'You can let your mind run away with you,' said Hal. 'There was a few people like that, you know. One day, one of them came over and said, "Hey, governor, I'm supposed to lead this next mission. I don't feel up to it. You lead and I'll fly your wing." The guy had not flown for four or five days, and he starts to think about it. And if you do that, all of a sudden you're not able to lead.'

Fighter-bomber squadrons like Hal's constantly sought out German men and equipment on the ground, attacking any caught out in the open with machine guns, cannons, bombs, and rockets.

Heading from Brittany to reinforce the German defence was Fritz Jeltsch, an eighteen-year-old mortarman who learned to fear these deadly 'Jabos'.

'When the invasion started in Normandy we were woken up about four o'clock in the morning. I didn't even know where

Normandy was.' Fritz and his unit moved toward the battle on bicycles, their supplies following behind in lorries. They soon came under attack from the skies, near Saint-Lô.

'The lorry was bombed and burned out. And this sergeant major, he lost his leg, I heard. The driver, he was killed.' The lorry had been carrying the unit's rations, and men struggled to retrieve what they could. 'When we had the food, it was half burnt.'

The lack of supplies was a constant issue during Fritz's time in Normandy. 'We couldn't get any supply. We only shot when we were in danger. We didn't have the ammunition.'

There seemed to be no shortage for the Allies, and Fritz's unit came under regular bombardment. One day, he and another mortar man dived into a foxhole to escape the shells. 'When he got up, both his cheeks were blown off. I had to put both my hands up (to hold his jaw), because it was just hanging on the skin on the bottom.'

Even calls of nature could prove deadly.

'I had to relieve myself. And about ten metres from me was a big tree. So I went behind there.' A few moments later, machine-gunners opened fire and shot the tree to bits. 'I was covered in leaves and little branches.'

Fritz survived that day, and had many similar escapes. His comrades were not so lucky. 'Our company . . . all got killed and wounded. The whole company.'

The Allies were suffering their own heavy casualties.

John Kerner was a US Army doctor. He landed in Normandy on D+1.

'I was originally assigned to a collecting company, which was supposed to collect people from aid stations. The training was that you'd pick up the guys, put 'em on a litter, carry them to the aid station, and then carry them on a litter from the aid station to the collecting company, which was absurd. That was what they'd done in World War One, which was absurd too, because people were dying on the way.'

Two doctors who had landed ahead of John were classmates of his.

'One of them was severely wounded and the other became a psychiatric casualty, and I was sent up to relieve the two of them because they didn't have enough doctors at that time. A lot of doctors got killed or wounded early on.

'The things that we'd been taught were World War One procedures, which obviously were foolish, and so the first things we did were, we got collecting companies to move their ambulances up to the aid stations so we could get people from the aid station to an ambulance, but then the other thing is, I don't know if you've ever tried it, but if you've tried carrying a wounded guy on a litter, and you're getting shot at, that's absurd. It's hard work to lift a two-hundred-pound man on a litter. Two people, it's hard. Even with four it's dangerous. I was with farm boys from the Middle West. Kansas, Nebraska. They decided that we could put litters on a jeep . . . and we'd drive out to the wounded . . . finally we could get a number of wounded people on our jeep . . . Now they use helicopters for that.

'The decisions to change it were made there in the field, by smart GIs.'

Not all of the casualties that John treated were soldiers.

'Someone came and said, "There's a bunch of civilians injured." I took one of our jeeps and some aid men and we went over . . . and the building was a fairly large building with a courtyard in the middle. We got there, and it was just a horrible sight, because the courtyard had a number of people in it who had been obviously severely injured.'

A German shell had caused multiple injuries amongst the civilians.

'As soon as we got there we saw that some people were more seriously wounded than the others, so I told the guys with me to look for the people who were alive who looked to be the most wounded, and try and take care of them first.

'What I picked for myself was a girl who was about the same age as my nieces, and she had obviously been severely injured, but I wasn't quite sure how. I think the blast itself of the shell had probably collapsed her lungs, and I was trying to start an IV on her as a small girl, and it was really difficult.'

As John tried to work on her, the young girl passed away.

'It was just an awful experience . . . as I talk about it now I can picture a man sitting in a chair who was dead. One of his legs was blown off. He obviously was sitting there, just sitting, and this shell goes off . . . there were a lot of people seriously wounded . . . it was really a horrible sight, and when I mention it, I can picture it as clearly as if it happened yesterday.'

The Cotentin Peninsula

As part of the US First Army pushed south towards Saint-Lô, other divisions attacked west and then north on the Cotentin Peninsula.

David Roderick was a squad leader in the 4th Infantry Division. He had landed at Utah on D-Day, and soon found that even more difficult days lay ahead.

'I only lost one man on the beach, and he was shot right through the eyes by a sniper. The next day I lost eight, which was half my men. That's one of the things that concerns me about the media and so forth when they show D-Day. Usually they talk about Omaha, and the carnage that was there, which there certainly was. But they make it look like we didn't have any difficulty, really.'

The 4th Infantry Division took 197 casualties on D-Day. 'But (then) we lost 50 per cent of our men within three or four days,' said David. 'I always say that our D-Day was the second day, because we had to wade through all of that water.' He was referring to the areas behind the beach that had been flooded to deny them as landing zones for paratroopers.

'The 22nd Infantry, and the 12th, which came in behind us, walked through that. It took us about seven hours to walk through that water.'

After crossing the flooded fields, David's unit got into a skirmish line, and prepared to go into battle the next morning.

'We jumped off to attack Azeville and Crisbecq.' These were formidable defensive positions. Both had complexes of fortifications that were connected underground, with smaller pillboxes out front, and communications back to artillery and rockets, making it a hellish proposition for attacking infantry.

'There was a whole extension of that fortification line that ran from Utah Beach clear up to what they call the Quenéville Ridge. It took us about three weeks to get through that ridge, one fortification after another.'

David gave great credit to their naval support off the coast. Though the navy suffered losses from both direct fire and sea mines, they kept the troops supplied and provided them with vital fire support.

'Our standard way of fighting was that we would have our artillery fire for fifteen mins to an hour on positions . . . and then hopefully we'd get the P47s, which we called Infantry Air Force. They'd come in and dive-bomb with their 500lb bombs, and strafe with their machine guns. And as soon as that lifted, we'd push off. But then, as soon as that (support fire) lifted, the Germans would come out of their holes, still waiting for you. And then, when you actually got to the fortifications, then they had radios connected with each other.'

The Germans used these communications to call fire support when they were in danger of being overrun. The defenders also had planned 'channels' for counter-attacks on the American flanks.

'For two days we lost a lot of men, but we didn't take (the positions). The third day we finally got in there.' This was accomplished by another battalion outflanking the Germans and coming in from their rear. Infantry kept the enemy pinned down while a tank destroyer manoeuvred into point-blank range, pushing its gun into the opening of the enemy pillboxes, and obliterating those inside. 'What was left, they'd come out. We used flamethrowers of course, too.'

With the positions taken, the men of the 4th pressed on towards their target.

'Our real goal for our troops on Utah Beach was to eventually capture Cherbourg and the harbor there at the end of the peninsula.'

The 9th ID landed on D+4 and was tasked with fighting its way west across the Cotentin Peninsula. Daniel Chester was an infantry soldier in the division.

'We went from the left side of the Cherbourg peninsula, and went from the bottom down there all the way up to the top.'

By 17 June the division had arrived at the coast by Barneville. It then turned north towards Cherbourg, a deep-water port that the Allies hoped to capture intact. With all reinforcements and materiel coming ashore via landing craft or onto Mulberry harbours, Cherbourg would significantly increase the rate at which the Allied armies in France could grow.

'We had no tanks,' said Daniel. 'I was about three, four days on shore before I saw an American tank. Meanwhile, the German tanks, they were having a hay day.

'The Germans used to use their 88s and shoot them in the trees.' This would throw out a shower of wooden splinters, causing injuries that would have been familiar to sailors in the age of sail.

'One time we were under shelling, so you'd go in your slit trench and lay there. And as we're laying there, suddenly you heard a thump, and after the shelling was over you look up, and over my right shoulder there was smoke coming up from a dud (shell) that landed about a foot from where our slit trench was. That was another time when God had his hand on me.'

It was one of several near misses for Daniel. On another occasion, he was entering a field in hedgerow country when his buddy spotted Germans lying in wait.

'As I was going through the entrance way there, he shouted, "Dan, look out!" And as I turned to him, there was a German at the opening in the other end (of the field) with his machine gun, and he shot across.'

The bullets hit Daniel's dog tags and scapular necklace. Miraculously, there wasn't a scratch on his skin. So far he'd been lucky, but with so much lead and metal in the air, it was often only a matter of time until some of it found its way into a soldier.

In one fight, Daniel took a piece of shrapnel to the jaw. He left the aid station as soon as it had been patched up and made his way back to his unit with two other soldiers. His unit needed every man that it could get, wounded or not. 'A platoon is forty men,' he said. 'At one time we were down to eighteen.'

Dominick Fiore, also in the 9th Infantry Division, had a close encounter with an enemy sniper. The German had been firing at his half-track before deciding to surrender.

'This guy's coming in, and I've got the gun on him, and I didn't know what to say. He didn't say nothing. Come in with his hands up on his head.'

A loud noise went off nearby. 'It scared the shit out of me,' said Dominick, and in that moment the German fell down, hit by a bullet.

'I must have pulled the trigger,' he said, and for years, Dominick would recall the man's pained expression. 'It was a horrible looking face that he gave. And I tell you what, man I was shaking like a leaf when that happened. I must have squeezed the trigger on that (rifle), and I'd swear to this day that I didn't. But I must have, during all this excitement. And boy I saw that guy's face for a long time.'

The experience had unnerved him, but combat has a way of changing a man.

'I was a rotten bastard. A lot of times them Germans would start running across the field, right? Well, I could have mowed them down no problem. Cause, you know, you get to the point after a while where you got pretty goddamn good at it. (Instead) I'd fire in front of them. They'd turn around and start running this way. (I'd) move the gun over and start firing at them again. They'd see those tracers going, they'd turn around and start running. I used to work them back and forth. You kept moving them. And then after a while they'd fall down, like you hit 'em.' The Germans would then make a final break for it, and Dominick would shoot to kill. 'They'd run right into it.'

Dominick was aware that this was a callous act.

'Now you talk about a rotten son of a bitch. That's the way you get. You get like an animal after a while. I would have never, never ever done anything in my life like that (before war), even to a dog, but I did it.'

Back on the east of the Cotentin peninsula, James Nannini was advancing with the 4th Infantry Division. Though the fighting was constant, day in, day out, it wasn't often that he got a good look at his enemy.

'I got two or three that I know of . . . I was shooting at someone, because he was shooting at me. He wasn't that far from me. My buddy was alongside of me. Now he shot at him too. Either he or I got him. One of us got him. But it didn't happen that often. We shot in an area where we knew that they were.

'There was another time . . . we were in a town. And I heard somebody on a motorcycle and I ran out. Somebody was leaving the town. I was able to rest my BAR on top of a little wall and I had a good shot at him, and I got him.' James then realized that the German was still alive. 'I ran out to get him, which was dopey. I mean, that's in no man's land. You don't do that. You expose yourself. Lucky I didn't get killed. But I got to the guy, and the poor guy, I felt sorry for him. He was crying. I lifted him up and we got help to him. That's one thing, we took good care of the prisoners. They were well treated. They were happy to get captured.'

James had little contact with the French civilians who lived on the peninsula. 'As we went into an area, they were coming out. You just felt sorry for them. You'd see families with little kids, and they'd have a wagon with all their belongings. It was heartbreaking.'

Contact with the enemy was far more common, and James recalled one battle in particular.

'All hell broke loose. We had machine-gun fire. Everything. The airbursts were terrible.'

'Airbursts' were artillery or mortar shells with fuses set to detonate above ground so that shrapnel rained on those below. One of these shells caught James and the man behind him.

'He got killed. I turned around to talk to him and he was laying down, and his eyes were closed. I tried to talk to him but there was no response. It looked like he was gone.'

James started yelling for a medic. 'There was blood coming down my leg, and there was a medic that came and he looked at it. I forget what he did. He said, "We gotta get you to the aid station." I think they did a good job. They saved my life. I could have bled to death.'

In battle, the line between life and death was measured in the thousandths of an inch. 'You saw goofy things. People that got it through the helmet and the helmet liner, and the bullet would follow the contour of the helmet (and miss the skull). Or sometimes it would go straight through. You see strange things.'

James was badly wounded enough that his time in Normandy was over. 'I gotta say I was the luckiest guy in the world because everything worked out good for me.'

John Witmeyer was on the Cotentin with the 4th ID. Like many soldiers he felt unprepared for the Normandy terrain. 'We had absolutely no experience. At no time in our training, three years or more, did we ever get training for the hedgerows. Any number of people were shot through the head when they'd go over a hedgerow, and that's how we learned.'

In such built-up countryside the 'front line' could become a jumble of units meshed together: friend, and foe.

'I had a sergeant, he used to smoke, and he jumped down about three feet from the field down to this sunken road, and he's leaning back against the side, and he had his M1 rifle cradled in his arms, and he was lighting a cigarette. And he looked up at the hedgerow on top, and there's a German officer climbing up about ten feet away. The German officer didn't even see him.'

John's sergeant fired, hollered, and came diving head-first back through the opening in the hedgerow. 'I went down there. And there was a German captain, dead. He was shot in the head. And I remember it so well because I sat down within three feet of him and opened my rations, and ate my lunch.'

John was becoming numb to the death of his enemy, but not to those of his own men.

'I sent a fellow by the name of Simpson and someone else across the road and told them, "Check that orchard on the other side." When Simpson raised himself up he got shot right in the head.' Miraculously, he wasn't killed. 'He come running back across the road bleeding profusely.'

Two Germans were then spotted running into a ditch. John took one of his best soldiers with him to clear them out. 'The grass was waving back and forth because these two German soldiers were crawling, and I started yelling for them to come out. Finally this guy's rifle come skidding across this road, and then his helmet. And next he came out, and I told him to come towards me fast, in German. And you do strange things when you're inhuman, and that's what I was by that point. I met him in the road with my fist. I was very upset with Simpson just getting shot in the head. He was a friend of mine. I had trained with him for three years.'

The other German didn't come out of the ditch. 'And he never will. You do things like that. You send people to their deaths. You send them to get hurt. It registers on you.'

John did everything he could to keep his men alive.

'I wouldn't let my guys stand up and urinate in hedgerow country, because somebody would throw a grenade.'

One day, a machine-gun position inflicted heavy casualties on his unit, and John led a small group to take it out. One of the soldiers was a small man from New York: Feriola. 'I took care of him like he was my son. I felt sorry for him being in the army, so I just adopted him, you might say.'

John found himself crawling through human waste towards the gun position. His company commander tried calling him back, but he pressed on behind a low wall.

'I took Feriola by the hand and I pulled him up on this wall, and the other two guys apparently stood up, and that machine gun cut loose.'

The bullets hit Feriola in the neck and chest. 'I still had him by the hand. I was cradling him in my arms and he was squirting blood on me.' Feriola died moments later. 'I know that's when I changed.'

It was a change that came over many soldiers in combat.

'First I had to change from a civilian to a soldier, and they did that in training, and then I had to change from a soldier to a killer, which is what you're there for in the first place.'

John called out to the other two men in his group and asked them how they were doing. 'They blew off the top of my head!' one of them replied. John helped the man, wrapping bandages around the wound. 'Last thing I said to Martin was, "You look just like my grandma."' The fourth member of the group had been hit in the chest. In just the blink of an eye, three of John's men had been cut to pieces.

'That's just one story,' he said. 'Every day is another story for the infantryman.'

Those days and stories turned John into a brutal man. On one occasion he took three Germans prisoner, but not all of them lived to see a POW camp.

'Someone started dropping mortar shells on us. So I told these Germans, "Lay down." And they're laying down there . . . and I'm squatting down . . . and one of these fellas is grinning at me. And I say, "Who you laughing at?" So the mortars stop, I told him to get up. Get up, and run. He did. And he probably run about forty feet and somebody shot him in the head. That's what happens in war. This is how you act because you're not exactly a human.'

Word of these actions was picked up by the men whose job was to preserve the soldiers' souls.

'One time somebody told me the chaplain wants to speak to you. I said, "I'm fighting a war, I don't have time for a chaplain." I'd already lost my religion back there when a guy died in my arms.'

Eventually the chaplain caught up to John. 'He said that grave registrations said there were an unusual number of people who were shot in the head. And I understood that, because I lost a couple of medics who were patching up German people when they got shot. And I would tell my guys, "When you fired out there and you knocked him down with your rifle, what were you doing? Were you trying to wound him?" (and they'd say) "Naw, trying to kill." So I said, "Well remember that when you pass him up." And some of them would do that. When they passed him up, they made sure he didn't shoot 'em in the back.'

The infantryman had developed a burning hatred for his enemy. 'I punched prisoners. I stuck bayonets through their neck. I did everything to them. I didn't piss on them laying on the ground, that wasn't the kind of anger I had. I was angry at the German soldiers, all of them, and I carried that with me in combat. And when they had a problem with a prisoner . . . I would persuade them to talk, persuade them to listen, or persuade them to die.'

John had no quarter for his enemy, but he had compassion for the locals whose homes had become battlefields.

'A young boy, ten years old or so, and maybe his grandfather, were coming down the road from the German side and I stopped them.' They gave John an explanation about where they were going and were allowed to pass through. 'And after a while they come back, and you're kinda dubious about them, and you say, well maybe they're gonna tell the Germans over here.'

But John let them through anyway.

The next day, while advancing, he found the old man and child dead in a ditch with their hands tied. 'Germans killed them. I was human enough to let them go by. They were so inhuman, that they thought they were perhaps working for us, so they killed them.'

255

It wasn't the only time that he saw civilian dead.

'I'm headed for Cherbourg . . . well this lady comes out and she's beating me on the chest. She's mad. French woman. I don't know what she's saying.'

The lady ran back into a house with a large hole in the roof. 'She's got a child in her arms about two or three years old. And she's blaming it on me. Americans had killed him.'

After battling up the peninsula, John's unit fought to take the port of Cherbourg, arriving on 22 June to find the German defenders well dug-in. It took three days of heavy fighting to overcome the defences.

'One of my guys got killed . . . and he's laying on the corner of this building.' Close by was an enemy pillbox overlooking a tank trap. 'After throwing a few grenades they surrendered that pillbox. About five Germans came out. And the last one was a sergeant. He had a bottle of wine in his hand, and he's looking me in the face from about twenty feet, and he drank from that bottle. Arrogant like, then he threw it away. If that had happened the next day he wouldn't have been living, but it happened that day.' One of John's soldiers then climbed on top of the pillbox to take the Nazi flag. 'He got hit five times in the back,' John remembered. The man did not survive his wounds.

It was one American death of thousands. Although Cherbourg was finally taken on 29 June, the port had been wrecked by the German defenders and it would be weeks before it was operational. The US First Army was being ground down fighting hedgerow to hedgerow, losing a massive amount of troops and materiel. It wasn't the stalemate of the First World War trenches, but neither was it the rapid advance of mechanized armies that had been envisioned.

Something had to change.

CHAPTER EIGHT

The Key

The Battle for Caen

'This young lad, he was burning. And he looked up to
a major that was there, he said, "Will you shoot me
please?" Because the phosphorus was eating away at his
body. So that was one of the first things I seen, which
really upset me. To see a young lad of about eighteen,
nineteen, asking to be shot.'

Douglas Rosewarn, 4th Battalion, Somerset Light Infantry

The liberation of Caen was supposed to have taken place on
D-Day itself, but weeks later the city was still in German hands,
with several panzer divisions in and around the area, including
those of the Waffen SS. To drive them out and destroy them was
the British main effort, with the first large scale operation starting
in late June.

There is still debate over Montgomery's expectations and
strategy at the time, but for the soldier on the ground, the 'why?'
is largely irrelevant. The rank and file are often unaware of what
is happening outside their own company or squadron, let alone

decisions made on a strategic level. Their concerns are surviving the day, finding something to eat, and hoping that they can get a few hours' sleep before they have to do it all again.

The tank crews of the Fife and Forfar Yeomanry had been fighting since early June. Caffeine and cigarettes were much needed to keep the weary men on their feet, and ease their nerves. 'For the English boys (tea) was (important),' said John Buchanan, who was twenty years old. 'They couldnae do without it. But if you were smoking it cleared your mouth, and you could smoke after it and enjoy your cigarette. I mean, there comes a time when you smoke, smoke, smoke, and your mouth gets really clogged up. A cup of tea washes that away.' It was a habit that remained with John for fifty-five years. 'It gives you something to do . . . as long as you were doing something you forgot everything else.'

'We had stacks of (cigarettes) in the tank,' said Roy Vallance, of the same regiment. 'You'd smoke probably forty a day.'

The men were lucky if they got four hours of sleep a night. They had been issued with amphetamines, but recollections differed on whether they were for emergency use only.

'I think we were ordered not to take them. I took them to try and keep awake. We were so short of sleep . . . I wasn't the only one taking them.'

'I remember using these pills,' said John Buchanan, 'but after twenty-four hours you flaked out.'

John Donnelly, serving in 1st Royal Tank Regiment, also received the pills. 'We were given them and told to take them. Just before landing we got them. They told us it would give us strength to get on through the nights. But after about the third or fourth night we were jiggered.'

There was also an official ration of alcohol. 'The rum ration, they were in one-gallon jars. Stone jars,' Roy Vallance recalled. 'The ration was a pint between twenty men.'

Conditions in the field for the tank crews at the time were understandably spartan.

'Each tank had a shovel, and in the ration packs there was loo paper. You simply took the shovel and found a spot. Later on, when we were resting, we would have loos of a sort. Thunderboxes, we called them. We buried (our rubbish). We weren't allowed to just throw anything everywhere.'

Aubrey Coombs landed with the 6th Battalion, Royal Welch Fusiliers towards the end of June. It was an unblooded battalion from top to bottom. When they came to relieve a battalion in the 15th (Scottish) Division, the combat-tested soldiers told them: 'Now you'll know what it's like.'

Aubrey remembered his first night in France well. 'We were looking into the dark, and every bush looked like a German helmet.' Over time he got to know the sights and sounds of war, including the different sounds made by each side's weapons. 'You learned to survive. You kept your head down and you never took chances.'

'You kept your head down, didn't you,' echoed Harry Martin, a corporal in 7th Battalion, Royal Welch Fusiliers. 'Eventually, it was a job of work. You had to look at it that way, but you still had to take care of yourself.'

In the fighting that followed, Harry formed bonds that lasted a lifetime. 'I've still got the same mates today, who were lucky like I was to come home. You lost a mate now and again, but it was all in a day's work, weren't it?'

'A day's work' in Normandy often involved taking part in a large-scale operation, such as Operation Epsom, a British advance to the west of Caen that aimed to circumvent the city, and take the bridges over the River Odon. 60,000 men and 600 tanks took part in the attack which lasted from 26 to 30 June.

'We formed up in the dark,' said Roy Vallance of the Fife and

Forfar Yeomanry, the leading regiment on the operation, 'before very long I heard over the (radio) that "So and so's brewing up, so and so's brewing up," I think I said to somebody in the crew, "What on earth are they brewing up for at this time?" Thinking they were brewing tea. But they weren't, of course. You realized possibly that the crew were in there . . . a lot didn't get out.'

Norman Bradley was a co-driver in the Fife and Forfar Yeomanry, and was in the second tank of the leading squadron. It was hit by the River Odon crossing and rolled down the embankment. Thankfully Norman's tank did not burst into flames, and the crew were all able to escape. Soon after the colonel came along. 'We were given a dressing-down for being in the wrong place at the wrong time . . . it was just unfortunate, but I remember him really dressing us down. And then of course they moved on and left us.'

'There were a lot of snipers about in that area,' said Roy Vallance, 'and I felt very sorry for the redcap (military policeman), who was stood at the ford supposedly directing traffic.'

Roy and others were told to dismount and clear the snipers from the woods. 'I remember crawling very rapidly along the ground, and the guy crawling beside me giving vent to the most awful language.' It wasn't until they got to the edge of the wood that Roy recognized the man. 'It turned out to be the padre.'

John Majendie was a company commander in the 4th Battalion, Somerset Light Infantry, and took part in the actions along the River Odon. 'It became known by the soldiers as Happy Valley, and a very short time after, Death Valley, because the Germans basically were on three sides of us. When we were advancing on the River Odon . . . I was just behind battalion headquarters and we had a stonk of shells landed among us. My own company clerk who was beside me, he was killed, and I got very slightly wounded in the hand.'

After being knocked out of the battle, Norman Bradley and his crew waited beside the river as the rest of the unit pressed on with their attack. As on D-Day, it was often the case that momentum in the assault had to be maintained at all costs.

'We had three or four days there, and we were taking shelter under a road bridge, and opposite was a farmhouse, where some old dear, who was English, had married a Frenchman during the First World War. So she did provide some food for us. But it was amazing, really, the number of German soldiers that were in this river. Dead, of course. They'd been shot out of the trees. Snipers, and that. And they lay there as we stood there for days.'

Norman and his crew eventually found their way back to the support elements of their regiment. 'The RSM . . . he was there of course. The greeting we got was something like "And where do you reckon you've been to then, bloody China? Here's a shovel, go dig some latrines over there." And that was the welcome back to the regiment that the five of us got.'

At the end of four days of fierce fighting, the British front had advanced only a small distance, but a narrow bridgehead had been established on the Odon. The German divisions in the area had been pushed back, but were far from beaten, and over the coming weeks this salient would see some of the heaviest casualties of the campaign.

Operation Charnwood

To the east of the salient created by Operation Epsom, British and Canadian troops launched Operation Charnwood, an offensive aimed at capturing Caen between 8 and 9 July. It was preceded by a massive aerial bombardment, with more than two and a half thousand tons of munitions falling on the city. Most of Caen's residents had already fled the fighting, but some 15,000 were still there on the night of 7 July. They suffered from the unimaginable noise of the explosions, fires, and blastwaves that sent buildings toppling into ruin.

Francis McGovern and his Halifax crew took part in the bombing.

'We made an attack on Caen in support of the invasion forces, and I think we were much criticized afterwards for the mess that we made, in so far that we took out the target all right – which we were told at the time was a steelworks on the banks of a canal, which the Germans had fortified quite heavily with anti-aircraft weapons, and weapons of one kind and another – and were making life quite difficult for the army and their advance. However, we took the place out, and from what I recall of it we simply left quite appalling clouds of dust and smoke in our wake, and the army were then complaining that we made life even more difficult because the roads that they'd intended to follow were simply strewn with rubble and all sorts of rubbish.'

Roy Crane's Typhoon squadron had been sent up to attack any Germans who tried to escape out of the city. 'Witnessing the bombing from the air, it was the most horrible sight I think I've ever seen. The whole ground was literally like a big volcano. It was erupting. And one felt, nobody could survive it. It would kill everybody. And we didn't see anything leave at all. I must say that it was one part of the war that was very unpleasant. Particularly knowing that there was a lot of French people there. I think it's the thing that I remember most.'

Roy's brother was outside of the city at the time of the attack. 'After the war, we were talking about Caen. He was in the Royal Engineers in Normandy . . . and I said to him, "Did you see anything of the bombing of Caen?" And he said, "Well I didn't actually see anything until two days later. We drove through Caen, and it was absolutely amazing how many people

Men of 12 Platoon, B Company, 6th Battalion, Royal Scots Fusiliers prepare to advance at the start of Operation Epsom, 26 June.

A Loyd carrier and 6-pdr anti-tank gun of the Durham Light Infantry of the 49th (West Riding) Division parked alongside a knocked-out German Panther tank during Operation Epsom, 27 June.

British soldiers with a PIAT gun in the ruins of
Caen watching for enemy movement, July 1944.

Troops of 130th Brigade, 43rd (Wessex) Division
take cover from mortar fire, 10 July.

One exhausted soldier gets some sleep in a slit trench in the forward area between Hill 112 and Hill 113 in the Odon valley, 16 July.

A sergeant briefs men of the Royal Welch Fusiliers before an attack towards Évrecy, 16 July.

Sherman tanks of the Staffordshire Yeomanry,
27th Armoured Brigade, carrying infantry from 3rd Division,
move up at the start of Operation Goodwood, 18 July.

A wounded soldier being carried out of the operating tent
at the 79th General Hospital at Bayeux by British medical staff.

American soldiers move through the battle-torn streets of
Saint-Lô in pursuit of the retreating German forces, 18 July.

American infantry during 'the breakout' of Operation Cobra,
which launched on 25 July in the area of Saint-Lô.

Men of the Durham Light Infantry move up during the fighting south of Mont Pinçon, 9 August. They were greeted with heavy mortar fire.

An injured German soldier from the 12th SS Panzer Division Hitlerjugend is captured by men of the 3rd Canadian Infantry Division on 12 August, near Falaise.

Allied infantry and armour moving past burning
German vehicles towards Falaise, 21 August.

Thousands of horses were killed in Normandy, many of them in the Falaise
Pocket. The plight of the animals moved many battle-hardened soldiers.

French civilians cheer as they return to Falaise on
19 August after its liberation by Allied forces.

American soldiers kneel in homage at the graves of their dead comrades near
Sainte-Mère-Église in August 1944. Allied and German graves, with simple markers,
were to be found throughout the Normandy countryside.

were still alive in all the rubble," because the place was literally demolished.'

Following the bombing, two British infantry divisions and one Canadian pushed on what was left of the city. In the rubble, the German defenders prepared to meet them.

Nineteen-year-old Gerhard Franzky, of the 10th SS Panzer, had already seen combat in Yugoslavia and on the Eastern Front. In late June, his division was moved to Normandy and took over from the badly mauled 12th SS Panzer. Now in the area of Caen, Gerhard experienced the brutal firepower of Allied bombing.

'I was sitting for hours, I don't know how many hours, in a manhole that I had previously put a mattress in, so I would lie comfortable, but scared. It was a rain of bombs. Artillery came later when the bombing stopped, because then they made a tank attack, and we were still there. They fired smoke grenades, so we didn't see what was coming. But you could hear the engine roar of the tanks. They came towards us, and the louder it got, the more scared you got. We all had a Panzerfaust, at least.

'Then the smog lifted, and the artillery was shooting, and they shot above us. In other words, now you know that we are clear.' Gerhard is referring to the creeping barrage that preceded the assault. Once the shells began to land behind the German lines, they knew that it wouldn't be long before their enemy appeared. 'When the smoke cleared you see between the tanks the infantry coming.'

Perhaps the advancing troops didn't believe that there could be any Germans left alive, because they came in bunched-up groups, talking, and without their weapons at the ready. 'They thought maybe they went to a picnic,' said Gerhard. 'And then we opened up when they were closing up, with a Panzerfaust, and we shot the first three tanks. And they can't turn around. They have to back up. Which is what they did. And so did the infantry.'

The soldiers dropped their kit and retreated. 'All you see is heels, running. That was the end for us. A time to take a breath. They took a pounding. That I remember well, and we were glad.'

Gerhard's unit was holding on in Caen, but their losses were high. 'We had a lot of casualties. A lot of casualties. You could only hope that you didn't get hit, that's all . . . Nobody can tell me "I wasn't afraid." That's nonsense. They're lying. You've gotta be afraid if you're human.'

Canadian Bill Lewis was part of a recovery tank crew..

'When the attack on Caen got going, we were really having a hard time. We weren't getting anywhere . . . I'd hauled about three tanks back in the morning. I would see the horrors that had occurred in the battle of that day . . . It was pretty horrible at times. Bodies were still left inside the tanks in all kinds of conditions. Blown to pieces, burnt out, or whatever the case may be, and I was hoping for the war to end as quick as possible.'

During one attack Bill's tank was stripped out and filled with ammunition to take up to the troops. '(The officer) said you'll get mentioned in dispatches. I said, "After I'm dead?" Anyway, you gotta do it in the army and that's it. So they loaded the tank up. What surprised me was then they started to put some on the outside – boxes of ammunition on the outside of the tank. OK, I thought, this is it.'

As Bill was driving towards the fighting he saw two men in RAF uniforms walking along the road. 'I said, "What are you doing up here?" He said, "We're souvenir-hunting." I couldn't believe it.'

He moved on to the rendezvous point where the tanks were waiting. They took his ammo on board then left him alone to wait for one more tank that was on its way to him. Bill saw an orchard nearby, and went to find something to eat.

'I'd no sooner got to the orchard than two Canadian soldiers come out with two German prisoners.' The Canadians wanted Bill to take the two prisoners back with him, but this was impossible. 'How can I drive the tank and keep an eye on prisoners? So they said, "You're not taking them?" And I said, "No. I can't do it." Well, they walked back into the orchard. The next thing I hear, bang, bang. And when I looked through there's the two Germans laying dead.'

Only moments later a bombardment of shells began to fall in the area. Bill spotted an old iron bathtub next to a building and pulled it over him. This likely saved his life. A shell struck the building, bringing masonry down on top of the tub.

'I was half covered in bricks and bits of wood. While I was there, I see a German half-track coming through loaded up with German soldiers. They went through and I cleared myself out and got in the tank.'

Bill had only just started back towards his unit when he saw a single figure walking around a field. 'He was one of our guys. His tank had been hit and the rest of the crew had been killed. He was in a state of shock and confusion, so I got him into the tank.'

As they moved along the track Bill recognized a pair of familiar faces. 'There's the two RAF guys lying dead on the side of the road. I assume that half-track full of Germans (had killed them).'

Bill survived a few near misses that day, but he was soon back in action. Two British tanks had lost their tracks in a minefield, and he was sent in to recover them. 'We were just unhooking the second tank when the shell landed in front of mine. It killed the British corporal, and badly wounded the British officer. Tore away half his stomach. I was just getting out of the tank, and I don't know what happened. I sort of went unconscious momentarily. But when I come to I'm head first down in the tank. My co-driver's screaming his head off, "I'm blinded!" Two Canadian soldiers who had got into the roof of a house across the way, they were killed.'

This first shell was only the beginning. More artillery and small-arms fire followed. 'The British officer was so badly wounded we didn't know what to do. We didn't think we could get him into the tank.' Despite the fire all around them, someone was thinking clearly enough to come up with a solution: there was a trapdoor beneath the tank. By attaching straps to the wounded officer, they were able to drag him under the tank and back to safety.

It had been a long day for Bill, but that night, he found that he couldn't sleep. His limbs kept twitching, and he reckoned that he must be on the verge of a nervous breakdown.

'About the fourth night, I hadn't had any sleep,' he said, and reported to the doctor. 'He felt my back and shoulders.' The doctor also gave him an injection. The next thing Bill remembered was waking up on a stretcher on the back of a jeep. He was passed through a number of aid stations and was eventually put on a ship for Britain that was packed with wounded. 'Next to me I got a German with his stomach in a glass container.' The jerking in Bill's limbs had come not from combat fatigue, but spinal injuries that would remain with him for life. His time at war was at an end.

One of the infantry soldiers advancing on Caen during Charnwood was William Snell of the 1st Battalion, King's Own Scottish Borderers.

'There was great big craters. Bombed-out places. The smell of death and cordite. By this time we'd got used to this. There was very few civilians about. There was one or two Germans still knocking about. We got in towards the centre of Caen. There was a little bit of street fighting. We consolidated and we were sent on patrol. We went through a brewery yard. There was about six of us and an officer. We were crawling under along the side of the wall, and we heard this rattling on the roof. The Germans were on the other side and they were throwing these stick grenades. Of course we all hit the deck, and there was all hell let loose. Eventually we got into a crater and I don't know whether they were afraid, or we were afraid. I remember Paddy Phillips jumping and running, and this officer what was with him. Paddy got hit in the back with a bullet. We went into a cellar, there was about four of us, and we holed up there all night, and things quietened down.

'Just before daylight we made our way back to Company HQ. And Paddy, he didn't know he'd been hit. He said that he felt sick, and they found a bullet hole in his back. The bullet had lodged in his stomach.'

William believed that there was one thing that united everyone in Caen: fear.

'We went to the catacombs where all the civilians were. Helped to sort them out. They were frightened. They were frightened, we were frightened. Took one or two prisoners, and they were frightened. I think everybody was frightened. But we were always told, you had to be frightened of being frightened.'

Hill 112

Erwin Rommel, who commanded the defence of Normandy, is quoted as saying, 'He who controls Hill 112 controls Normandy.' Whether or not those were his words, Rommel deployed several of his best units in the area, southwest of Caen, including the 2nd SS Panzer Corps, made up of two SS panzer divisions and an SS heavy tank battalion.

The men that would be tasked with pushing them back off 112 were largely new to action, at least on this scale. The primary British formations which took part in the battle were three infantry divisions, 15th (Scottish), 43rd (Wessex), 53rd (Welsh), and the 11th Armoured Division.

The Hill itself (named 112 for its height in metres) was more of a plateau and had controlling views not only to the south of Caen, but of much of the surrounding 'tank country', which was more open and allowed for large formations of armour to move in concert, and maximize the range of their weaponry. On 28 June British infantry had advanced on Hill 112, as part of Operation Epsom, but only managed to secure its northern slope before being pulled back because of their exposed position. They attacked again between 10 and 11 July in Operation Jupiter. In the end the hill changed hands several times in more than a month of fighting, in which over 10,000 men lost their lives.[1]

John Majendie, an officer in the 4th Battalion, Somerset Light Infantry, described taking part in one of the attacks on 112 during Operation Jupiter.

'The attack started with a very heavy creeping barrage from our own guns. A very heavy artillery barrage indeed. Our own divisional artillery fired 23,000 shells in twenty-four hours.' The SLI were also supported by a squadron of the 7th Royal Tank Regiment. John described the advance as 'very much stop and start.' The Somersets moved through pastures and fields of corn, which came up to the men's chests. They were under fire and after a couple of hours, before they were anywhere near the plateau of the summit, they had already suffered heavy losses. 'The platoons which were normally thirty strong were down to about ten men. The CO decided it simply wasn't on to go any further . . . A normal infantry battalion was about eight hundred and thirty strong, and we actually had five hundred and twenty-five casualties killed, missing, and wounded.'

Thomas Peace was an officer in the 5th Battalion, Wiltshire Regiment, who advanced on 112 on the right flank of the

Somersets. 'We had our first experience of these nebelwerfers. I remember seeing one salvo come over right in the middle of a platoon about two hundred yards in front of me. I thought, "Oh God, that's written them off." In fact, they all got up after it. My recollection is we suffered about two hundred casualties . . . Nobody got anywhere seriously at 112,' he said, meaning that no battalion made a successful attack that ended the battle.

Arthur Jones served in the 5th Battalion, Duke of Cornwall's Light Infantry. They had pushed through the Somersets at dusk and set up in what became known as Cornwall Wood.

'We were formed up all afternoon in this wheat field on a reverse slope . . . it was absolutely appalling. You had no cover. You couldn't dig in. And Gerry was just plonking mortar bombs down in amongst us, and the casualties was, well, there was so many people on the ground they couldn't miss nothing at all. My old company, B Company, got clobbered. Practically wiped out. The feller that took the Bren over from me, the company commander, and most of the NCOs, and three parts of the company were killed on the initial attack.'

A request came back from the Cornwalls asking the Somersets for anti-tank weapons.

'Our CO sent me,' said John Majendie. 'I went with about six chaps with half a dozen PIATs. We got back to our own positions . . . when suddenly two tanks came up from behind us. We thought at first that these were tanks coming up to relieve the Cornwalls, and then they started firing their machine guns straight ahead. They came about twenty yards to the left of where I was dug in.'

A Somersets' soldier had a lucky escape when the tanks ran over his slit trench but he emerged unharmed. One of the tanks disappeared, but the other came back towards John's position. Illumination flares went up into the air, 'and an anti-tank gun got a direct hit, but unfortunately, (it was) on a Churchill tank that had been knocked out earlier in the day.'

In the confusion, the man who had fired the flare was mistaken for a German and was killed by one of his own men. 'It's the sort of thing that happens,' said John. Another anti-tank gun got a direct hit on the tank, but the round bounced harmlessly into the sky. 'Eventually it got into the arc of fire of the gun that was with me, and I fired the last remaining (flare).' But the flare was a dud, and the tank escaped in the darkness.

Thomas Peace recalled that the battlefield proved a steep learning curve for some soldiers. 'Despite all their training, they'd been prancing about on the skyline, they'd dug slit trenches about a foot deep, thinking that was enough . . . The shelling was intense all night. One of our FOOs, he spotted German troops forming up for an attack, and he called for artillery fire. I'm going to be quite honest. If they'd come straight at us, I don't think we were in any position to resist a night attack. But they crossed our front, and that's where this FOO got them. From captured German documents, I believe this was meant to be a thrust to the sea. And it was that FOO, and the guns, who saved us.'

'(The next day) a squadron of the Scots Greys were sent up through us to try and drive the Boche tanks back,' said John Majendie.

Godfrey Welch was one of these tankers. 'Our B Squadron, nineteen tanks, was to go up to these woods with a company of infantry and take the woods, which was across about four or five hundred yards of open ground. You're belting away with everything you've got . . . You're using your own weapons to get the infantry in. You're only doing about two mile an hour because infantry are well loaded with their equipment.'

The Scots Greys made it into the woods, but German armour was waiting for them. 'The other end of the wood was dug-in

Tigers, 88s, nebelwerfers, and the Jerry infantry, and they opened up. We just bought it, there was no two ways about it. We lost a lot of people. I think nine out of nineteen (tanks) were knocked out, and the mortars were playing hell with the infantry.' As shells hit the trees they threw out a wave of lethal splinters. 'The infantry took an awful belting,' he said.

Godfrey's own tank was struck by an 88. 'It came in the hull just behind me, and hit Pete Stevens.' The tank was in flames. The crew had only seconds to get out. 'I turned around, and the officer went to bail out. You could see the tracers of (a machine gun) going through him.' This left Godfrey with two choices, neither of them good.

'You're sitting in a furnace. And the thing is, are you gonna sit in a furnace, or take your chances out there with the Spandau (machine gun)? I can remember looking through the turret, and the fire, and seeing a lovely blue sky and white clouds.'

Godfrey decided to take his chances and was immediately struck by a bullet. 'I fell on the ground, still trying to get my breath back, and by this time (the tank's) a ball of fire.' The driver, Pete Kemble, had also escaped. 'When I looked back he's in one of the German weapon pits, taking cover.' Godfrey joined him, and there followed a lull of sorts. 'The 88s stopped but the mortars kept going.'

This opportunity to evacuate the wounded was seized. Casualties were carried out by some as others provided covering fire. Godfrey and Pete were given a Bren gun. As they got low on ammunition, Godfrey had to scour the battlefield for more. During this time they were still under concentrated mortar fire. 'We heard this one coming, and we knew it was ours.' The round hit the top of the trench and knocked both men out.

The story that Godfrey heard later was that, when Pete had regained consciousness, he thought that Godfrey was dead, and left, before returning with the reserves to find Godfrey's body. 'He brought them up to where I was laying, and they found me still at the bottom of the weapon pit. Next thing I know I came to in a half-track.'

Godfrey had shrapnel injuries and was eventually flown back to England. He was awarded the Military Medal for his actions that day, and returned to action when his wound had healed.

Arthur Jones was also in Cornwall Wood during that action.

'I still have nightmares about it now. When it got light there was this wood. Only a small wood. And Jerry was only a hundred yards away, and he was firing. Tanks were firing into the trees, and there was no cover. Nobody had chance to dig a hole much. The casualties with the shrapnel raining down, it was so bad there. Our gun, all our people went. I don't know what happened to them really. There was only me and a chap called Hunt left on this anti-tank gun.'

Arthur came across his old rifle company in the woods. 'There was about twenty of them there. Some were dead. Died during the night. Others were severely wounded. The padre came up in a carrier. And we helped put them on stretchers and get some of them out. All of this was going on under appalling shell fire and mortar fire. It went on all day long.'

'They really suffered badly, the DCLIs, the Cornwalls,' said Thomas Bryan of the 7th Somersets. 'I used to feel terribly sorry for them. They always seemed to be going into the attack.'

Dick James, the twenty-six-year-old Commanding Officer of the Cornwalls, was killed while trying to spot for the artillery. '(He was) virtually decapitated by a machine gun,' said John Majendie, who was a friend of his. Finally the order was given for the Cornwalls to pull off the hill. Arthur Jones and a friend made their way out of the hellish woods.

'We ducked under a knocked-out Sherman halfway down,

and there was some of the crew that had been burnt down beside of us. That stuck in me mind for a few years.'

John Majendie watched the Cornwalls retire from the top of the hill. 'I'm not being rude about the Cornwalls, they had a terrible time . . . they came back at a run, at the double . . . our own CO went out and said, "The first Somerset who goes, I'll shoot." They were stopped, collected, sent back. They only had about two officers left.'

The Somersets' anti-tank platoon commander went with them. He found a gun that was serviceable, but there were no crews left to man it. A private soldier volunteered and was given a three-minute lesson on how to use it. As a reward, the officer opened a ration crate and gave the man fourteen men's daily ration of cigarettes. Inexperienced and alone on a gun facing Tiger tanks, it's doubtful that the soldier ever had the chance to finish them.

It was eventually decided that to keep the Cornwalls on the hill was futile. They withdrew under cover of smoke and dug in to the left of John Majendie's positions. Their casualties were so heavy that their battalion was now down to a composite company. 'They'd had a very rough time indeed.'

'There was dead and dying all around there. It was a terrible sight to see,' said Thomas Bryan.

'On the second day the lance corporal, I was with him all the time, this young lad. This one day, oh we were being mortared heavily. Oh, the fear. I'll never forget the fear of it to this very day. That young lad, oh he was telling me, "I want to see me mam again." And of course I was about the same. We were crouching down . . . we hear a ear-splitting bang. Me ears are still ringing to this very day, that's how I am, you know . . . They had to come and dig us out.' Thomas suffered what would today be diagnosed as a traumatic brain injury. 'They said I'd be like this. I can't gather me thoughts properly.'

Douglas Rosewarn was sent to the Somersets as a casualty replacement. During his first action he was shaking with fright. 'As the war went on we got used to it. It was just another day. You never thought much about it, you know. You just went into action where we had to. You just got used to it.'

Douglas spoke of one casualty that he would never forget.

'A young lad in our company was carrying a phosphorus bomb in his pouch. And a bit of shrapnel knocked the phosphorus bomb and set it off, and once the phosphorus starts, you can't put it out. This young lad, he was burning. And he looked up to a major that was there, he said, "Will you shoot me please?" Because the phosphorus was eating away at his body. So that was one of the first things I seen, which really upset me. To see a young lad of about eighteen, nineteen, asking to be shot.'

'He was well, just burning to death,' recalled John Majendie. 'He shouted out, "Shoot me, somebody." And one of the officers in the company shot him. We saw the flames go up and wondered what it was.'

'We went back on the hill again and took over from the Monmouths,' said Arthur Jones of 5th Cornwalls. 'And I remember one position we were in, we took over a gun that was down in the side of a hedge. In the middle of the field was one of our chaps that had got killed. He was on his knees with his backside stuck up in the air. It used to be odd to see this feller there every morning.'

Any movement outside of the trenches would instantly bring down mortar and sniper fire. This presented a predicament when men needed to answer a call of nature. 'You had to do it in a biscuit tin,' said Arthur.

During this time they received a number of replacements, many of them eighteen years old. One of the green soldiers didn't listen to the advice of the veterans and got out of his trench to 'go to the bathroom'. 'Jerry started to mortar us, round our position,

274

and it got so bad that it was knocking the trenches to bits. I think we had a casualty or two. So in the end we decided to move back down the hill.'

Stretcher-bearers were in constant demand on Hill 112. John Majendie recalled their unending bravery. 'You'd hear this shout, "Stretcher-bearers", and they'd get up out of their trenches and went forward to attend to the casualties. They were a wonderful lot of chaps.'

When John thinks back on Hill 112, his emotions are mixed. 'One has feelings of guilt, sometimes . . . I remember so clearly a little British ambulance with the Red Cross came up the road from behind us. And, we never thought to say, "If I was you I wouldn't go any further," because ahead of A Company there was nobody between us and the Boche . . . this little ambulance trundled past us, we never saw him come back, and I don't know to this day where he went. I suppose we weren't quite compos mentis, and things happened.'

After the war John met some of the Waffen SS soldiers who had fought against him. 'We had a get together in Bayeux, and we had a dinner, and we went up to 112 together.'

One of the German soldiers had been wounded in an attack and left behind. As he was trying to make his way back to friendly lines, he came across a British soldier who was also wounded. John recalled what the German had told him. '(He said that) we put our arms around each other and helped each other down to our own regimental aid post.'

The pastures, cornfields, and woodland surrounding 112 were littered with the detritus of war. 'All you could see lying around was dead men, dead cows, pigs, everything,' said Douglas Rosewarn.

'When we came off Hill 112, out of a hundred and twenty men, there was only twenty-seven left. There was not one officer.

They had all been either killed or wounded. The company commander was a sergeant.'

While battles like Hill 112 are far less known by the public than those on the Normandy beaches, they were no less bloody: the 43rd Division suffered 2,000 casualties in two days of fighting on 112, and 7,000 casualties in total: almost half of the division's strength.

Infantry soldier Arthur Jones believed that without the support of the artillery, things would have been even worse. 'My honest opinion is, if it wasn't for the artillery, I don't think we'd have ever got off the beaches.' The rate of fire by the British artillery was so impressive that several German prisoners of war believed that the British possessed 'belt-fed artillery'. Rather, it was the skill and effort of the Royal Artillery gun crews that was responsible for this high rate of fire.

Arthur was equally full of praise for the RAF. 'The Typhoons saved our bacon over and over again.' Kenneth Trott was one of these Typhoon pilots. The day after Operation Jupiter ended in stalemate on 112, so too did Kenneth's war in the air.

Prisoner of War

On 13 July, Kenneth Trott prepared to take his Typhoon up for one last mission before he rotated back to England for leave.

'And I said to somebody, "Thank God it's Thursday the 13th . . . I wouldn't like to be flying on Friday the 13th!" Which was a fateful thing to do, because I didn't fly any more after that.' With a couple of Bayeux cheeses in his cockpit, which he had planned on taking back home to his parents the next day, Kenneth took off and headed to the south of Caen. He and his wingman spotted a half-track, and went down to attack while the other members of the flight provided cover. 'Our cannon fire

was going down all around it . . . I saw two people run away . . .'
Kenneth then asked his leader for permission to do a second run.
'He said, "For goodness' sakes no, we're in the middle of thirty
109s."' German fighters had swarmed the Typhoons.

'We got up, and I couldn't see the wing commander, but what
I could see was a gaggle of 109s.' He turned straight towards the
enemy. 'I made an attack. As soon as they saw me coming . . .
they came back at me. And they were flashing past, four of them I
think.' Kenneth disappeared into cloud cover, but his instruments
were faulty. Flying without them in the cloud seemed a more dangerous proposition than the enemy fighters, and so he broke out
of the cloud bank. His wingman was nowhere to be seen. Only
after the war would Kenneth learn that he had been hit by flak
and forced to return to base.

'As I came out of cloud I spotted another 109 on his own . . . so
I made a head-on attack, and really, head-on attacks are not a good
proposition . . . I was doing four hundred an hour, and he was no
doubt doing three or four hundred an hour . . . I pulled the stick
over, but the Typhoon was a sluggish aircraft. My wing collided
with the 109's, and that's when I went out through the cockpit.'

The violence of the impact launched Kenneth through the
canopy. He was knocked unconscious, but his parachute was
fitted with an emergency device that deployed when it reached a
certain altitude. The pain from the canopy filling with air jerked
him back to consciousness.

Kenneth was met on the ground by German soldiers, one of
whom spoke basic English. When he tried to raise his arms in surrender, he found that one would not lift beyond a certain point.
This injury stayed with him for life.

'There was some French children looking on . . . and suddenly
one of the Germans fired a shot in that direction, and they all
disappeared.'

Kenneth felt well treated by his captors, who asked him questions about his unit but did not press him when he refused to answer. He was held in a school classroom, and noticed several British names on a blackboard: they belonged to men taken prisoner before him. He added his own name and service number to the list.

Later that day he began to cough up blood. He was taken to a field hospital, where he met a captain from the Welch Regiment who had been shot through the stomach. Kenneth required an operation on a hematoma on his spine. He saw out the rest of the war as a prisoner in Stalag Luft III.

After the war, Kenneth found eyewitnesses who had seen him collide with the Luftwaffe fighter. They told him that the German pilot had come down in a field, and that he was an old man. 'Of course, old men used to be twenty-nine in those days.'

Operation Greenline

On 15 July, Operation Greenline was launched by the 15th (Scottish) and 53rd (Welsh) Divisions to the west of Hill 112. Its purpose was to hold German divisions so that they would be unavailable to counter coming operations by the British at Caen and the Americans at Saint-Lô.

Taking part in Greenline was Norman Griffin, a nineteen-year-old soldier in the 7th Battalion, Royal Welch Fusiliers (RWF).

'Our first real attack was on Évrecy . . . we made our way to Hill 112, and that was probably the first major experience we had of battle.'

The village of Évrecy had already suffered greatly. On the night of 15 June it had been heavily bombed by the Allies to deny its important crossroads to the German army. Of the 430 French civilians who lived there, 130 died that night.

'Every house was flat,' said Aubrey Coombs of 6th RWF. 'There wasn't a house standing.'

'We were advancing to the perimeter of the hill overlooking Évrecy,' said Norman, 'and we were doing this in conjunction with the Churchill tanks, which were in the same fields, dug in at hull down position. The intelligence was not as great as one would like to have thought . . . it was originally anticipated that Évrecy was going to be taken quite quickly.' Instead it became a prolonged and bloody battle. 'We lost our company commander, and we lost an awful lot of people in that area killed and wounded.'

'We dug in,' said Aubrey, 'and we could hear these voices coming towards us. And a corporal says to me, "Taffy, that's Welsh, isn't it?" And I was hoping it was, but it wasn't. It was German. They told us to hold fire, but somebody pulled a trigger. With that, these men come towards us with their hands up.' It transpired that the Germans belonged to a party that were escorting prisoners from 7th RWF back to their own lines. 'The bullet had hit the sergeant major of A Company, of the 7th Battalion, in the foot. But he said, "Oh boys am I glad to see you!" So he didn't mind.'

'We were at that time using many of the trenches that had in actual fact been dug by the Germans,' said Norman Griffin. 'They had obviously been dug in for a very long time there. They were excellent trenches. Half the trench was covered with heavy logs.'

The downside of using these trenches was that the Germans knew exactly where they were, and could call in their artillery accordingly.

'We took an awful hammering in terms of 88s and German artillery. It was quite hairy. We lost quite a lot of people.'

'We were on there for quite a few days, and that was where you really got shelled,' said Harry Martin, of 7th RWF. 'Moaning Minnies as we used to call them. They used to send six at a time . . . and 88s, and the 105s . . . There was a wood on one side (of the slope), and that got down to stumps.'

The heavy shelling caused cases of 'shell shock' amongst the men.

'If you got a big barrage, some went what we call bomb-happy,' said Harry. 'They couldn't help it. You just had to cope with it. If you were strong enough to cope with it, you coped with it, but not everybody could do that.

'If they saw movement then they'd shell that area. You'd keep your head down. That was the job. Keep your head down. We got caught out one day, and I dived into a trench, and I hit my face on the side of the trench as I dropped in it, and broke me false teeth. And the biggest laugh was that while I was waiting for them to be repaired I used to get two slices of bread while the others were on hardtack biscuits.'

As well as artillery fire, the British forces were also up against SS panzers. Robert Smith was a reconnaissance sergeant in the Royal Engineers, attached to one of the Welsh battalions.

'They required a defensive minefield to be laid in front of their position, and I was attached to them as sapper advisor. Whilst we were engaged in this, the battalion was very heavily attacked by infantry and six Tiger tanks, and were partially overrun. The counter-attack by a sister battalion, however, cleared the enemy. This was my first taste of action. Strange enough I didn't seem to be particularly concerned . . . I think I had so much faith in the infantry lads around me.'

'(They) had created quite a lot of havoc,' said Norman, 'but with the reinforcements coming up, the German prisoners then started to come through. They looked pretty shattered . . . they were young men like we were. They'd obviously had quite an experience . . . I think probably their demeanour was one of relief to be out of it. There was certainly no arrogance or anything.'

'They were no different to us,' said Trevor Edwards, of the Royal Welch. 'Young lads. They'd ask you for a cigarette. (You'd) have a fag with them and talk with them. There was no hate or nothing I don't think.'

During the fighting, Trevor received a light shrapnel wound and was sent to the regimental aid post.

'When I got there I was ashamed really, seeing lads really wounded. One lad in particular was a mate. A Wrexham boy . . . Jack was lying on the floor, and the MO and his aide were taking shrapnel off his back. The shrapnel ripped his back straight off, and they were with pincers, getting the fabric (out of the wounds). They were picking bits and pieces of his tunic out of his wounds. I had this little finger wound, I felt ashamed.' Trevor had known Jack since 1940. '(He was) a conscript like me, on the same train coming from Wrexham together.'

'We had the three battalions in the brigade,' Norman Griffin explained, 'all Royal Welch battalions, 4th 6th and 7th . . . and of course, the problem was, as Évrecy was going to be the target of the Royal Welch Fusiliers, the casualties that occurred at Évrecy . . . were extremely heavy . . . The consequence of that was, because it had been a Territorial (Army) brigade . . . the casualties were then relating back to the townships in Wales. For example, a town like Newtown, a very small Welsh town, was heavily populated with soldiers from the regiment. So when this happened, of course then the casualties were notified back, and quite obviously there was a great deal of mourning and concern back in the towns. And I think this was obviously relevant to the other battalions, and other brigades as well.'*

* After hearing this from Norman, I checked the war memorials in the villages that are within a few miles of my home, and found the names of five Royal Welch Fusiliers who had been killed during the two days of

The make-up of brigades in the 53rd Division was soon changed to avoid this happening again. 'In that way any casualties in the future would be much more dispersed over the whole country, rather than just in the isolated townships of the individual Territorial regiments.'

'We had to do away with our D Company,' said Aubrey Coombs, '(they) put us into A, B and C, because there wasn't enough men. We were down to fifteen (men) a platoon. It should have been about thirty-five, something like that.'

Trevor Edwards had served in 8th RWF before being drafted into the 7th Battalion. 'D Company lads weren't as familiar to me as my 8th Battalion lads were, because previous to when I went to France, we weren't long associated. It was more or less a rush job, and you didn't know these lads.'

Trevor would get word on the grapevine about his friends from the 8th, many of whom were from the same town as him. Several of them were killed and wounded during Greenline. Casualties amongst the RWFs officers were so high that the brigade had to borrow officers from the Canadian Army. 'We had six Canadian officers and every one of them got killed,' said Aubrey Coombs. 'They were brave officers. Unbelievably brave.' Aubrey explained that snipers were often to blame for the officers' deaths.

'When we were moving forward snipers used to pick off the officers. Then they'd go to the sergeants, and then they'd work down.' The battalions soon made changes to try to mitigate the sniper threat. 'They decided then to take all the (rank insignia) off. And they give the officers rifles instead of revolvers, and they'd put their map case behind them.'

Operation Greenline. One can only imagine the effect that this had on the close-knit communities who had already lost so many of their men to the Great War. GJ.

This worked for a while, but then the enemy found a new way to identify the officers. The RWF found out how when they captured and interrogated a German sniper. 'He said, "We look for men with little moustaches." Most officers had a little moustache, and anybody with a little moustache, they'd pick him off first.'

Despite the high casualty rate, the brigade's officers continued to show exceptional bravery. Aubrey recalled that one officer, Lord Davies, went into no man's land to evacuate French civilians from the firing line, but was caught by the SS and taken for interrogation. 'He was took into a room, and when he went in, this major of the SS had been in college with him! So they had drinks together. (We) recaptured Lord Davies, but he got killed in Holland.'

The front line was a hard and dangerous place, but the men still retained their sense of humour. Aubrey recalled one incident, a miraculous escape, that still made him laugh more than sixty years later.

'The Canadians were on our left, and there was a farmhouse in front, and the Germans had been using it as an OP to shell them, so they asked us if we could send a patrol out and demolish it.'

A patrol of fusiliers stripped most of their equipment, removed their helmets, and blackened their faces.

'There was a lane going down the road and there was an orchard below, and the Germans were in the orchard. And so our pioneer platoon had put three tripwires across there, with explosives . . . and they had a Bren gun looking down (the road).'

The patrol, from 15 Platoon, passed through Aubrey's 14 Platoon and went forward.

'And WG now, he was a little bit slow. He got out of the trench and went with them. And when he got near the farmhouse he was making a terrible noise, and the sergeant told him to be quiet. He had all his kit on.'

When the sergeant discovered the identity of the noisy soldier he sent him back to his own platoon. 'He went back now, run back, but he run in the wrong direction. He run towards the Germans, right down to the orchard, and (then) he came up this lane, and the Bren-gunner could hear him coming up . . . and he was preparing to open fire. And with this, who should come towards him but WG, and he stepped over the three wires and didn't trip anything!

'He said, "I'm glad to see you, I've been lost, I've been with the Germans down the bottom!" And they didn't even stop him or anything!'

Casualties

'What if I get hit?'

This is a question every soldier will ask himself in war. The answer can have a huge effect not only on his morale but also on the army as a whole. If a soldier knows that any wound is likely to be fatal, with him being left to die slowly on the battlefield, he will be far less likely to expose himself to risk. If, on the other hand, he knows about – and trusts in – the casualty clearing chain behind him, he will be more willing to do what the army asks of him.

The emphasis put on the care of the Allied wounded in World War Two was unlike any war that had preceded it. Huge numbers of skilled servicemen, and massive amounts of logistics, were provided not only for Allied wounded, but for the enemy, and for civilians.

A soldier badly wounded in Normandy would likely have gone through the following phases: first aid by unit medics on the battlefield, treatment at a regimental aid post, evacuation to a field hospital, evacuation by sea or air to England, and further surgeries then convalescence at a hospital or series of hospitals in the United Kingdom.

William Wood was a dental technician in the Army Dental Corps, and operated in No. 32 Casualty Clearing Station.

Although he was sometimes called upon for other duties, William's primary work in Normandy was with facial injuries. 'If shrapnel or a bullet had gone in at one side and taken the whole side of the face out, our job was to make sure that that patient could be sent back (to England). One of the main things that we did, we used to make a metal band which we fastened onto the head with plaster of Paris bandages, and then . . . we'd suture through the tongue, and fasten it onto this metal bar, and that kept the tongue out so that they didn't choke. They were mostly conscious, the people with facial wounds. Very few were unconscious. And of course we had to make sure that they didn't see any sign on our face that they were so badly wounded. I think to see a face badly wounded is one of the worst. And so we'd always remember that, because they were waiting for one little hint about how badly they were wounded. And as a lot of the nerves were severed, they wouldn't get a lot of pain in many cases. They were sort of numbed.'

Medics were instructed to collect as much of the shattered face as they could, 'because when it came to the day that they had to start building back, they needed every little bit of bone they could find to build the face back to something like normal.'

Having served in the Royal Army Medical Corps in Egypt, Amy 'Pam' Dunnett was no stranger to the cost of war, but she and the other members of the 3rd Casualty Clearing Station thought the Battle of Normandy would be different.

'Really I don't think that anybody knew what to expect very much. We landed on this beach, and we were there for some time, and then a truck came and took us up to the site for the

CCS . . . that's where we put up our tents and received our first casualties.'

Pam's 3rd CCS and the 10th CCS would leapfrog each other to keep close to the front line as it moved forward, so that there was always one established station to receive casualties.

'We never stayed more than ten days in any spot . . . There was the large tent where we had the reception tent for the casualties. I was in charge of that. And then there was another tent for surgical operations, and then there were two very long tents that would hold about twenty beds for the wounded that had to be nursed there for ten days before they were fit to evacuate.'

Pam's role in the CCS's reception was to prepare the casualties for surgery. 'Later, when they were so busy, I worked in the operating theatres. And on one occasion I worked for fifty-six hours without a break. (Women) were almost always at base hospitals, a certain distance back, but we were very much frontline.'

Joan Nicolson was a nurse in Queen Alexandra's Imperial Military Nursing Service, based at No. 106 General Hospital, Bayeux.

'The stretcher-bearers went out at night, and they would bring in just one after another of ambulances with very shot-up people, or people they'd got out of no man's land, and they would just lay them in rows up and down. We had two or three sergeants in the unit who would then come, and they would walk up and down, and they would decide who could go to the theatre, or what we could do.

'You got some terrible shocks as you went up and down the rows. You'd see somebody with a funny eye looking across, and you'd think, head injury. And you'd pick up their head and the back would fall off, or something dreadful like that. Awful things happened. You were doing, really, around the clock work for many weeks. And in the end you almost felt that the world had gone mad. It was really very bad for about five or six weeks, until the advance had moved forwards. You were utterly exhausted. I think that one was really deeply shocked. You couldn't really know what to expect. As the matron said, because you were young, you just got on with it.

'The fighting was going on all around us . . . to begin with, and then slowly, as the weeks went by, the advance moved on. To begin with we had shrapnel come down on us . . . our particular unit wasn't bombed as such. It was just fallout from other areas I should think. We did get shrapnel coming through our tents, and things.'

Conditions at the hospital were spartan. 'For quite a long period we only had one water bottle of water a day. And that was to drink, and to wash, and everything, because the Germans had poisoned all the water wells. And the tankers that came for the hospital we needed for the wounded. In a way, I suppose it was quite a good war, because they were able to fly quite a lot of people out after initial treatment. Those that could be flown out were flown out, and there was a continuous movement of this.'

Joan cared for both Allied and enemy soldiers. 'The ones who were really quite terrifying . . . (were) the Russians, they were White Russians working with the Germans . . . and they were terrifying people, because they seemed to have no manners, or morals, or anything else. They would steal from each other. We found it was increasingly difficult to nurse the young Germans. The Hitler Youth, because they really hated you, and they thought you would kill them, so they tried to prevent you from helping them . . . they were so indoctrinated. It was terrifying to see them. (To) see young men, in very bad agony, and yet they tried to refuse treatment. The way that was overcome was very interesting.'

German POWs were allocated to the wards to both help with

the massive workload, but also reassure newly captured wounded Germans that they would not be mistreated and killed by the Allies. Joan was incredibly impressed by the two German orderlies who were assigned to work with her. Her impression of the German soldiers as a whole was that, despite the Allied landings and advances, they still believed in victory for their side.

'You got the impression that they were exceedingly well trained, and strong, and they believed I'm sure, implicitly, that they would still be able to drive us out.'

One day, as she was taking some air, Joan had a strange encounter with a German officer.

'I was out walking round the perimeter of our field hospital and found a high-ranking German in a ditch being looked after by one of the orderlies who worked with us.' Joan went back to the camp and told the guards, who went out to collect the German, who was then put into a tent under guard. 'It was very hot, and the (guard) fainted, and the German general or whatever he was crawled out of his bed and gave him some water and was reviving him.'

Like many families during the war, Joan had a sibling who was also serving.

'Strange thing was that my brother didn't even know I was in the army. He was with the Royal Artillery . . . On one occasion one of the girls in my unit came back to me, and she said, "Have you got a brother in the army?" So I said, "Yes I have, but last I heard of him he was in Iceland."'

Joan was given directions and caught a lift towards the front. 'When I got there my brother wasn't there. A Canadian was, and I asked him if a Royal Artillery unit had been there, and he said yes.' The officer gave Joan a lift in his jeep to the unit's new location. 'And sure enough, my brother was in a ditch with some other fellow officers eating sardines out of a can with his fingers.

And he looked up, and of course he didn't know I was in the army at all . . . and I think he thought he was hallucinating, because they'd been bombed out of Caen. And he swore for about five or six minutes, just swore. Anyway, it was a great reunion. After that, whenever he could get back at all to see me, he did.'

Although many members of the medical staff did not discriminate when it came to their patients, there were others who believed that some did not deserve their care.

'Towards the end of our time in Normandy . . . they brought a very young boy who couldn't have been more than seventeen in, who had been very badly roughed up in one of the military camps.' The young soldier had a card that said Deserter. 'I'd just spent about ten minutes reassuring this child that he would only feel a prick in his arm, and then he would go to sleep, and we would get some of the worst of his injuries treated . . . he was completely disintegrating as a person, and it was horrible to behold . . . and the surgeon, came in and picked his (deserter) card up, and threw it down on this boy again, and said, "Might as well have wished you'd died." And it upset me very much, and so I asked him to come outside the tent . . . and said I was sorry, but I did not wish to work with him any more, and so of course I was in grave trouble, because it was considered insubordination. And his rank was major, and mine was only lieutenant. So then I had to go before the colonel in charge of the surgical division . . . and he asked me what had happened, and I explained . . . and said that I believed that we should be sanctuary for such people, and there was very little point in bringing them in if we weren't going to help them. I've always believed to this day that I was in the right.'

Joan did not believe that she was discriminated against as a woman in the army. 'There were only very few, or relatively few, women over there, so of course we were made much of by anybody who wanted female company. So I think we were probably in rather a good position,' she laughed. 'Could really call the shots you might say. I think some girls had an unhappy experience from it, you know, things went slightly wrong for them. In as much as there were a great many men, I think, without their wives or without their girlfriends, looking for release more than relationships. In that respect, I really did have my head screwed on. I thought we were in enough trouble already without getting into any further involvements.'

However, Joan did meet a man in Normandy. 'When I first met David I said it didn't really matter, because, you know, things were too busy to meet anybody properly, and it was better if we didn't. However, he pursued it, and we went on and then, eventually decided that we would get married.'

Maurice Tondowski was a Polish Jew in the British army. His road to that occupation included service in the French Foreign Legion in Algeria, then imprisonment and slave labour after the collapse of the French government. Freed by the Allies in 1942, in Normandy he served as an interpreter. He recalled one incident when he was part of a 'clean up' after a large operation to dislodge Germans near Caen.

'We took out the badly wounded men – Canadians, Poles, and Germans as well.' Many of the wounded had waited a long time for treatment, and gangrene had set in the wounds. 'I remember we took them with stretchers day and night to the operating theatre, it was also in a big tent, no buildings. We cut them off. The legs. We took (them) outside to bury them in the night, but we had to go back quick and pick up more legs. (We) didn't realize that we didn't dig it deep enough. In the morning we came and saw dozens of legs sticking out and we had to re-bury them.'

One German soldier was in dire need of a blood transfusion. 'He said no, he'd rather die. I said, "Why?" and he said, "It's Jewish blood," and he died.'

Cecelia Christie served as a psychiatric nurse in the British army. She was part of an advanced party to set up a psychiatric unit in Bayeux. Before that establishment could come online, Cecelia nursed casualties in the 79th General Hospital.

'We stayed there for several weeks working with our general battle casualties. It was all under canvas. Large tents made into wards . . . we slept on stretchers. We had very primitive sanitation. We did very urgent general duties of all types of casualties, both British soldiers and German soldiers. Often you had a row of 7th Armoured Div soldiers on one side of your ward, and on the other side you had a panzer division's casualties, so that you were nursing both British and German in the same ward. It's typical of that sort of war situation where one minute they're killing each other, and the next they're lying side by side, offering each other sweets and cigarettes, which officially they weren't supposed to do, because it was very strictly no fraternization. We had German prisoners of war who were acting as ward orderlies, cleaning up, and doing odd jobs.'

Cecelia spoke fluent German. 'It did come in handy, as you can imagine. The German casualties were extremely hostile, and many times they were very, very young, sometimes fifteen, sixteen years of age with very severe injuries. A lot of them died. But they were still hostile right up to the last gasp, some of them . . . calling us all kinds of unpleasant names despite the fact that we were nursing them. But on the whole (the Germans) were amazed at the amount of general nursing care they were getting, because I think they felt that they were going to be shot as prisoners . . . a lot of them were . . . calling for their mother, or their sister, or their wife.'

Trevor Edwards, of the Royal Welch Fusiliers, was wounded in the fighting west of Caen.

'I got blown up. We were moving up . . . we were getting mortared and shells. I was blown off this carrier like a ragdoll. I had what they call a deflated lung through blast.' He was evacuated to England with a collapsed lung and shell-shock. He developed pneumonia, and spent two weeks in a coma.

'We had a telegram from the War Office,' said Trevor's wife, who came to the town where he was hospitalized. 'They gave me bed and breakfast. The Red Cross people put me up. I was there all night. I was with him all night. He'd come round now and then, but far and few between. I was in this ward, with all the men that had been wounded . . . I went into the corridor then (with the doctor), and I said, "Is my husband all right?" He said, "Whatever you do, don't get him in bad tempers." He said, "A couple of years, and he'll come round to his normal self." Which he did eventually. But oh, you wouldn't have given tuppence for him, he was that ill.'

She was heartbroken that Trevor was injured, but relieved that he was alive. 'Our Ron didn't come back. My brother didn't come back. And me mam said, "Well you've got (your husband) back, we haven't got our Ron back." And I said, "I know, Mam, but look at the state of him." And she said, "Oooh he'll come all right, he's a strong lad. He can pull through anything with good backing." And he pulled through it all right.'

She recalled one day when she brought their son into the hospital. 'I sneaked our Michael up, who was about eighteen month old. Oh that brightened his day up when he saw that child.'

Operation Goodwood

On 18 July, British and Canadian forces launched Goodwood, an armoured thrust intended to capture any parts of Caen that remained in German hands, and fix the panzer divisions so that they could not contest Cobra, which was soon to be launched by the Americans to the west.

Goodwood was one of the largest British operations of the war, involving around 1,200 tanks. More than 2,000 heavy bombers preceded the attack, followed in turn by a massive artillery bombardment.

'I've never seen so many planes in my life,' said Berkeley Meredith of the Staffordshire Yeomanry. 'They were going over in a continuous stream out and back. There was a tremendous noise, both from the planes and from the bombardment.'

John Donnelly was with 1st Royal Tank Regiment. 'We had to withdraw so many hundred yards. These boys come over, the RAF, and honestly, you thought you coulda brought them down with a catapult. They flattened (Caen), but we were told afterwards the Jerries had seen us moving back. They knew something was happening.'

The bombardment destroyed much of the historic city, which had already taken severe damage.

'What a mess,' said John. 'I don't think there was anything standing. It looked grotesque.'

John Court, of 3rd Royal Tank Regiment, was also taking part in the operation.

'As far as the eye could see it seemed to be just tanks waiting to move forward. I can remember standing outside the tank and hearing the drone of the planes coming over. And first of all the pathfinders came in, and dropped all these flares, and then wave after wave of bombers coming over, and it was a fantastic sight, it really was. And to see the ground ahead erupting, it didn't seem as though there was a square inch of ground that wasn't sort of heaving. It was a fantastic sight. And then our guns started up.'

Some of the salvos dropped short and caused some casualties amongst the men who hadn't mounted their tanks.

John's squadron then went into the attack.

'I didn't think there could be any opposition whatsoever . . .

and suddenly a mortar opened up a couple of hundred yards ahead of us. Well, they were very, very brave men. To have seen a complete line of tanks moving towards you, and to open up with a mortar against that sort of opposition, well, I think about eight or nine tanks just slew their guns around and blasted it out of existence, but I thought they were very brave. They could have just stood up and surrendered . . . I thought that was fantastic, to have the guts to do that.'

Other German soldiers decided it was better to surrender than die fighting. 'I remember seeing one or two Germans coming forward with white flags. They seemed to be very, very dazed.'

Roy Vallance, of the Fife and Forfar Yeomanry, had reservations about the coming operation.

'We weren't very happy about the whole thing, because we weren't having any infantry with us. We were told that the air bombardment would be so heavy that there would be no opposition.

'Once we got through the area that had been bombed we spread out . . . and we started going down the valley . . . and suddenly the tanks started brewing up all around. My own reaction was to tell the driver to speed up and go flat out. I wasn't certain where the fire was coming from . . . it was an open area and I didn't know where I was going . . . I was thinking, What can I do? I daren't stop. It would be fatal.'

Roy's tank came to a railway line where there was a deep cutting, and took cover. 'I could see over the cutting top, but the tank was completely hidden.'

'We went through the 13th/18th (Hussars) and made our way across this plain,' said Berkeley Meredith. 'There was a tremendous number of tanks in this battle. And there were many, many knocked out. We'd reached a railway embankment when we were disabled. We had an armour-piercing shell through the side of the tank, which entered the engine. We were very, very lucky, because normally a tank brews up. It catches fire.'

Berkeley and the crew bailed out, but got back into the tank when they realized it wasn't going to go up in flames.

'There were a couple of Germans on the other side of the railway embankment who popped up occasionally and tried to lob grenades into the turret. This was infuriating because we couldn't depress our gun low enough to fire back.'

Hans von Luck, commander of the 125th Panzergrenadier Regiment of the 21st Panzer Division, arrived back at his unit from Paris as the attack was underway.

'I saw all my staff . . . very depressed. I asked them what happened. They informed me of the heavy bombardment, and the artillery barrage which had just finished.'

Hans asked one of the officers about the state of the battalions. He received no reply. 'This man had lost his nerves, and didn't know what to do. I had to relieve him immediately. I myself went in my (formal dress), in a MK IV, and drove very slowly in the direction of the 1st Battalion.'

He saw signs of the bombing. Worse than that, he saw the rapid advance of Allied tanks. 'Half of this village was destroyed. The other half was still intact. So when I came to the west end . . . I was absolutely frustrated seeing the whole ground covered with British tanks, of which about twenty had already crossed the main road (and were heading) south.'

Hans was heading back to organize his regiment when he saw something that could slow the tide of British armour.

'I suddenly saw an air force 88 battery with all their guns pointing into the air. I stopped and ran over to the battery. There was a young lieutenant commanding this battery, and I said, "What are you doing here?" '

The officer told Hans that he was part of the anti-aircraft defences around Caen.

'So I informed him about what was going on on his left flank. All the British tanks. He didn't know that, because he was in the middle of the village. So I said, "You are going to fight these tanks." Well, I got a flat refusal. He said to me, "Tanks are your job, my job are the planes." So again, I said, "You have to fight the tanks." Again I got a flat refusal. So I took my pistol . . . (and told him), "You will be a dead man, or get a high decoration." He decided for the decoration.'

Though technically in different chains of command, Hans had 'convinced' the Luftwaffe officer to follow his order, and led him to an advantageous position for the 88s.

'I went with him to the northern edge (of the village). There was a big apple orchard. I said, "That is the right place to file up your four guns." Within seconds they had killed about sixteen tanks, and they fought the whole day . . . (until) the Armoured Guards division advanced and took the village.'

'I could see the tanks all round,' said John Court of 3rd RTR. 'I remember hearing a big bang, and someone said, "Monty's tank's been hit." I can remember seeing this figure run across in front of me, and I recognized him as Monty, and he climbed on the front of the tank. I remember swivelling the periscope around, and it seemed that everywhere I looked, every tank was burning. I just slapped it in reverse and backed out.'

When John's tank resumed the attack they were struck on the turret. The shell didn't penetrate the armour but the commander was wounded by shrapnel that hit his head.

'We got down behind a ridge. A small ridge.'

John heard over the radio that another tank had been hit, killing several. One of the crew had lost his legs, and the voice on the radio announced that he was staying with him.

At the end of the action, John counted only thirteen tanks remaining in the regiment.

'Fighting was grim,' said John Donnelly. 'After Caen we met as a regiment. And when you looked around . . . you realized how much you'd lost.'

Goodwood secured the areas of Caen that had remained in German hands, but there is debate over how successful it was, given that it did not decisively drive the enemy out of the wider Caen area, and cost of thousands of casualties, and hundreds of tanks.

Norman Bradley, of the Fife and Forfar Yeomanry, lost comrades during Goodwood.

'It's one of those things I find a bit difficult to talk about. There was a lot going on, and I used the machine gun in the hull of the tank.'

Norman was asked by his interviewer what he was firing at.

'People . . . It's a difficult one to say and talk about really. We saw tanks on fire . . . you could just see tanks burning, and it wasn't long before ours was burning . . . I think we ended up with three 88mm shells . . . one after the other. I would think it was the same gun . . . They hit the turret . . . The turret crew, I think they had it first . . . they were killed.'

He had to get out quickly before the Sherman went up in flames. 'When I got out I was fired at by a machine gun. I fell in the corn and got into a ditch. There was a guy out of the Guards Armoured Division also in that same ditch. I lay there for a number of hours.'

Norman eventually made his way back to where the survivors of his regiment had gathered. The tanks had driven under the wings of crash-landed gliders close to Ranville, six miles northwest, in an attempt to hide them from prying German eyes. Perhaps they had been spotted by forward observers, or perhaps an aircraft saw the tracks leading through the corn, but the field came under an intense attack by the Luftwaffe. Norman and his best friend in the regiment dived under a tank for cover.

'We lay side by side under this Sherman . . . I'd been through the Coventry blitzes, and I have tried over the years to lay one (experience) against the other, but this was concentrated. They knew the tanks had gone back there. A lot of the turrets of the tanks were left open, and when the Germans came over and they bombed this area, the burning wings of the gliders dropped in the tanks that had survived the battle, and added to the pandemonium, and all of the wheat and cereal fields were on fire.'

Norman's friend was severely wounded, and he received shrapnel wounds to his leg and face. They were collected by members of the Royal Army Medical Corps, and Norman was driven to a field hospital by ambulance.

Decades after the war, whilst visiting France, Norman ran into an old friend from his home village. He remarked that it must have been forty years since he'd last seen him. 'And he said, well I've seen you. In fact, I think I've still got your dog tags.'

Norman's childhood friend had driven the ambulance.

Exhaustion

Goodwood was not the end of fighting for British forces in Normandy. More battles lay ahead, many of them in support of American operations that were about to take place at Saint-Lô, some twenty-five miles to the west of Caen.

John Buchanan, a tank gunner in the Fife and Forfar, got his second panzer kill at the end of July.

'The Germans had counter-attacked us, and (our) infantry were falling back. They were pointing (at something). A MK IV tank came out of the sunken lane to turn into the field that I was sitting in, and it got sort of jammed. The chap couldn't see me, (but) I could see him. And he got his leg out over the turret to get out and guide his driver, and then he saw me . . . I can still see the expression on his face today.' John fired a high-explosive shell. 'It hit just below where his foot was, and when the smoke cleared he was gone. The tank was there, but he'd disappeared.'

Tank commander John Donnelly had developed a reputation in the squadron for being so cool in action that he must be mad.

'But I wasnae mad. I was frightened, maybe more so than them. The biggest part was trying to not show it to your crew. I felt, well, if I show fear it's going to spread through the crew.'

John must have been well trusted by his unit's leaders. When a new officer was assigned to them as a casualty replacement, John was asked by his commanding officer to take him in his tank so that he could watch and learn.

'So we went into action one day, and he came out all right.'

After the evening meal that day, the gunner came to John and told him that the officer hadn't cleaned his mess tin. John told him to put it back in its place in the tank as it was.

The next morning at breakfast 'he come around and he says, "Sergeant, nobody's washed my mess tin." I said, "Everybody washes their own plate, sir." He says, "God, this is bloody ridiculous." But after that he was all right. He mixed in with the rest . . . And, poor soul, after about two or three weeks he got a tank of his own, and lost his head the first day with an AP (armour-piercing round). (It took his) head right off his shoulders.'

Ronald Hann was an infantryman in the 51st (Highland) Division, and often worked with the armoured regiments.

'You can believe me, or believe me not, but I remember in one particular period after the breakthrough in Caen, where we had to take tanks with us . . . we were specifically told that we must have a section of infantry in front of the tanks, and a section of infantry either side of the tanks, as they were very valuable. So obviously we weren't so valuable.'*

Combat troops like Ronald had little time to rest.

'I had eight hours' sleep and seven meals (one) week. You may get an hour and a half (to rest), and you'd get up again and move forward.'

After one particularly intense period of combat, Ronald was shocked to see how much his appearance had changed.

'I had a large mirror which I had appropriated from somewhere. I can't remember now. I took it out and I looked. My God, is that me? Bloodshot eyes, heavy growth of beard, and absolutely shattered. But, the human body being what it is, within a few days you're right as rain.'

Ronald had fought the Germans in North Africa, Italy, and now France, but he did not hold a hatred for his enemy.

'You tried to kill them because they were trying to kill you, but that was what it was all about. Once it was finished with, it was finished.'

At the end of Goodwood, John Court had counted only 13 tanks remaining in his regiment, 3rd RTR. His own tank had been hit, and his commander injured. John was given a new tank commander who had learned how to deal with enemy infantry from his time in the desert. 'This commander, he was one of the old school. He said, "See these slit trenches? Drive over them." As you hit the slit trench you pulled the lever and slewed the tank to fill the slit trench in.' This was to entomb any soldier waiting to shoot a Panzerfaust at the rear of the tank as it passed.

---

* This may have been down to the number of tanks that had been lost in operations like Goodwood. With that being said, the author can confirm that the practice of having infantry walk ahead of armoured vehicles was still in use some seventy years later.

John's next action after Goodwood was in support of the Guards Armoured Division.

'We got into the village . . . there was a lot of infantry fire, and suddenly there was a terrific bang in the tank. The whole tank filled up with smoke, and someone yelled, "Bail out! Bail out!" One of the front of the houses had collapsed across the front of the tank, and I said to my co-driver, "Let's go out through the escape hatch." When I got out the commander was laying on the ground, not a mark on him, but he was dead.'

John had been in action since the desert, and this long exposure to combat caught up with him in the closing stages of the Normandy campaign.

'I was so tired . . . I remember them saying, "Start up, driver," and I thought, Who's he talking to? He's not talking to me, who's he talking to? And there was a terrific bang. I think either a mortar or a shell had dropped beside the tank, and again, I heard this voice again, "Come on, start up, driver." And I thought, He's talking to somebody, I don't know who he's talking to.

'The next thing I remember, I'm in a British ambulance, I'm going along, and the orderly in the ambulance is saying, "Hold on to this." '

John was given a bag of blood to hold for an infantry officer 'with half his arm blown away. And I can remember him saying, "This has buggered up my game of golf." '

Their destination was an American hospital at Saint-Lô. John was impressed with the American construction of the camp, including the latrines. '(They) had proper pans on. Complete latrine, with lights and everything. Fantastic.'

'I can remember this major said, "Well, if you were one of our fellows we'd send you back to the States." But I can remember also thinking, What the hell am I doing here? There's nothing wrong with me, what am I here for?'

John recalled the other patients on his ward.

'It was filled with American soldiers that had been caught in their own bombing at Saint-Lô.'

Many of the nurses had boyfriends at the nearby airfield, and these pilots would buzz the hospital, flying low, just over the tents. This proved terrifying for men who had been wounded by aerial attack.

'All the patients, they'd all be diving out of beds and running across the fields.

'I used to feel sorry for them . . . I thought it was terrible, the fact that (the pilots) were just showing off to the nurses.

'I got to know one of the nurses . . . She used to sit on the bed at night time and talk to me. And I couldn't sleep, and she used to talk and talk and talk. I learnt more about Chicago and America than I'd ever known before. She was great.'

John remained at the hospital for two weeks.

'They gave me a piece of paper. It said, "In our considered opinion, this man is no longer fit for active duty." They put some long (medical terms) underneath I can't remember now. I suppose basically I was shell-shocked. I was thinking to myself, There's nothing wrong with me.'

John was then transferred to a British general hospital at Bayeux. 'The matron there was a dragon. My god she was a dragon. I got out of there and went to our tank delivery squadron.'

John caught a lift on a replacement tank and made his way to catch up with the unit. 'What did grieve me, and I couldn't understand it . . . they took me down to lance corporal again. They took my second stripe. That grieved me because I thought, Well I didn't deserve that.'

John was taken off tanks, which always grieved him, and spent the rest of the war in a variety of roles. In cases like his, the attitude of fellow combat veterans was often more compassionate than army officialdom.

Roy Vallance, of the Fife and Forfar Yeomanry, recalled an incident at Hill 112.

'The commander, he became a medical case. A nervous case. He was an excellent chap, but as soon as we got into action he just went to pieces. He couldn't do his job. He got down in the turret to hide.'

Roy was sympathetic, 'It was obvious he couldn't go on . . . He was obviously ill.'

Arthur Thompson was serving in the 2nd Battalion of the East Yorkshire Regiment. Though Normandy was his first campaign, Arthur gave the impression of being a 'natural' soldier who was looked up to by his comrades, and respected by his commanders. During weeks of fighting, Arthur's company, which should have numbered some 120 men, had been ground down to almost nothing.

'Well at that time, all we could find was four of us . . . and we had to hold this high ground.' Most of his company had been killed or wounded, but others had left their lines out of their own choice. 'It came out that there was an officer, two sergeants, and a lance corporal which had done a bunk. They'd gone, you see. I gets word (ordering me to go and) see if I could find (them). Well I went, and I found them. But instead of running back our way, they'd run towards the Germans. They were in a dugout there, but they wouldn't get out. They were all crying, you see.'

Like Roy, Arthur had sympathy for the clearly terrified men. 'It's all right people talking about people running away, but there's something to run away from. It's terrible. Nobody knows what it's like. Once the nerves go, that's it. You can't do nothing about it.'

He had no luck convincing the men to come with him, and returned to his company HQ alone.

'I shouted but I couldn't get no reply, so I makes my way to the slit trenches . . . and the first thing I come to, he's just sat there like a statue, and I'm shouting at him, no answer, so I touch him, and he just fell over. He's dead. They were all dead.'

Arthur made his way back to the three remaining men on the high ground. Soon after, an explosion riddled his chest with shrapnel, and blew off his right leg. After bandaging the stump himself, Arthur called to the other men and asked them to bring him water. 'Well, they started crying . . . They were saying, "Well what we gonna do now? What we gonna do now?" I said, "Well, I can't do no more for you now, I've had it. That's it."'

Arthur explained why it was that some men acted this way while others did not.

'I'll just tell you something you see a lot of people don't understand. A lot of people, you get this in civilian life as well, a lot of people can be led, but they can't do anything for themselves. They can be led, and they can be good. But when it comes to doing something for themselves, they're lost. They've had it. And that was the same with them. When I was there leading them they were all right.'

One of the young soldiers used to follow Arthur around 'like a lamb'. 'That lad saved my life. He went (back) and came back with two stretcher-bearers, but they were only two small chaps, and they couldn't pick me up to get me on the stretcher.' Arthur rolled onto the stretcher instead, but they'd only just started back when the shelling began again. The two men dropped him and ran. At some point they must have come back to collect him, because when Arthur came to he was with the medical officer and one of his old friends, who gave him a cup of tea. Arthur then began his evacuation to England, his war over, and his life changed for ever.

James Blinkhorn was also serving in the 2nd East Yorks but

had a different experience of men breaking under the strain of combat.

'I only ever saw one that panicked. The morale was very high. We'd been under constant shelling . . . I suppose his nerve just went. He was cracked up. He was quivering like jelly, you know, so they had to send him back.'

James was understanding. 'It could have happened to anybody, really. We'd been in constant action all the time. Something had got to give. We didn't look down on him at all.'

The British army executed more than 300 'cowards' during the First World War,[2] and while progress had certainly been made in understanding the psychological effects of combat, they were still not seen in the same light as physical wounds – hardly surprising, considering that there is a great deal we still do not understand about these conditions. Some commanders opposed treating mental wounds as equal to physical, believing that healthy soldiers would 'play the system' to avoid action on the front line. There is no grey area about a bullet wound to a leg; a mental injury is hard to diagnose. Has the soldier taken all he can take, or does he simply want to avoid further risk? There was also some hostility to the field of psychiatry. In 1942, Winston Churchill wrote: 'I am sure it would be sensible to restrict as much as possible the work of these gentlemen, who are capable of doing an immense amount of harm with what may very easily degenerate into charlatanry. The tightest hand should be kept over them, and they should not be allowed to quarter themselves in large numbers upon the fighting services at the public expense. There are no doubt easily recognisable cases which may benefit from treatment of this kind, but . . . it is very wrong to disturb large numbers of healthy normal men and women by asking the kind of odd questions in which the psychiatrists specialise.'[3]

In spite of scepticism, psychiatric units were set up close to the front lines with the aim of returning men to their units wherever possible. Patients wore military uniform, and their treatment mostly consisted of occupational therapy and physical training. Diet and rest were very important, and sometimes involved sedation. This is reflected in the term given to such patients, 'exhaustion cases'; by mid-July, they were 15 per cent of British casualties. Although there was some success in returning men to their units, many could not return to combat.

'We had hundreds of battle casualties who broke down,' said Cecelia Christie, a nurse in the 32nd General (Psychiatric) Hospital. Many of these casualties were veterans of previous campaigns. Dunkirk, North Africa, Italy, Sicily, and the last straw was (Normandy), and a lot of them cracked up. And quite a lot of them were senior NCOs, who just about had enough. They were highly experienced, battle-experienced soldiers. A lot of them broke down. Infantry NCOs. They'd had enough. And a lot of them were genuine, scared, what was known as "effort syndrome". All the panic symptoms of fear. Stress, anxiety, simulating heart attacks . . . all the symptoms of a heart attack. And they had a pretty rough time. Some of them were pushed around by the MPs. In fact I was so angry with the MPs I kicked them out of the ward.' These psychiatric patients were eventually shipped back to the UK. 'A lot of them ended up in psychiatric hospitals having completely broken down.'

Other casualties suffered from 'battle neurosis'. 'They were treated with . . . a form of psychiatric treatment to get a person to relive their stress. They were given an injection of Pentathol, and then the psychiatrist would talk to them while they were under the influence of the Pentathol. It was known as the truth drug. The soldier would then probably, totally relive his battle experience. And it was quite amazing what they went through.

But they got it out of their system, and afterwards, they were receptive to psychotherapy.

'In those days battle neurosis was rather frowned on as being cowardly. Shell-shock, bomb-happy, all sorts of adverse labels were attached to it. Because of the recognition of true psychiatric problems in the field, the whole of the appreciation of psychiatric illness was changed. People realized that you do look and you do feel with mental illness, and psychiatric illness.'

Cecilia recalled that any soldier with a self-inflected wound was treated as a prisoner by the army, and offered an explanation why some of the men might have injured themselves.

'A lot of them did it out of sheer fear of going up the front line again. That was their only way out. And obviously they were treated as prisoners. It was a punishable offence. But the battle neuroses were then treated as sick people.'

She believed there were reasons why some men felt they had no way out.

'A lot depends on leadership. If you've got first-class officers, NCOs, who have strong leadership potential, and set a good example, the chaps behind are going to gain a lot from that. Again, if they've had continuous bombardment, and continuous frontline fighting and bad conditions, the stress is going to crack them up . . . but it's very difficult to define what's cowardice . . . and what is fear and stress.

You always give the patient the benefit of the doubt, because you can so easily be wrong.'

Treating the patients was a delicate balance.

'You had to be fairly firm with some of them. Certainly sympathetic. Listen to them. Socialize with them, mix with them, talk to them. Listen to their stories. Listen to them talk about their families. It helped tremendously. Even keeping in touch with them sometimes afterwards when they got back home. They wrote to you. You wrote back letters . . . but they needed a lot of moral support. They were well looked after by all qualified psychiatric sisters and psychiatrists, and they had regular interviews with a psychiatrist. There was lots of projects to keep them active . . . physical exercise, good diet. And gradually they were all evacuated back to the UK.'

Sometimes an improvement could be seen as quickly as a few days, 'but the majority of them didn't want to go back to the front line. As their condition improved they were reassessed, and those that had to go back, went back. But by and large, the majority of them came back to the UK to psychiatric units.

'I think the majority of them felt they'd done their bit, because they were all hardened veterans from all the other areas of warfare. A lot of them, I think their attitude was "I just couldn't take any more."'

The series of British operations in and around Caen had been incredibly costly not only to the British and Canadian armies, but to the civilian population. Caen was a D-Day objective that had instead taken seven weeks to secure, and much of it was reduced to rubble by Allied bombing and bombardment. Montgomery's approach has been much criticized, particularly the use of bombers, and the timeline of operations. However this is often in comparison to the bold and risky ventures of the German army in the early stages of the war. It must be remembered that Montgomery was, in essence, fighting a different kind of war.[4] Rather than risking expending what was by 1944 a limited manpower pool, he hoped to employ superior Allied resources to 'let the metal do it rather than the flesh',[5] and keep the best German divisions fixed around Caen. In this respect he succeeded and now, after endless weeks of fighting hedgerow to hedgerow, the Americans were about to break out.

CHAPTER NINE

The Breakout

From Operation Cobra to the Falaise Pocket

'The mess, it's hard to describe. People, horses, vehicles,
anything. It's just one mesh, intermingled, you know?
Dead bodies, dead horses, dead vehicles. This one burns,
this one blows up. A terrible situation, let's put it that way.
I was glad to get out of there.'

Gerhard Franzky, 10th SS Panzer Division

Saint-Lô lies around forty kilometres south-west of Omaha
Beach. Today, you can make the trip in forty minutes. In 1944,
it took some forty *days* before the first American troops set foot
in the city. This is testament to the ferocity of the fighting in the
hedgerows, where a good day's advance might be three hundred
yards.

Resistance was no less fierce when the First Army reached
Saint-Lô towards the beginning of July. It was defended by the
3rd Parachute Division and the 352nd Infantry Division, and as
the British had discovered at Caen, the Wehrmacht's troops were
experts at turning towns — even destroyed ones — into fortresses

defended by machine guns, snipers, armour, anti-tank weapons, and artillery. As at Caen, American forces tried to blast their way through the enemy using massive formations of bomber aircraft, but one lesson that can be taken from the Battle of Normandy is that, for all the fire power that the Allies possessed, it came down to the rifles and bayonets of the infantry to drive the enemy out.

As the British held much of the Wehrmacht's armoured and SS divisions around Caen, the US First Army planned an offensive to punch through the enemy lines on the western flank. The name given to this attack was Operation Cobra, and after several postponements due to bad weather and the bombing of friendly troops, Cobra was finally launched on 25 July.

The epicentre of the operation was Saint-Lô, which (like Caen) was an important transport hub. If the Americans could break out here, there was the promise of the more open countryside beyond, bringing with it the chance for rapid advance, and the deployment of the US Third Army under General Patton which could advance on Paris.

Saint-Lô would pay a heavy price for its value on the battlefield: 95 per cent of its buildings would be destroyed in the coming fighting, and more than 400 French civilians would die.

Operation Cobra

While many men arrived in France with their units, other soldiers, like infantryman Anton Jaber, filtered through as individual replacements. Anton arrived in Normandy in mid-July. 'We went to an area, it was just a field, where we pitched our tents, and we stayed there until our name was called. Every morning they'd call out people.'

Anton's first taste of combat came when a Luftwaffe fighter strafed the replacements' camp. '(It) scared the hell out of me. I'd just turned nineteen years old, and here's a plane coming down with the machine guns firing . . . it's scary.'

One morning in July, Anton finally heard his name called. He was assigned to Company E of the 120th Infantry Regiment, soon to be thrown into the jaws of battle.

Supporting this regiment was Frank Denius, a forward observation officer for the artillery.

'We got into position where we able to begin this attack. On July the 24th, in the field where we had dug in our foxholes, we were visited by General Lesley McNair, a four-star general. And he came forward to observe. At that point in time the 119th Regiment was selected to be the spearpoint regiment in the attack at Saint-Lô.'

To precede the assault, 1,800 bombers would drop their payloads mere miles in front of the American ground troops. 'That early morning of the 24th, the frontline troops, including my artillery party, we pulled back from our frontline penetration about a half, to three-quarters of a mile, to give a little more cushion for the bombers. Unfortunately, when the attack came the next day, some of those bombs fell short, and one of them fell close to General McNair's foxhole, and he was unfortunately killed. My observation party were probably fifty to seventy-five yards away in a foxhole from where General McNair was.'

Anton recalled the bombing that day: one of his first on the front line. 'It was like a movie. And then all of a sudden, they were dropping them across the field from where we were!'

Bob Miksa, of the 723rd Tank Battalion, was also present: 'I was standing on my tank, I was watching it. I was about three miles away from Saint-Lô and my pants were just shaking, you know concussion and everything, because they just kept dropping bomb after bomb.'

'It was a most incredible sight,' said William Gast of the 743rd

Tank Battalion. 'You heard this rumbling, and you looked up in the sky and the sky was full of (bombers). We just thought, Oh this great! Well, it seemed there was some smoke or something had drifted up towards us. So where did the bombs fall? Right on us!'

One of the airmen flying that day was Edward Nacey. 'We participated in that. Unfortunately it had problems. It was a poorly planned mission, and poorly executed in many respects. The bomb line was a road between the German defences and our forces which was marked by smoke. And so the first wave of bombers that went over bombed the correct target, but as the bomber stream kept dragging out and getting longer and longer, and the smoke moved, some of the bomb groups dropped short. And they did kill some of our own troops. One of the sad things that happens in wartime.'

P47 pilot Hal Shook was also involved – but this time on the ground. 'They had a big raid, and twenty-five hundred birds coming in from the UK, B17s first. And we were pretty close to the front lines, and I could hear them coming, and all of a sudden all hell broke loose on our airfield. A B24 dropped its bombs right on our airbase, and we lost five airplanes and a couple of pilots.'

'That was horrible,' said William Gast, recalling the first day's bombing. 'But do you know what? It happened again the next day!'

The attack on Saint-Lô had been rescheduled for the 25th, and another massive formation of bombers came over to soften up the German defences.

'I was standing out beside my tank,' said William, 'just observing this gorgeous sight of aeroplanes and everything, and it was a really nice day. And when the bombs started to drop . . . the next thing I remember I was inside my tank with the hatch closed, and I don't remember touching the tank.'

The falling bombs broke the nerves of some of the men. 'I remember a fellow . . . he was from Philadelphia. He went stark raving mad. They had to haul him away.'

Anton Jaber was also watching the bombers. 'They moved us up on a road, and it had a little ditch on each side of it. And we were standing up there waiting, and you could see the planes coming open, and you could see the bomb bay doors open, and you could see the bombs falling. I was petrified, and somebody said, "Hit the ditch!" I didn't get hurt, but some people in front of me, and some people in back of me did. I had never seen more than one or two dead people, and this ground was littered with dead soldiers where they had dropped the bombs on 'em. And F Company was supposed to spearhead that attack (on Saint-Lô), and they got hit so hard that E Company had to do it.'

'They dropped bombs within I would say a couple of miles right in front of our area,' said Frank Denius. 'As soon as the bombing was over we jumped off on the attack.'

Despite the friendly casualties it caused, the bombing was successful in weakening the Germans' defences. 'We were able to break through the German lines,' said Frank.

As they pushed towards the town, he saw the destruction wrought by the massive Allied firepower. 'Saint-Lô was destroyed completely by bombing and artillery. We had never seen anything like this. And certainly not in front of us immediately. And we really didn't know how destructive it would be. You can just think of all of the bomb craters. And we're not talking about two or three miles away. We're talking about within half to three-quarters of a mile where those bombs were falling in front of us. And the sound was deafening.'

Frank called in artillery on areas where they thought that the bombing might not have been successful. 'I never elected not to fire artillery in front of our advancing units. I directed artillery fire in advance of them whether we thought the Germans were there or not. I always felt like it was one of our duties as artillerymen to protect the infantry not just in defence, but in attack. And we did that. We lay down barrages in front of our infantry constantly. And we did so even at the Saint-Lô breakthrough. We took no chances. We protected the infantry, and we protected the success of our attack.'

Frank was asked if he walked forwards with the advance. 'I crawled!' he replied with laughter.

The land they advanced across was shattered. Trees were torn up, buildings torn down, the countryside pockmarked with craters and littered with dead livestock.

'It just looked like a tornado or hurricane had just swept through and demolished everything within sight.'

Medic Raymond VanDuzer recalled the smell of death at Saint-Lô. 'You know, a dead body out in the open, you can smell it for a long way from where they are.'

David Roderick, of the 4th Infantry Division, had watched and waited for the last bomb to drop on the town. 'As soon as that happened we jumped on the tanks and away we went. All hell broke loose. There was little groups of Germans still around. We fought all night. We'd stop just long enough to knock out a group of them and then we'd get back on the tanks, and we'd go on again. And that was kind of hairy, that night. There was a little road that we went down, and we were waiting there temporarily. And all of a sudden there was a German walked out on the road.' The enemy soldier was unarmed, and surrendered to David and his men. 'He could talk a little English. And by motions, and by what he said . . . we knew there was some other people over there behind the hedgerows. We ask him how many, and he said twenty. So we said what the heck. Let's send him back over there by himself. Why should *we* take the chance?' The gamble that the

German would keep his word and not simply vanish paid off, and he returned with twenty-two more soldiers. 'We lined them up, and disarmed them, and sent them back to the rear.'

Anton Jaber was getting his first taste of combat. 'I didn't know whether I'd make it through there or not, because I wasn't used to that kind of stuff. Discipline and stuff like that I was used to, but I wasn't used to (combat).'

In times like this, it was natural for a young soldier to want to be in close proximity to his comrades. 'Bunching' was common amongst green recruits, but could draw the ire of more seasoned veterans, who knew that it made them easier targets for enemy fire.

'That first attack that I was in, I was scared, and I'm not gonna lie about it,' Anton said. 'There was a guy, laying up against a hedgerow there, and I didn't wanna be by myself. So I moved up there close to him, and he told me get away from here, I don't want you up here.'

Donald Evans, of the 66th Armored, saw his fair share of action before Saint-Lô, but even he was shocked by what he experienced during Cobra.

'The first day in that, or the second day, was the worst day I'd ever put in in my time on the front lines. It was horrible. The Germans had tanks that were dug in and the air force couldn't knock 'em out. It was just Germans everywhere. We were out on a road and we couldn't advance, and the Germans just kept shelling the road.'

That night, 'I got out the car to dig in. I was just so exhausted. Most of the guys were.' In this state of fatigue they soon gave up on their foxholes. 'We said we'll just take what comes tonight. So I just crawled under the vehicle to sleep for the night. And then the German Luftwaffe came over dropping them little butterfly bombs.'

Things didn't let up the next day, either.

315

'Our vehicle got knocked out and I bailed out of that. And I don't know what happened to the other guys at the time. But I got out of the fire, and they were just firing everywhere. I mean it was mortars and artillery, and dive-bombing. I went down the hedgerow. Half-tracks were sitting there and there wasn't anybody in 'em. I crawled up in there. It had a post in the middle and a .50 calibre machine gun on it. When I got up in there, there was a kid just kinda cowered up in the back. I knew the kid's first name . . . (it was) his first time in combat. And he was just scared to death. He was scared to even move. And I talked to him, and he wouldn't talk.'

Donald periodically fired bursts into the hedgerow in case the Germans were advancing. He was eventually joined by an officer who was looking for men to go on a patrol.

'I didn't want to go down there, and the first word that came out of his mouth was "Evans". And he said, "Evans, you stay on that .50 calibre." I drew a sigh of relief then. He took the kid, and they went down there and there was a lot of firing. And the kid came back with a big hunk of shrapnel coming out of his mouth.'

After a while Donald left the half-track and moved up the hedgerow, where he found another two men 'cowered up'. 'And they were new guys. They were new to combat. And I knew that if we didn't get out of there we were gonna die. They were too scared, they would hardly even talk. I said, "I'll lead the way, you follow me."' They finally came to an opening in the hedgerow. A shell landed behind them and blew Donald through the gap. 'And I knew that I was wounded, and I didn't look back. I didn't know what happened to those other guys.' Donald was collected by medics and taken to the aid post, then put on a jeep that took him to a second-line medical unit.

'All you see in there is litters. And in the center of that they're operating. They have a wood form there where they can pick your litter up and just sit it on that form, and then the doctors would work over you. They look at you, and they look at your dog tags.'

His clothing was cut away and he was given a shot that knocked him out. 'It's the greatest feeling.'

Surgeons then removed shrapnel from his back, legs, and hands.

'When I woke up I was naked under the blanket, and I was on a litter out in a field under this other big tent where they put the guys after the operation. I had no idea what time it was, only that it was daylight. And somebody's come by, and kinda check a little bit. And then the cargo plane would come in, a C47, and land alongside that tent. And then they'd pick up that litter and take it in the plane. You flew over that area that you'd just fought over. I was looking over it and I just couldn't believe it. How bad it looked.'

Fighting alongside the infantry was William Greer of the 315th Engineer Combat Battalion. 'We went into a little apple orchard, and it was pretty open. All of a sudden these machine guns and firearms started, and mortars. We started getting mortar fire on us. I was firing. The squad leader, it looked to me like the whole back of his head blowed off.' William used the dead man's body as cover while he returned fire. Around this time he realized that he'd been hit, and sought better shelter. 'I went through this hedgerow, and I see a dead German there.' Close by was a ditch, where a young lieutenant was being chewed out by a squad leader.

'(He was) telling him to get us out of there. He got us in there, now get us out. And this lieutenant, he was just really scared to death.' The lieutenant had a blond moustache that usually looked almost white, but that day, it somehow appeared darker. William realized it was because the officer's face had gone so pale with fright.

'I told him, I said, "Lieutenant, I'm hit." And he said, "Well

317

you gotta get out of here, everybody's on their own. We gotta get outta here." And of course that's when this sergeant started in on him again.'

William made his plan to escape. 'There was a Mexican boy there. He was the scout. And he'd never got hit. So him and I, he said, "Well we're gonna get out," and I said, "OK, I'm gonna go with you." We got out on this road, and started down that road, and we didn't go too far and this machine gun cut loose. I wasn't zigzagging or anything, I just started running.' William was able to make it around a curve in the road without any of the bullets finding their mark, and was later evacuated to England for treatment.

Daniel Chester, of the 9th Infantry Division, was also wounded in the battles around Saint-Lô. 'I was out on patrol with three other men, and a German barrage was laid down on top of us. The guy on my right got killed, and the guy on my left got killed. And the guy on his left got his leg blown off. And I got shot in both arms and legs with shrapnel. We laid there and finally our people came up. They got us, and they got us onto a jeep.' Daniel slipped in and out of consciousness. When he arrived at the aid station he could hear German voices. 'And I thought, Oh no, I've been captured!' The voices belonged to prisoners acting as stretcher-bearers, but his wounds were so severe that he never returned to combat.

Raymond VanDuzer was a medic in the 28th Infantry Division. After arriving in Normandy on 22 July, his unit went straight into action on Operation Cobra. It was the kind of situation that called for a stiff drink.

'When we first went into the hedgerows I had access to (medicinal) alcohol, and I had this lemon drink, powder drink, and I mixed it in with some of that stuff. I became intoxicated, and that was the night that the Germans flew over and were strafing the troops.' Fortunately for Raymond, he came through the scrape without either a wound, or a court martial. Soon they encountered the German ground forces, and Raymond dealt with his first casualties.

'I had a lot of wounded. Machine guns would tear them apart. When a guy gets a bullet in his chest, it's only just a little (hole), but on the back it would be big. Really a big-sized opening in his back. And so we knew, when we saw the little hole in the front, flip him over.

'When you're hit with an 88 you're gone. Bandages wouldn't do you any good. I had a case which was very bad. It was a tank and the guy got hit, and the tank was burning, and he was inside. This guy was hollering. I had to go in, and I went in the tank to get him, and I couldn't get him out. I think of it like a chicken. The skin was sliding off. I had to take my belt off and put it underneath his arms and pull him. That's the way I pulled him out. And I got him out on the ground, but I knew he wasn't gonna live, and I give him some morphine to try and comfort him.

'He didn't live.'

Richard Ford, a junior officer in the 29th Infantry Division, had been injured in earlier combat, and came back to his unit just after they'd gone into Saint-Lô. 'And I thought, Boy, you were lucky again, because that was a vicious fight down there.'

Their next objective was the town of Percy, fifteen miles to the south. Along with three other men, Richard was sent to check the area for a suitable defensive position. After finding what they needed, they headed back to bring in the rest of the platoon.

'They hadn't walked five yards down that darn gone lane when they all got nailed.'

The experienced Germans may have recognized the recon for what it was, and waited until they had a greater number of soldiers in their sights.

'We were trapped. They were all around us. And I thought, How the hell am I gonna get out of this?' He sent a runner to bring back reinforcements from the battalion. 'He came back a little while later and he said, "They can't afford to send anybody up to help you."' The only option was to sneak out of the encirclement in ones and twos. We finally did, but I lost several guys that day. When I got back to that company commander I chewed him out.'

The officer explained that a higher level of command had 'nixed' the plan to send help. 'And I said to him, "Who the hell's running this company, you or the battalion?" It's a wonder they didn't court martial me right there, but I could care less.'

Soon after, Richard was wounded a second time. 'I'll never forget the name of that place. Percy. That was the end of me there.'

During the fighting around Saint-Lô, Walter Ehlers and his men discovered a group of dead paratroopers. 'We came across a bunch of American soldiers who had been lined up and shot. There was about ten of them in a row there. They'd been executed, and all their boots were missing. We discovered them during the breakthrough. It was unbelievable.'

The state of the ruined town shocked him. 'What a mess that town was. We had Germans come out of it. Kids, almost. They couldn't hear you. From the noise of the bombs. It was just unbelievable.'

It was a bomb that gave Walter his second wound of the campaign. He didn't know if it came from the Luftwaffe or an Allied plane. 'All I know is that we got bombed,' he laughed.

Walter was taken to a hospital in Cherbourg.

'First they put me in a bed next to a guy. And he's laying there, and every time he breathed, blood would come out of his stomach.

The next guy laying next to him, he was in a half-body cast from his waist up.'

The soldier had lost his facial features.

'All he had was tubes for sucking food. He'd been burned in a knocked-out tank.

I saw so many other wounded in there that were so terribly wounded, I just couldn't stand to be in that hospital.'

After pulling shrapnel – and a lot of 'hamburger meat' – out of his leg, the surgeon told Walter that he was the first person that he'd ever operated on, and asked if he could keep the shrapnel as a souvenir. 'I said, "Yeah, but you can never operate on me again!"'

Henrietta Harkness served as a nurse in the 24th Evacuation Hospital. She came ashore at Omaha on D+6, and started receiving casualties within a day of landing. The hospital was originally at La Cambe, near the beach, then moved to L'Épinay-Tesson, on the road to Saint-Lô, near the front line. While at La Cambe, the 24th received more than 1,100 casualties. In the fighting around Saint-Lô, this increased to more than 2,700. The roar of nearby artillery and bombers was constant as the medical staff went about their life-saving work.

'I think the biggest battle I remember was the battle of Saint-Lô . . . I started to take care of soldiers. Because the war was going so slowly a lot of them were depressed. They wanted to go back (to their unit), but they weren't capable of going. The doctor told me I should do what I was taught in training . . . I had no doctor to assist me because they were too busy with surgery, so I gave them a sedative . . . and then that way they were rested. I was able to send some of them back to the front line. Some of them wanted to go. Some of them I didn't think were secure enough to go. I had one who begged me to stay with him.'

The soldier would follow Henrietta around as she made her rounds.

'I happened to have a German prisoner who had his leg in a cast, and when I gave him his medicine he spit it out at me.' The American soldier 'practically choked him to death. He said, "No Kraut is gonna spit in my nurse's face!"'

Henrietta didn't take it to heart, and had no problem caring for German soldiers. 'It was just another patient. Really didn't bother me. He probably thought I was poisoning him,' she joked.

After they received surgery, Henrietta prepared the wounded for evacuation to England.

'I had corpsmen there, and I had an ambulance (at) the back of the tent, and I would tell them, "Evacuate so and so" . . . I never knew where they went, where they were taken . . . my job was just to see to it that they got on the ambulance.'

Myron Guisewite was the co-pilot of a C47. During the initial invasion he flew paratroopers into Normandy. Now he ferried the wounded back to England.

'Every ship had a nurse, and every ship was equipped with stretchers two or three high, where we put the wounded on, and the nurses took care of them on the way back to the hospitals. At the time I was looking at every bunch that came in on my plane. I was looking for my brother because he was in the invasion force under Bradley, and he was wounded twice in Normandy. Every plane trip I had I looked for him.'

Julia Myers was an army nurse in Ellesmere, England, and received soldiers wounded in Normandy. 'They were the first soldiers that we got to take care of. They had various wounds, but to us it was just the grim results of what the war was really like. This was our first time seeing wounded soldiers. We were upset to see those wounds . . . I still think about the bravery of those men. They were so brave.'

'(It was) scary as hell,' said Jack Davis, who was fighting with the 5th Infantry Division. 'The casualties were terrible. If you made it, you were considered damn lucky.'

On 28 July, Jack's unit made an assault on a piece of high ground held by the Germans.

'Hill 183 was a bloody battle. That was our first attack and we were up against the 3rd and 5th Paratroop Divisions. The British attacked at the same time and they came up the road between Caen and Saint-Lô. We had opened that road up. I remember the British going by and they knew who we were, because we had fought alongside of them at Caen. And we had liaison with them. They hollered out, "Is that the 10th Infantry?" They said, "Good show, blokes!"'

By the end of July, Operation Cobra had broken out beyond Saint-Lô and taken Avranches. With the German left flanks now in retreat, the US Third Army was activated on 1 August, and soon launched into Brittany.

Jack's 5th Infantry Division would become a part of Third Army, but first he had a reunion to attend. 'I had a friend in the 3rd Battalion, I was in the 1st. He came over to see if I was still alive, and he had this canteen of Calvados, and we drank it. He wandered off, went back to the 3rd Battalion, and I got sick. I didn't dig a foxhole, and I puked all over my field jacket. The next day the guys said, "Some bombing last night," and I said, "What bombing?" I never heard it.'

Prisoner of War

On 2 August, Typhoon pilot Roy Crane was flying over the 'Suisse Normande'. Unlike the bocage close to the coast, this area had rolling hills that were often cloaked in forest. Pilots like Roy had to keep pressure on the retreating enemy and provide close air support to the troops on the ground. 'The Germans' concentration in that area was clearly formidable,' he said. 'The worst problem was dug-in Tiger tanks . . . and they were invariably in woods.'

Although pilots could take targets of opportunity, intelligence played a large part in planning missions. Pilots were often given aerial photographs of their targets, or information from the forward units of the army, pinpointing the positions of the enemy defences.

'You knew which corner of the wood it was, but you couldn't actually see the tank when you went in to attack.' Once on target, the Typhoons fired rockets so powerful that they could flip over even the heaviest German tanks. 'You never fired rockets at troops or lorries. You purely fired cannons, because you had incendiary high-explosive shells. You kept the rockets for armour.'

As the Germans retreated their divisions choked the few roads leading to comparative safety. They were nose to tail, and Roy would fire a pair of rockets at each vehicle.

'We attacked armoured vehicles along a road . . . north of Falaise. We absolutely caught them sitting in a valley, a fairly wooded area, and having attacked those with purely cannon, we turned and we flew up the valley.'

Roy's squadron climbed to come in for another run, but before they could come back down for this second attack, his aircraft shook violently. 'I was hit on the port wing . . . so I turned immediately for my own lines . . .' Roy was hoping to ditch his aircraft in friendly territory, but the situation quickly went from bad to worse.

'As soon as I turned I was hit again, and the aircraft just went straight for the ground. I found out later that half the tail-plane was shot off.' Over the radio, other pilots in the squadron told him to bail out. 'Somebody called, "For God's sake, get out,

Roy!" I jettisoned the hood and pulled my radio socket out, (and) released the harness. I went out like a bullet. I didn't even have to climb out of the aircraft, I just shot out.'

As he came down on his parachute, Roy heard his aircraft explode in a nearby field. Having bailed out so low, he was only in the air for a few moments before he landed in trees at the bottom of the valley he had just attacked. 'I saw a lot of soldiers running, and my first thought was, they were ours.' He was mistaken. In fact, he might have landed in the worst possible spot. 'It turned out that I'd landed right in the middle of an SS camp, and well, you couldn't expect them to be very jolly if you're shooting at them one minute and in their hands the next.'

The point of capture is always dangerous, and made more so if someone is carrying memorabilia taken from the enemy.

'I had in my boot a German dagger that my father had given me from the First World War, but even worse, I had some German ammunition in the top of my pocket, because I'd acquired a German Sten gun that I used to go rabbit-shooting with in Normandy. They wanted to know where the gun was, and why I'd got it.'

The soldiers took Roy's watch and the photos of his new wife. They also distributed his cigarettes, 'but didn't give me one!'

Roy soon had more pressing concerns than stolen smokes. 'One German came and just took hold of me by the scruff of my neck and took me and put me against a tree. And another one came, and was just starting to lift a gun, and there was a lot of shouting took place. I turned around and could see one German soldier talking to another one.'

Roy was wearing a khaki uniform rather than RAF blues. He had been told that this was because American soldiers had mistaken British aircrew for Germans and shot them as they came down on parachutes. But now the khaki posed its own danger.

If the Germans took Roy for an SOE agent parachuting behind the lines, they might kill him because of Hitler's directive to shoot such 'commandos'. Of course, the SS men might just want to take revenge on one of the pilots who had caused such devastation to their divisions.

'There was a big conflab between them and another German, who was clearly not in army uniform. He was in air force uniform. And he turned out to be the man in charge of the guns that had shot me down, and he had run down the hill from where the guns were, having seen me on the parachute.'

The Luftwaffe officer's intervention saved Roy's life. He was taken from the SS, and up to the gun position. He remembered them as 'Quite a good crowd of chaps actually. They were entirely different to the SS people.'

Accompanied by the Luftwaffe officer, Roy was politely interrogated at a chateau before being taken in the direction of Falaise. The roads were packed with German vehicles and tanks. 'Some Germans standing alongside the road waved us down. So he pulled in, and the Germans shouted something, and this German from the guns got me out of the car . . . he pushed me in a ditch and jumped in on top of me.

'Then there was a tremendous crescendo of cannon-fire, and of course I looked up, and you'd never believe it. There was a squadron of Typhoons!' They worked over the trapped vehicles, destroying several. 'And they came back and back. Firing rockets. Cannon-fire. I thought it would never end.'

The Typhoons finally peeled away, but that wasn't the end of the danger for Roy. For a second time, he believed he would be shot out of hand by men who had just lost comrades at the hands of the RAF. 'I thought, Well this is curtains, I've had it . . . they're bound to (kill me). Anyway, this German, this air force chap, he got me straight into the staff car.' The man who shot Roy down had become his guardian angel. 'My father said that there isn't a good German, but I can tell you that chap saved my life.'

Remarkably, that day was not the last time that Roy came under attack from Allied aircraft. With other POWs on a train to Frankfurt he was attacked by American fighters, then while in the city he experienced bombing raids by the RAF. He survived both, and was liberated from the POW camp in 1945.

Mortain

Fritz Jeltsch, of the 352nd Infantry Division, had been fighting the Americans for weeks. He was told by military police that the American forces employed hardened criminals, who would be given a pardon if they could prove that they'd killed a certain number of Germans. 'We never took much notice. I didn't believe it.' This changed when he came across a dead comrade who was missing his army identification. 'I heard a loud cry come from that direction just a few hours before, but didn't take much notice. A very short cry.' The soldier had not been killed by a bullet, but by blade. 'They chopped his head off, because if they would shoot they would cause a sensation. They just chopped the head off with a very sharp knife, silent.'

The American soldiers may not have been hardened criminals, but by this point in the campaign they were certainly hardened soldiers. Frank Denius had been in near constant combat for almost two months.

'After the breakthrough at Saint-Lô, the next five days we were in a defensive position defending and straightening our lines.' Frank finally got to take his first shower in two months. His unit was also treated to a USO show, where he got a kiss from famous singer Dinah Shaw. His comrades asked him which he liked best: the shower, or the kiss. 'I called it a tie.'

After being resupplied and taking on replacements, Frank's division was sent to the small town of Mortain, where they relieved the 1st Infantry Division.

'On that Sunday around noon . . . we marched up a hill just on the east side (of Mortain).' This piece of high ground, known as Hill 314, had dug-in positions, and the soldiers of the 1st Infantry Division told Frank that they hadn't seen a German in five or six days. For soldiers who had been almost continuously fighting since D-Day, the quiet hill sounded like a little piece of heaven.

Hill 314 had steep slopes, with a plateau on top. 'On the east side it's a sheer cliff,' said Frank, 'and on the other side are forest and a couple of trails up that hill. It was an artillery observer's dream, as far as the location, because you could actually see 360 degrees completely around. You could almost see the Atlantic Ocean at (Avranches) which was about twenty-five miles away. On a clear day you could just see forever.'

Frank could not know that Avranches was the main objective of the German counter-attack, and Hill 314 was about to play a key role in the battle. For months the German High Command had held back several divisions in the Pas de Calais area, where they expected a second Allied landing. With the breakout at Saint-Lô, it was finally realized that Normandy would be the decisive battle in France, and these formations were belatedly released for action. Hitler ordered them to make an attack that should drive the Allies back into the sea.

On their first night on the high ground, the men defending Hill 314 heard trucks, and caught glimpses of infantry dismounting from the vehicles. 'They were coming to within a mile of the bottom of the hill,' said Frank. 'When the opportune moment came, we started directing artillery fire on those Germans.'

The fire missions were successful, but the Germans now had

no doubt that the hill was occupied by American forces. Soon after, the Luftwaffe began strafing the hilltop, and on the morning of 7 August, the Germans attacked en masse. It was the first assault in a battle that raged for six and a half days.

George Wichterich was in the 823rd Tank Destroyer Battalion, 30th Infantry Division. 'When they put us in position in Mortain, and they pulled the 1st Division out, we asked them how was things going. They said, no problem. And about two o'clock the next morning we could hear some people talking in a funny language coming down the highway. With .50 calibre machine guns we chased them back that night. The next morning we went out and looked on the road and they had one or two dead, but they had removed anything else that we had caught during the night.'

George and another soldier took a jeep to their command post for orders. 'All of a sudden tracer bullets start hitting in front of the jeep. We drove through this ambush that they had set up, and the jeep stopped. Wouldn't go any further. So we bailed out.' This was when George saw that a bullet had gone through his rifle. 'We got with the 1st Platoon. This lieutenant, Springfield, eventually he had his leg blown off, but we stayed with him for about two weeks when we were surrounded in Mortain.'

George and this small element of the 823rd Tank Destroyer Battalion were positioned on a hill overlooking a likely enemy approach route. 'You could see a highway around the front of us. They'd come around with half-tracks, and various other things. Even had a half-track with the Red Cross on the sides of it, like an ambulance. We knocked that out, that was full of ammunition. And if we'd knock out a vehicle we'd hook a half-track to it, haul it out of the way, and they'd come with some more.'

The Germans had been able to advance unseen largely because of the weather. For much of the campaign, movement by the

Wehrmacht during daylight hours had been suicidal, but on the 7th there was a heavy mist lying across Normandy, hiding the attacking divisions from the eyes of the prowling Allied fighter bombers.

John Golley was in the cockpit of a Typhoon, scouring the area for any sight of the enemy. His squadron finally spotted a break in the cover and dived down to investigate. What they found astounded them. Hundreds of armoured vehicles were packed along the roads, but who did they belong to? The Typhoons made a second pass through the break in the cloud, then a third. Finally, there could be no doubt.

They had discovered a full-strength Panzer division.

'(It was) something like three hundred tanks, a thousand vehicles, maybe ten, twelve, fourteen thousand men, all along this road hoping to crack the American lines and drive a wedge between the British and Canadian army, and the American army.' This had to be stopped. 'Every Typhoon in Normandy was scrambled, and we went in to attack this panzer division. We made the first attack at about quarter to twelve. Our job was to blow the lead tanks.'

If the Typhoons could achieve this then the following vehicles would be trapped in a deadly bottleneck. As the day went on, the mist shrouding the countryside burned away, leaving the panzers as easy targets for the fighter-bombers. 'There was twenty squadrons of Typhoons in Normandy . . .' said John, 'we kept up a cyclonic roll of attacks from midday until four in the afternoon under a blazing sun.'

It was another example of the wisdom of Allied planners in putting airfields on Normandy soil. The Typhoons had only a ten-minute flight from Mortain to the airstrip to be refuelled, rearmed, and sent back into the fray. After the war, John was given photos of the effects of the attacks surreptitiously taken by a French schoolteacher: German heavy tanks had been blown onto their sides by the force of the rocket blasts. 'It was a great day,' he said of 7 August, '(the Typhoon) really made its name there as the most lethal air-to-ground fighter to come out of World War Two.'

But while the support of fighter-bombers proved deadly, they couldn't account for every vehicle or soldier, and the Germans were still able to make inroads into the Allied lines.

'We got orders to retreat,' said tank driver William Gast. 'That was a very tough battle. That's where I was wounded. I got a piece of shrapnel in my back, and they sent me back to a field hospital.'

As the American troops were pushed back, Hill 314 was cut off and isolated.

'We'd been completely surrounded by the German forces,' said Frank Denius. 'As long as we held (the high ground) we could defend Patton's supply lines, as well as defend the area to the Atlantic, because we had perfect observation.'

The 120th Infantry Regiment received a radio call from General Eisenhower: hold Hill 314 at all costs. With such good fields of observation, Frank was able to direct massive amounts of artillery on that first day of battle. 'We completely dominated that area . . . and the Germans kept attacking. We wounded and killed a lot of Germans. They were unsuccessful in even advancing halfway up the hill in most areas.'

For the second time in Normandy, Frank and his radio sergeant Goldstein had to take over after their lieutenant was incapacitated. The first time this was because the officer had been killed, but not the case on Hill 314. In his interview, Frank requested that the details of the man's incapacitation be kept off the record. What can be said is that once again it came to nineteen-year-old Frank to direct the artillery in defence of the infantry.

That night, the Germans attacked his foxhole. 'It was difficult to turn the radio on, because if you turned your radio on you disclosed your position. And the Germans were nearly on top of our foxhole. But we were able, with hand-to-hand combat, to fight those Germans off.'

Frank and Goldstein then pulled back to direct fire onto the attackers wherever they appeared. The time and skill they had put into the pre-recorded firing positions now came into their own.

'All we had to do was call the emergency barrage number at the location where the Germans were.' These emergency barrages were on targets such as likely forming-up points and avenues of approach. 'The significance of the pre-set barrages was that, after we'd been on the hill for two days, our radio batteries were beginning to get low, and the only communication we had with the division artillery and battalion HQ was by radio. By being able to use the emergency barrages it shortened the timing and use of the radio.'

The Germans were experienced fighters and began to avoid the pre-recorded areas, forcing Frank to make longer radio calls while he adjusted the artillery fire. 'We were doing this day and night.'

The Germans were bringing their own guns to bear, and Hill 314 was being hit by strafing runs, bombs, artillery, mortars, and small-arms fire. 'We were beginning to take a lot of casualties. The medics were just so good at helping our guys that were wounded.'

The details of the long-running battle were understandably difficult to recall.

'It's just difficult to describe the battle at Mortain and 314 because of the intensity. For six and a half days it was fighting all the time. When you're in combat on a constant basis, your body, your mind, and I like to think, in the 30th Division, our hearts, were always prepared for what was to come. And you are totally involved and immersed in what you're doing, and you give little consideration to other factors. The weather, your body feelings, you don't think about hunger. You think about staying alive, and doing your job, and protecting your fellow soldiers. And that's what we did. You're not thinking about yourself. You're thinking about your buddies.

'There's no way to describe what your whole existence is, and what your life is like, because you're just dedicated to the fighting objective that you had, and that's your sole objective.'

The stout defence of Hill 314 earned the admiration of the German attackers.

'On the third day the Germans sent a white flag to Hill 314. We waved them up. We stopped them mid-way up that hill and they congratulated us on the bravery, and said that they would go on an all-out attack and annihilate everyone on the hill unless we surrendered.'

The commander of Hill 314's defenders declined. True to their word, the Germans then launched a massive attack. They finally withdrew at around midnight, after eight hours of fighting. It was not the final assault on 314, but Frank noted how the German attacks became shorter after that day: 'I don't think they gave up, I don't think that at all, but I think they saw that they could not make it up the hill.'

Frank gave full credit to a second FOO team that was operating on the other side of the hill. 'They did a marvellous job.'

Under siege on the hilltop, the men of the 120th were running dangerously low on ammunition and medical supplies.

'Eisenhower tried to supply us with airdrops,' said Frank. 'And the C47s came over and dropped literally thousands of parachutes with ammunition, medicine, and batteries, but because of the German anti-aircraft guns around the hill, the planes had to fly extremely high, and the parachutes floated away from the top of the hill. We were able to get some of that supply from no man's land by fighting out into that area, but so much of it fell in the hands of Germans.'

On a hunch, Frank and his sergeant placed their radio batteries out in the sunshine. 'We didn't even know the word solar,' he said, but it produced a few minutes more charge.

'The other thing, that was probably the first thing in the history of warfare, and probably the last . . . we needed medicine so bad my battalion commander radioed me and said, "We're going to try something. We have propaganda shells back at the artillery battalion." And those propaganda shells aren't high explosive.' They were stuffed with propaganda leaflets that would flutter down into the hands of the enemy. On Hill 314, they served a different, life-saving purpose.

'They took the propaganda leaflets out of the shells, stuffed it with cotton and put in morphine and penicillin, and I directed those artillery shells into our position on the top of 314. We dug them out of the ground. The impact could mash the medicine, but we were still able to get some penicillin, and some morphine. History says maybe that wasn't a total success, but I can still see the smiles on those guys that were wounded.'

On the afternoon of the seventh day, the enemy began to withdraw from the base of 314. 'By this time elements of our 119th Division, and elements of the 35th Division began to reach us.' Through heroic resistance, Hill 314 did not fall into German hands. It was a pivotal moment in the Battle of Mortain.

Tank driver Bob Miksa had survived D-Day and fighting through the hedgerows, but at Mortain he was wounded for the first time.

'We finished for the day, so hunkered down, and these two Stuka bombers dropped the flares and lit up the whole area. They come in and start strafing, and they were after my tank, and I just happened to be right next to a truck that had a load of gasoline cans and ammunition.'

The Stukas scored a hit on the truck. 'It exploded right next to me, practically. The flames from the gasoline shot over, right on top of my tank, so I helped to put the fire out with extinguishers and blankets and in the meantime these (Stukas) kept coming around, firing away. I had to get the tanks out of there so I drove my tank out. They were following me with this Stuka, I think they were 20mm shells. I finally got out and parked my tank in a dark spot and ran back to get the other guys out. I ran in front of most of them and they followed me out. They figured I saved the five tanks and some lives, so they figured it was worth the Silver Star.'

Bob was also awarded the first of two Purple Hearts that he would receive in the war.

US army doctor John Kerner was at Mortain.

'In the midst of the battle I had an aid station set up . . . and into this aid station one later afternoon, early evening, came a couple of men carrying a ladder, and on the ladder was a woman who was obviously in great distress. As they got nearer it was obvious that she was in labour.

At my aid station I'd put up a small tent . . . so I put her in there . . . and when I examined her she was close to the end of labour, but she was in labour with a breech, and a complicated kind of a breech. So I got two aid men, one who could speak a little bit of French to instruct her, and another just to help me hold her, and I delivered this breech baby by methods I had learned as an intern. Breech deliveries can be complicated . . . and also it's common, because the baby's head come last, the baby will very often die in the process.

'But I delivered the baby and the baby was fine, and so was the mother. Fortunately I didn't have to do anything surgical. We put the mother and the baby in the ambulance that we had . . .

and got them out as fast as I could, because I didn't want them to get hurt, because as they were leaving there was still fighting going on around us. It was quite a dramatic experience, as you can imagine.'

In John's unit was a soldier nicknamed 'Gangster', who had been a rum-runner during Prohibition. When they heard that there was a unit cut off with large numbers of wounded, John and Gangster loaded up a jeep with medical supplies to make a run through the German lines.

'We took off at full speed, and it was early in the morning and I guess the Germans were eating breakfast, but one of the things that I remember, it was a beautiful sunny morning, and there was an American GI dead in a foxhole, with flaming red hair, and I'll never forget that sight.

'Gangster had surprised the Germans and they didn't expect anyone coming from behind them, and we got through pretty fast before they began shooting at us.'

They arrived at a stone quarry filled with wounded men. 'It looked like the Civil War as far as I could recall, because there was just a field of people. The two of us went to work and we worked all day using our supplies, and into the night. And to the best of my recollection I probably passed out (from exhaustion) somewhere in the night time, but (Gangster) kept working all night.'

Fighting against the Americans was Gunter von Waskowski, an artillery officer in the Wehrmacht. For the Battle of Mortain, his unit was spread out across several divisions.

'I think we were part of the (116th Panzer Division). And of course, that (operation) was a failure. I was personally . . . cut off several times. We moved mostly at night, really. Our whole unit moved at night, because during the daylight you couldn't move. You were shot to pieces by the Typhoons, or any other Allied aircraft. The offensive, I think it was near Mortain, stopped. We couldn't get any further. Mainly American troops were against us. We were able to get some success with our 88s against American tanks. But in general, after three or four days, we were retreating.'

The German counter-attack had failed, and the Allies now had a retreating enemy in their sights. While the German army was hindered in their movements by Allied fighter-bombers, Patton's Third Army began making a rapid advance, as the British launched similar operations from the west. If British and American forces could meet in the south, they would enclose some fifteen German divisions. Many of these formations were already severely depleted from the previous two months' fighting, but now, the Allies had a chance to wipe them out of existence.

This battle became known as the Falaise Pocket.

The Falaise Pocket

Ian Hammerton was an officer in the Westminster Dragoons, and had been in Normandy since the beginning of the invasion.

'One of my sergeant's crew, from D-Day onwards, would not get out of his tank. And for weeks, something like three weeks I think, he could just not be persuaded to leave the tank at all. He was in a bit of a state . . . Everybody took a hand in trying to persuade (him). He finally disappeared when the RAF bombed us.'

Ian recalled that day. 'In the course of the afternoon, just as we were brewing up some tea, we saw a wave of Lancasters and Liberators come down very low . . . you could see the pilots. We also saw the bomb doors open. We cheered them on their way, but then we saw the bombs leaving their bomb doors. All we had time to do was just drop everything and dive under our tanks . . . It dropped all around us, and it was pretty horrible.'

A second wave of bombers were coming, and Typhoons were

'snooping' around the bomber formations to pick off anything that tried to escape.

'We just about got inside and the second lot came over, and I think that's the only time I've really prayed over the radio, because we knew if the enemy knew about this they'd be right through us like a dose of salts.'

A second wave bombed short, then a third. 'There was shrapnel whizzing around, and we were literally biting the dust and breathing it in.' In an attempt to stop the friendly bombing, brave pilots of the artillery spotter aircraft put themselves in harm's way, flying under the bombers and firing flares. 'Eventually the fifth wave came over, didn't drop anything, and we saw it turn around.' A lot of damage had already been done. 'The poor Poles suffered. Their B Echelon was practically eliminated.'

Ian and his dragoons were part of the Canadian-led Operation Totalize, which aimed to capture ground north of Falaise and lasted from 8 August until the 10th.

'Monty's moonlight was used.' This was a term for search lights shone onto low cloud to light the battlefield. 'And also Bofors guns firing tracer every minute on the axis of advance so that we could keep direction. It was totally impossible with the dust from the bombing, and the guns, to see.' Ian was at the head of the column with one tank ahead of him. 'In the course of the night he wandered off to the left. We got stuck in a crater. (Our bombers) were supposed to be using anti-personnel bombs, but this was a whopping great crater, (and) in trying to reverse out of it the track broke.' Ian described that night as 'horrible'.

Three or four days later they found the troop's missing tank. 'They'd all been killed. Two of them, or perhaps three of them, trying to get out of the turret. They were just cut down, and there were bits of flesh dangling all over the place. The driver and the co-driver didn't get out at all. All that was left of them was from the waist down. My squadron commander had forbidden me from going to see it, but I felt I had to. The (self-propelled gun) that caught them had also been knocked out, I'm glad to say.'

As the Canadians and British pushed on Falaise, and the noose around the German army got tighter, it became almost impossible for them to resupply.

Ernst Eberling was a pilot in a Luftwaffe bomber squadron. 'We got food and ammunition and fuel, and had to throw it to the German troops. We learned we had to drop our things between three fires, in a triangle. But when we came there, there were fires all over. So the first night we didn't know where to throw. Then a German group went in with green and red fires, and the next night we dropped (on the correct site). It was dangerous, especially at our aerodrome, because (Allied) night fighters were there. We lost some airplanes, but on these three flights (into Falaise) we didn't have too many losses.'

P47 pilot Hal Shook was also in the skies over Falaise.

'That was a hot son of a gun,' he said, recalling the amount of anti-aircraft fire. 'If you go straight and level you're gonna get hit for sure . . . If I see flak coming I turn into it, because everyone would turn away from it, and they'd expect that. So I turned into it.'

At the same time as he was manoeuvring his aircraft, Hal was navigating to his target using a paper map. On one mission over Falaise a burst of flak hit his aircraft, but the damage was light. 'And so I make my run. I always hold it to the last minute and go in as steep as I can, and bend that thing out. I kicked the throttle up, but nothing was happening. I couldn't throttle up, and I also couldn't throttle off.' Hal's speed was stuck at 200 mph, which made landing a dangerous proposition. 'I came over the field and I just turned the fuel off.'

Hal came in hot, but he was able to set down on the airfield, and walk away. It was a situation that would have proved fatal to anyone but an exceptional pilot, but that's what he was. Indeed, Hal was once described as 'the best pilot in any man's air force.'[1] He survived World War Two, and served in Korea and Vietnam.

Typhoon pilot John Golley was also in action at Falaise, but found it different from earlier battles against the Wehrmacht.

'Mortain was a battle with very live Germans firing all the time, and advancing. We were attacking an advancing army. We had no compunction. Falaise Gap, it was total annihilation of German forces caught in a trap. Personally, I didn't like the Falaise Gap. My degree of sensitivity revolted because there was so much horse-drawn transport. You couldn't miss, really. It gave me no satisfaction. It's not that I'm a terrific sportsman or anything, but I can't bear horses to be clobbered.'

'It was slaughter, from the Germans' point of view,' said George Clubley, also a Typhoon pilot. 'In the few days I was there for it, it was exciting because it was a matter of how quickly you could get back, re-arm, re-fuel, and get back to it. There were many tanks, and personnel carriers getting the army people out. And I can recall one or two incidents of tanks trying to get out, you could see the people, their crews, and they were being slaughtered by rockets coming from all over the place. It really was quite horrific.'

But George felt no compassion for the trapped German forces. 'I don't know whether I'm unfeeling there, but this was our job. I eventually ended up in Germany after the war, in peacetime, and I got on very well with the Germans, but this was different. We were fighting. And as far as we were concerned they were the enemy, and the more of them we could knock out the better.'

Kazimierz Budzik, a Polish Spitfire pilot in the Royal Air Force, shared this feeling. 'We just destroyed them,' he said, firing on 'anything that was moving.' During these attacks, German soldiers would put their hands up in the air as if trying to surrender to his aircraft. 'At that time we still had that anger of what they'd done to our (country). So we showed little mercy. They were massacred. It must have been a horrible thing.'

But despite their losses, the Wehrmacht continued to mount a resistance.

Anthony Bashford was advancing with the 4th Armoured Brigade.

'We had passed through the Polish Armoured Brigade, who fought ferociously at the time. One passed burning Sherman after burning Sherman and thought, it couldn't get any worse.'

Antony's own tank was hit in the fighting. 'There was an enormous bang . . . somehow nothing else happened after that, but the sergeant had disappeared out of the tank. The tank had slewed round, and the rest of the crew were busy getting out. There was a lot of small-arms fire going on.'

A nearby tank from his troop had also been hit, and the commander's leg had been amputated. 'He just died of loss of blood,' Anthony said, rueing their lack of medical training. 'We never ever had first-aid instruction. We all had first-aid dressings. We never ever knew where to put it or quite what to do with it.'

Gerhard Franzky, a soldier in the 10th SS Panzer Division, was one of those attempting to escape the pocket.

'(We were) surrounded by not only US, but British and the Polish troops.' They had lost all of their radio equipment by this time, and had to rely on runners. 'Usually the runners didn't even come back. My first radioman, he got shrapnel in the back. We had to leave him in the basement of a house, where I found a weapon, because I didn't have a weapon any more. All I had was a pistol. The mess, it's hard to describe. People, horses, vehicles, anything. It's just one mesh, intermingled, you know? Dead bodies, dead horses, dead vehicles. This one burns, this one blows up. A terrible situation, let's put it that way. I was glad to get out of there.'

'We got one gun and one tractor out,' said artillery officer Gunter von Waskowski. 'When we came into St Lambert, the place was full of blown up horses, dead soldiers, equipment. Chaos. Complete chaos. We didn't know where to go. We came onto this big plain . . . It was a big field. It was absolutely chaos. Then the shelling started. We were under fire, I believe they were Polish.'

Gunter compared the situation to the infamous Highway of Death during the First Gulf War. 'But (Falaise) was on a much larger scale.'

'We were surrounded,' said German infantryman Fritz Jeltsch. 'It was awful. We were so close in, like rats. We went across a potato field, and they were shooting from every direction.'

Fritz was sitting on a lorry when the man behind him was hit. The soldier fell off, and was run over.

'Everybody was for himself,' said Fritz. 'My mate, he was just walking in front of me, and we were attacked again. A (shell) splinter hit him on the head. He fell on me. I pulled him back, and I put him on the side. An ambulance came along. I was crying. I said to the ambulance man, "Can I put him in?" And he looked out, the first aid man, he said, "It's too late. He can't be saved any more. Just save yourself." I left him before he died, and that was on my conscience for years. I couldn't do anything about it.'

After escaping Falaise, Fritz was taken prisoner by the French Resistance between Rouen and Amiens on 31 August.

'We didn't know what would happen to us. We didn't know whether they'd shoot us or not.' The next day Fritz and the other men were handed over to British soldiers, and put in a temporary POW camp. 'From there we marched on to a different camp.'

The POWs were eventually loaded onto empty lorries returning from the front.

'I remember we went through Caen. The French were throwing stones and bottles, and calling, "Raus, raus!" Out, out! The British chaps on the back of the lorry, they just laughed a bit . . . they were just grinning and didn't do anything about it.'

A 'coloured' soldier then fired over the head of the crowd to stop them. 'That coloured chap, he tried to protect us, because we were helpless.'

Closer to the coast, the POWs got a change of guards.

'The British soldiers, they came from Liverpool. They came on the lorry.' One of the soldiers was a short man with an angry disposition. 'And that little chap came on the lorry and tried to pinch everything that we got. Put it in a sack.

'Next to me there was a married man. He had a ring on, and he couldn't get it off. And he was so angry, he put the pistol on his chest, that little Liverpool chap.

'When he couldn't get the ring off he spit on his fingers, and still couldn't get it off. So he left it.

'They pinched all valuable things and put it in a bag.'

One of the German POWs could speak English. 'And when we came to the camp he was complaining to the camp commandant. And the camp commandant, he said, "I will do everything possible to find the chaps who are responsible for that."'

The items were not returned, but Fritz and the other men on the lorry had at least escaped Normandy with their lives.

Gerhard Franzky also survived Falaise.

'On the 20th of August, (the Wehrmacht) made a counter-attack from the outside (of the pocket). Part of the 2nd Division and other units opened up (a gap). I mounted a P4 tank, on which also the well-known Papa Hausser was sitting. And we got out of that mess before the Allies closed it all together.'

Paul Hausser (nicknamed Papa) was a senior member of the Waffen SS, rising as high as army group commander. He survived the war, and was the founding member of a group which sought to rehabilitate the reputation of the SS in later years.

One wonders what Hausser's thoughts were that day. For Gerhard, Falaise clearly signalled the end of the Third Reich.

'Even as a young man, I'm not stupid, and I can see the writing on the wall. I mean, by no way did I think that we would win the war at that point.'

Things had looked very different just four years before.

Klaus Steffen had served in the swift invasion of France and on the Eastern Front. After Russia, he was hospitalized with jaundice and continued to suffer from medical conditions, but in the summer of 1944, Germany needed every man that it could muster.

'Things looked very bad. Of course they had been looking very bad in the east, as we knew all along. We were called out, and a division was formed of all people who were declared fit for garrison duty. The commanding officer of the division was the brother of Field Marshal Kluge, and he had a wooden leg. So that shows you what sort of division that was.'

In mid-August this 'division of cripples' – the 226th Infantry Division, in which Klaus was an NCO – was sent to France.

'When we disembarked from the train we came under heavy fighter-bomber attacks. I think our strength was halved before we even fired a shot.' Their situation did not improve, and Klaus's unit was in constant retreat. 'On the 1st of September the battery commander, myself, and another corporal went on an advanced reconnaissance. We were walking through this village where the people looked absolutely aghast at us. Not threatening, they just couldn't understand how we were going through, and we couldn't make out why. And as we came out of the village, marching along this road, my battery commander said, "Look over there, there must be some tanks from the 1940 war." He was just putting his binoculars to look at them when those tanks opened fire.'

What they had mistaken for light tanks from earlier in the war were in fact British armoured cars.

'We dived into the ditch beside the road but they kept shooting over our heads. We crawled out of that into a sugar beet field. And all of a sudden I heard a groan. My battery commander had been hit in the leg. He said, "Come on, this is no good, we'll give up." So we just laid there and eventually they came, and the first thing they did was look after the battery commander. Tore his boot off, and dressed the wound. They took care of him, which rather impressed me, I must admit. And once that was done, and they searched us . . . out came a whisky bottle, and we all got a shot of whisky. Which I thought was rather strange under the circumstances, but it left a lasting impression on me.'

Thanks to his mother, Klaus had grown up with fond feelings for Great Britain.

'During the war, my mother religiously listened behind drawn curtains to BBC German broadcasts. A, to find out the truth. And B, that the connection on my mother's side has been very strong, in that her grandmother came over with Prince Albert when he married Princess Victoria, and became governess to the children. So, through the whole family, ran a strong Anglophile streak.'

Under the Nazi regime, such activities could have landed his mother in a concentration camp. 'Listening to BBC broadcasts was a rather dangerous affair, but she didn't care. My father was worried, but she wouldn't be told not to do it. She just did.'

While Klaus was a prisoner of war he received a letter from each of his parents.

'The one from my mother started, My dear son, know that

I know that you are in England. I know you will be safe, and nothing will happen to you. That was the first sentence in that letter. So that just shows you, there was a certain feeling towards England. A friendly feeling. Admittedly, we were never bombed or anything in our home. Our village was far too small. Had we been living in Berlin or Dresden or something it may have been different. I can only talk as things were in our home.'

Tragically, Klaus's parents would not survive the war. 'She and my father were both killed by the Russians when they came in.'

Though a large part of German forces had been caught in the Falaise Pocket, there were other soldiers in France who were not encircled.

Eighteen-year-old Hans Behrens had been sent to the country at the end of July, but rather than going into combat, he was sent to the east of Reims for training.

'It's unbelievable when I think of it today. By that time the Allied forces were well advanced . . . We were still sitting down on desks, learning Morse code.' The young troops were not in the dark about what was happening at the front. 'News came that things were not going so well. Troops coming back. And the French staff in the kitchen, and people we met outside, got a bit more irritated.' At the end of August, as the front collapsed, the young trainees were ordered back to Germany. 'One night we retreated. We left everything. We walked fifty kilometres that night. I remember falling asleep hanging onto a cart that was drawn by a horse. The following day there was a French lady and I gave her a letter. An IOU. Could I have her bike? I mean, I was just scared. I just wanted to go home. I cycled only a little while, and the war had overtaken us. (Artillery) came in. It was pretty awful for an absolutely green recruit to be thrown into this mess. Out of our company of two hundred and fifty odd, only twenty-eight survived.'

Elsewhere, Gunter von Waskowski and his few remaining men made it from the Falaise Pocket to the River Seine. 'We only got out using hand-made rafts. We cut down trees, bound it together, and then steered over. Some people tried to swim over and of course they were taken away by the (current). I don't think we saw any of them again.' The same was true of his division at large. 'Most of (the army) stayed in the pocket. It didn't come out.'

As the Allies squeezed the pocket to nothing, the advancing soldiers saw the devastation wrought by their artillery and aircraft. John Wilson was with the 51st (Highland) Division: 'I never saw anything like it in my life. Dead Germans, and tanks, equipment, God it was absolutely incredible. Absolutely incredible.'

'(It) was a terrible sight,' said Wallace Jeffrey, an RAF radio-man and fighter director. 'You couldn't walk through there without stepping on flesh, or bodies. It was a gruesome sight.'

Michael Bendix, of the Coldstream Guards, went through the Falaise Pocket. 'It was perfectly appalling, the carnage the Germans had suffered. Absolutely dreadful.' He recalled the state of the German prisoners. 'They were just sort of like automatons really. They were in a complete daze.'

'On this road there was open spaces like a moor,' said Eric Hooper of the Durham Light Infantry. 'There was horses which the Germans had for transport, they were running about with their backsides hanging off, there was cows lying dead, there was German soldiers lying dead and wounded, there was transport burning. It wasn't a pretty sight.'

Frank Collins was part of an RAF forward control party. More than fifty years later, the things that he saw at Falaise still haunted him. 'I think even today, the devastation of this has a profound effect (on me). I saw people coming out of burning tanks with their bodies alight, their clothing alight. And for me, I think that was possibly the worst part of the war.' Tanker Anthony Bashford

347

also found it difficult to speak about. 'The dreadful stench that arose was quite . . . just lasted . . .' His voice trailed away.

While the German army was being pulverized at Falaise, on 17 August the 6th Airborne were finally released to advance to the mouth of the Seine. Resistance member André Geloso was quick to offer his services to a major in the 6th Airborne when, on 23 August, they arrived near Bonneville-sur-Touques.

'I explained who I was and all that, and he said you would be very useful if you packed your bags and came with us. And that's what I did. Showed them any artillery positions and things like that. The night before went very smoothly really. The major was next door to me, came early in the morning at five o clock in the morning. He said, "André, the last Germans have left." We know the British army is just on the other side of the river. Go to the river, shout in English and say it's all safe to come. So I went down there, spent about an hour, it was a bit eerie because we didn't know where the Germans were and where the British were, we were right in the middle. I never got a response and I came back to the house and said, "I can't see a soul," and later on it was swarming with British soldiers. They probably saw me from the other side and thought it was a trap of some sort and they never responded.'

André had waited almost four years to see the day of liberation.

'(It) was marvellous. My wife went to Deauville to see the Belgians, because the Belgians were liberating Deauville, so she went here. When she got back I had disappeared and gone with the airborne. I was with them for quite a while, about three weeks, and it was quite interesting. I saw the town of Beuzeville taken by the airborne. Very smooth. They said, "We're not going in tonight because we don't want to risk lives, we're going to go in the morning." I said, "Well I'd be very pleased if you would because I know some friends in Beuzeville, and I bet they'll be on the edge of the road to greet the British and I'd like to be one of the first to enter Beuzeville." He said, "That's quite easy – you get in one of the first half-tracks."

'I had an absolutely marvellous time, I saw my friends and they were surprised to see me there. We went on right up the River Seine on the edge of Rouen. It was terrible there, there was a whole division of German tanks there, who came to cross the bridges and the bridges had been blown and they couldn't cross and then, of course, the RAF strafed all those tanks and it was a terrible mess really.'

The battle of the Falaise Pocket marked the end of significant German resistance in France, but it was not the complete encirclement and destruction of the forces trapped within that some had had hoped for. Still, by late August, the Allied forces had advanced across most of northern France. On 25 August, French troops under US command liberated Paris; by 31 August, with the conclusion of Operation Paddle, Allied forces had secured the entirety of the Seine's west bank.[2]

Operation Overlord came to an end on 1 September. The Battle for Normandy had lasted two months, three weeks, and three days. During the fighting, some 15–20,000 civilians lost their lives. German military losses were 23,000 dead, 10,000 of them in the Falaise Pocket. They also suffered some 67,000 wounded, and 200,000 missing or captured. Allied losses were more than 50,000 dead, and over 200,000 other casualties.

Gordon Penter was one of those casualties. He lost many comrades when he landed with the South Lancs on Sword Beach. A little over two weeks later, his company was practically wiped out in one of the campaign's largely forgotten battles, at Le Landel. Gordon suffered severe facial wounds during that action, and was captured and transported to the Rennes Military Hospital in Brittany, which was used to treat Allied POWs. When

Gordon staggered from the ambulance, it was a British major in the commandos who ran out to help him. Gordon then slipped into an unconscious state that lasted for two days. When he woke up, the major was by his side. '(He was) pushing butter down through the side of my mouth . . . he was marvellous to me, this major. I thought, This is keeping me alive.'

There were only seven doctors, including captured American and British medics working under the supervision of a French chief consultant, and it was common for patients to help the overworked staff.

'It was hell in that prisoner hospital . . . when I was a boy I'd watched this picture called *All Quiet on the Western Front*, when the leading chap there was put in a ward of twelve beds, which was supposed to be the dying ward, and anybody that went in there sort of never came out.

Well you can imagine my horror one day when I was put in that type of ward. There was Americans, and myself, and a few more British, and we were put in this ward. And each morning, when I woke up, there was two or three gone. And the chap (in) the next bed to me, I always remember, he was a Texas chap. He was a wonderful chap, but he'd been terribly wounded in the stomach, and he had all sorts of tubes in. And we were supposed, in my weak state, to make sure he kept them in. And it was impossible, and he died one day. It was very sad that, because he was a smashing chap.'

The ward gradually emptied as men succumbed to their wounds.

'In the end most of them were gone, and I was amazed to find, like this chap in (*All Quiet on the Western Front*), that I survived.'

But Gordon was not out of danger. 'The next thing we knew was a huge air raid on Rennes. American bombers. And three bombs hit the hospital. After they'd passed over it wasn't long before we heard that the Germans were pulling out.'

Gordon was able to get out of bed and to a window. It was 4 August.

'And there was an amazing sight. Coming up the road was this huge American tank division, and on one of the tanks, sitting . . . on the gun, was General Patton. You couldn't miss him. He had a silver helmet and two silver Colt (revolvers).'

Gordon was taken to a US medical facility before being evacuated to England. To his delight he found himself in a hospital across the street from his home, and was soon reunited with his family.

Such a reunion was denied to tens of thousands of others. For those that did survive the Battle of Normandy, their lives had changed for ever.

CHAPTER TEN

After Normandy

'I had nightmares . . . of the dead I saw laying on the beach, and the people dropping. And then, what I really had nightmares about, was why was I so fortunate to be a survivor? When all those other men were wounded or killed. I mean, it still haunts me to this day. But at the same time I think I'm lucky. Very lucky.'

Russell Clark, 116th Infantry Regiment

Many of the soldiers who saw victory in Normandy did not survive the war. The battles in the west continued for eight months, until the unconditional surrender of Germany in May 1945. Some soldiers who had been wounded in Normandy returned to action and were wounded a second time, or more; others returned and were killed. Troops who fought relentlessly in Normandy saw action in Belgium, Holland, and in Germany itself. They fought forest by forest, river by river, town by town, and house by house. By December 1944, the 50th (Northumbrian) Division, which included the 9th Durham Light Infantry, had seen so much action and suffered so many losses that it was broken up amongst other formations, and became a training division in England.

Gordon Penter had fought in Normandy with the South Lancs, and did not agree with some of the criticism levelled at the British in later years.

'After the war, many Americans said we were too cautious, and we didn't take enough chances, and we should have gone forward, and this and that. But when I look back at the casualty records of divisions, especially infantry divisions . . . when eleven months had passed (from Normandy to VE-Day), the casualties turned out to be 15,000 (per division), which of course is about the same (strength) as the division itself. But these casualties are mainly borne by the 4,500 men of the infantry companies, so you can see there's a turnover of just over three. And when you think of those casualties, it's hardly right to say that we didn't take chances . . . the heaviest casualties were definitely in Normandy.'

Gordon recalled one story from the regimental history when, at the end of the war, a sergeant major remarked to the company commander that they were the only two 'originals' who had made it all the way from Normandy to VE-Day. 'Some of them had been wounded and come back, but they were the only two . . . that got through without a scratch.'

American losses were equally heavy, and it is miraculous that any man who landed with the 116th Infantry Regiment not only survived D-Day, but further battles such as attacks on the Siegfried Line, and the advance into the Roer valley.

Harry Parley, who had landed on Omaha with the 116th, recorded an interview with his son many decades later, and recalled the ghastly moments of his war.

'I could see where the tanks had ridden over the bodies. Which at the time, I could withstand the look. But when a tank crushes a body and then the track is stopped and it makes a turn. That could bring your breakfast up. I don't know why I told you this. I just want you to know. I wanted you to know that it wasn't . . . it wasn't too easy.'

Harry found the sadness of war as difficult to deal with as the horror. 'You'd be running along the road in the midst of a battle. You were told to follow the road down to the next farmhouse and join such and such a squad. You were running there in the marshes, and puddles of old rainwater, with the brambles covering the body of the GI. And you saw yourself in that. And I used to be sad. And I used to say to myself, "His family will never know how he wound up. They will always wonder, How did he die? They will never know that he died face down in some dirty ditch water."'

Harry was a changed man when he came home. 'I was left, I think, a little less than normal. You've got to pick your own percentages. It makes you a little crazy.'

But he chose to see a positive aspect in this change. 'It helps because it's a crutch. And any time you want to lean back and dredge it up into your mind, there was nothing, absolutely nothing to worry you in your present life. Cause if you could dredge any part of this up and say, "Listen, I went through this," there's nothing that can worry you. Actually, you can use this. You can psych yourself into any condition you want. It's helped me through a lot of my life just by dredging up this craziness and using it as a weapon. I can raise more compassion immediately if I want. We were once addressed by Eisenhower, and he summed it up by saying, "If you are killed in this action coming up, you're gone, (and) you will be a hero. But if you live through it, there is nothing, nothing that will ever bother you again."'

Medic Russell Clark also landed with the 116th on Omaha. He fought across Europe for four months until he was badly injured while rescuing men from a burning tank. 'I got two out, but when I went back in to get the other two out the tank blew up. That's the last thing I remember.' He was taken back to England, and then the United States, for treatment. As well as a severe concussion he had a broken left ankle, a broken left leg, a broken hip, numerous broken ribs, a broken left arm, and a broken collarbone. 'That leads me to believe that I must have landed on my left side. I don't know how many yards I was blown. Probably quite a distance.'

Russell spent almost two years at Walter Reed National Military Medical Centre. After his discharge he pushed himself to live a full and active life. 'I played football, I played basketball. In fact I was dumb enough that I enlisted in the (Army's) Inactive Reserves. I was called to active duty and sent to Korea, and served a hitch there. I was with a MASH unit.'

He thinks a lot about what happened to the men he treated on Omaha Beach. 'I often wonder how many of them survived. And where they live. And . . . yeah, I think about it a lot. I knew a lot of them were very, very young men. Some of them were wounded so bad that I took care of them, but it was questionable whether they'd survive. But those that I knew I couldn't help, that was one of the hardest things I had to do, was crawl away from them. Couple of the things I said to them, I'd say, "You just hang in there, I'll be back." Knowing full well I wouldn't be back. It was impossible to get to all of them that were going down, and that sticks in my mind. That there were many men that maybe I could have helped, but I couldn't get to them.'

Like many soldiers who returned from the war, 'I had nightmares . . . of the dead I saw laying on the beach, and the people dropping. And then, what I really had nightmares about, was why was I so fortunate to be a survivor? When all those other men were wounded or killed. I mean, it still haunts me to this day. But at the same time I think I'm lucky. Very lucky.'

It was a hellish experience, but not one that he would change.

'I consider myself honored and privileged to have been able to serve my country and to serve my fellow Americans. I was fighting so that we had our freedom, and could retain our freedom. I don't regret a thing I did.'

Bud Lomell climbed the cliffs at Pointe du Hoc and destroyed the enemy guns there. For his actions that day he was awarded the Distinguished Service Cross. He became a lawyer, and gained a reputation as a 'fierce advocate for women in trouble' and a pro bono defender of the poor. When a Jewish colleague was refused admittance to a private lawyers' club, Bud told them, 'I didn't climb the cliffs of Normandy to find fascists in my own back yard.' When told that he had done more to win D-Day than any other man than Eisenhower, he was quick to correct them: 'I lost half my men. What more is there to know?'[1]

Psychiatric nurse Cecelia Christie, speaking fifty years after the end of the war, understood the impact of losing men one had responsibility for. 'I've met, quite recently, a colonel . . . who said, almost in tears, "I had to send a chap up the line, and he was killed, and I've never been able to get it out of my mind. I still live it." Another army officer told me that he still relives being in a particular battle in a field where they were being sniped, so he still had that feeling that he was never really safe . . . lots of them say they still have this feeling. Either a guilt feeling . . . or a feeling of stress.'

Cecelia was not immune from trauma.

'I can't see a soldier or hear a military band without being choked. And I wasn't involved in the front line, but because of seeing all these injured soldiers in Normandy, hundreds of them that we couldn't really do a lot for that were going to die anyway, I myself am almost uncontrollably emotional about that sort of thing.'

John Witmeyer of the 4th Infantry Division was wounded

several times during the war, including a stab wound in Normandy. After he was wounded again on the French–German border he was given command of a company of men suffering from battle fatigue.

'Today we call it PTSD . . . no doubt, in my own mind, I carry some PTSD if you wanna call it that. I don't think anybody could serve in combat – especially if you served two hundred-plus days like I did – and say that you haven't absorbed some of that in you. Unwantingly, unwillingly, it's in your brain.'

John turned from a soldier to a killer on the battlefield. Now he had to learn how to be a civilian, and to live with the things that he had done in war.

'I brought a lot of the war home with me. I still have it in my head. Done a lot of things, atrocities, and shouldn't have done, and feel sorry for them now. I have a guilt complex.'

Some nights John would drive to a secluded spot and sit alone. 'I couldn't stand to be around people. I was afraid to be around people. And that's what these guys are talking about with PTSD. We didn't get any treatment and what not. I'm glad they didn't do. Guys come back, and you get in a fight, you'd wanna kill the guy. You really did. It wasn't what you wanted to do, it was what came out of ya. And if they had asked me, what did I learn in the military, I learned a bunch of ways to kill people. Who wants somebody who can do that?'

John killed many men in the war, and at least ten within arm's length. Some were prisoners. 'If you laughed at me, that was death for you. If you were German I'd say, "What are you laughing at," and I'd shoot them in the head. I told them to run. I always gave them a chance. And that's terrible. It's terrible to talk about. I feel the heaviness in my chest and I've got a headache. And it gets worse than that. It gets worse than that. My guys killed a lot of people when they were surrendering, or surrendered. I hated them,' he said of his enemy.

Medic Raymond VanDuzer was taken as a POW during the fighting in Germany, then freed by American troops. When he returned home his dog was waiting for him: 'he was spellbound. It looked to me like some of his hair had grown gray. It was great to see him.'

Raymond enjoyed his time in the service, and even contemplated re-enlistment. That was not to say that he was not scarred by war, and he had to change his life to adjust to that. 'I stopped drinking. I wasn't a good boy, then. I just learned, don't worry about it. It'll work out. Whatever happens, you can take care of yourself. Improvise, you know?' He suffered with nightmares, and was later diagnosed with PTSD. 'I take some medication now for it. That's helped me a lot.'

When infantry officer David Roderick came home, his family noticed the change in him. 'I was having bad dreams, and that sort of thing.' His mother-in-law insisted that he go to the Veterans' Administration for help. 'So I finally did, and they sent me to a psychiatrist who gave me an evaluation.' He was diagnosed with 'anxiety', which today would likely be labelled as PTSD. It remained with him his whole life. 'If I'm sitting here, or in the kitchen, not thinking about anything, "boom", artillery lands in the backyard. No sounds, or anything. No sight. It's just an image kind of thing. And that's sixty years ago. I still get that. But after you've been constantly through that stuff, it just lives with you.'

John Kerner served as a doctor in Normandy. 'I got home a little depressed because of the shock of going through all this.' During a period of leave in San Francisco, he met the woman who would become his wife. 'She helped get me out of the depressed state.' John helped deliver a baby in the middle of the Battle of

Mortain. He became head of ObGyn in a California hospital, and delivered many more. He also wrote several books about his experiences.

Some British soldiers were unhappy about the circumstances of their discharge, and the aftercare they were given on their return – or lack of it. Norman Madden landed on Gold Beach. In March 1945, during combat in Germany, a mine blew up his tank and shattered his leg. That was the end of his army career – which he would have liked to have continued.

'I feel very bitter now, especially when I look around at today and they talk about stress, and understanding. There was no understanding (when I demobilized). Not only me, thousands of us come out like this. You were just thrown out. There was no thought how you were going to cope, nobody to give you a voice. There's your railway ticket, you're on your own. You never existed. And I just wonder in meself, how people of today when they say they've got stress, how would they have managed in the war. Because I think it was so cruel, throwing you out. You'd done your job. Through no fault of your own you get injured, and you're just put on the side. No help. No nothing. I thought I could have had advice given to me . . . (but I got) no help in anyway, which I think was wrong. I just felt like you're just thrown out, they couldn't care less. I've always felt, and I always will, (that) you're just an object that was no good . . . I don't think the aftercare was there . . . I don't think they treated us right. I don't think anyone will convince me any other (way). They treated us terrible.'

Infantryman Anton Jaber was discharged from the US Army in November 1945. After growing up in an orphanage, and not being taught anything by the army except how to kill, 'it was like starting all over again. I didn't learn anything in the army that qualified me for a job outside.' After a couple of years as a civilian he decided to re-enlist in the military. 'I joined the air force.

I figured if I was gonna go to war, I might as well go where it's a lot easier than the infantry.' Anton served in Korea, and remained in the air force until 1972.

William Gast's tank came ashore on Omaha. During his long months in combat, he didn't think much about the future. 'You lived day by day. It was just a day-by-day survival.'

The William who landed on D-Day was not the man who returned home. 'I went in as a kid and I came out as a well-seasoned man. I learned comradeship. We had affection and affiliation then with each other that hardly anybody knows today any more. It really makes me sad for what we did, what we went through, and those who gave their lives for what is happening to this country today. It makes me very, very sad. Our whole country was different then. We were a united country. We went through good times, wonderful times, and it has just turned a huge percentage of our people into greedy individuals, and it is a sad, sad situation.'

The years went by for the veterans of Normandy, but the memories of comrades never faded.

'You never forget, especially your buddies,' said Bob Miksa, who came ashore with the 743rd Tank Battalion at Omaha. '(It feels) just like yesterday or last week and that's what hurts. As you're growing older you think more about it. When I was younger it was a bit in my mind but as I'm older I'm thinking more about it and it hurts a little more.' Bob was asked how he got over these traumatic experiences.

'You don't.'

It was a pain he had to carry for the rest of his life, but to him, it was a price that had to be paid. 'It was worth it.'

Ramsey Bader served in the Essex Yeomanry. His father was from Sierra Leone, and had also served during wartime. Ramsey said that he only came across one case of discrimination due to his skin colour during his time in the service, but things changed when peace came.

'After the war, then I think I had the same problems again, that nobody wanted to employ you. And yet I'd served my country, but at least now, looking back over the years, I still feel, meeting other coloureds, and meeting other people, we all fought for the same cause.' Ramsey's brother fought in Burma; he was a decorated sergeant major. 'We served along with all the other people who fought. Perhaps a lot of people don't even know today. But they did fight for, what today is, the survival of mankind, because if Hitler had won the war, we wouldn't be here today.'

For many soldiers the army was their home, their family, and their purpose. Leaving the army wasn't a case of taking off a uniform, but losing their entire existence.

Robert Blatnik was wounded both physically and mentally during his many years of combat. After appearing in front of a medical board he was discharged from the army.

'I said, "That's a lot of bullshit, I'm good for service. I want to go back to my outfit."' His pleas fell on deaf ears. 'I didn't know what the hell to do with myself. I was with my mother, I said, "Ma, I don't know what's going on. I belong in the army."' Blatnik, a recipient of the Silver Star, decided to dedicate himself to the American Legion, and veterans' affairs. It was a path that many other veterans chose to follow.

Walter Ehlers joined the infantry with his older brother, Roland. They served in the same regiment, but only Walter survived the assault on Omaha Beach. Over the course of the war Walter was wounded four times, the last of which ended his time in the army. For his actions in Normandy, he was awarded America's highest reward for bravery, the Medal of Honor.

'My life didn't end with my military service. I spent

twenty-nine years working for the Veterans' Administration. I interviewed veterans all the way from the Civil War to the Persian Gulf War.'

Walter was a firm believer in the importance of learning from history. 'History is good for all children to know as much as they can about their country. And to understand exactly what made it as great as it is, and that's our constitution of the United States. Our constitution is the best in the world. They don't seem to understand that when we made that constitution and Bill of Rights we already had those freedoms. This meant everybody, regardless of race, colour or creed . . . We, the People. And also, that's what the presidents and our legislative body should know. We, the People are the government, and we put those guys into office, they're working for us, not we for them. They're working for us, and they better start shaping up. I think we've got the best country in the world. Only thing is we've got to shape up a little bit.'

Walter was a man of strong faith before and after the war. Others, like Donald Evans, who served in an armoured regiment, found their religion whilst on the front line.

'Before I went to the service I never went to church . . . (but) when you're over there you pray, you pray, you pray all the time, man. When the shooting's going on, you pray! "Lord, you get me out of this and I'm gonna be good," this kind of stuff. But when the shooting's over it's the same old story.

'The only thing that I regret is that I was not a born-again Christian when I was in the service. And it's not to say that if I was a born-again Christian, God would spare my life. But life would have been a lot easier, because God would have helped me carry the load.'

Donald had been wounded during the fighting at Saint-Lô. After treatment in England he was returned to combat, seeing action in the Battle of the Bulge and Germany, where he was injured for a second time and taken prisoner. Donald saw out the rest of the European war in a German hospital. VJ-Day was also special for him, but perhaps for different reasons than many other soldiers: it was the day of his first date with the woman who would become his wife.

Jimmy Wilkinson served with the Durham Light Infantry in several theatres of war. His recollections of North Africa are vivid, but 'I don't remember a lot after D+4. From outside of Caen, I can't remember a thing. I sort of blacked out again, and I don't know what happened.' Jimmy went back to work in the mines after the war. He continued to suffer with periods of blackouts. 'I took a bad turn, and I completely blacked out, and I had to go to hospital. And what they said in effect was that I'd burst a blood vessel, and it was affecting me memory. I wouldn't do anything about it, because I didn't want people to know. I couldn't see, but I could tell what was happening. When I drove over a pavement, I knew that I had to keep to the left, but I hadn't the sense to stop. It was rather strange.'

It is possible that Jimmy was suffering with a form of dissociative disorder, described here by the NHS: 'Some people dissociate after experiencing war . . . Switching off from reality is a normal defence mechanism that helps the person cope during a traumatic time . . . Someone with a dissociative disorder may also have other mental health conditions, such as . . . Post Traumatic Stress Disorder.'* Jimmy admitted that after the war he 'never enquired anything about the army. I wanted to forget it.'

'I've got some bad memories,' said Trevor Edwards, of the Royal Welch Fusiliers. 'When I got home I couldn't settle. (I had) a temper. I couldn't adjust for a bit. That's gone now. All bar this

* https://www.nhs.uk/mental-health/conditions/dissociative-disorders/

memory of burying the dead. That's never left me, and never will.' After the war, Trevor worked in the Brymbo Steelworks for thirty-four years. Sometimes his wife would notice that though he was physically present, his mind was elsewhere, thinking back to his days at war. 'You can't help it,' he said. 'All soldiers have got it.'

'You miss your comrades,' said Harry Martin, also of the Royal Welch. 'In the army, you're with men. And you get good friends, and your comradeship, cause you're all doing the same job together. When you come out of the army you lose all that straight away. But I have still got friends that I was with. You was never without anybody wherever you went. We were all friends. And when you come home, and especially now, I'm on me own, because I lost my wife ten years ago. I don't let it get me down. I'm all right.'

John Court fought in North Africa and Normandy in the Royal Tank Regiment, and found it hard to adjust back to 'mundane' civilian life.

'I was so unsettled, I couldn't settle at all. I felt absolutely lost. It's a terrible feeling, it really is. I can imagine anybody that comes out of the services feeling very lonely. You miss your comradeship, and the fact that you're doing something in a big organization . . . To me, the army and civvy life were two entirely different things . . . You were very conscious also that an awful lot of people were getting jobs that hadn't been in the army . . . it is a resentment, and it's very hard to overcome it.' But he did not regret his wartime service. 'In some respects (the army was) one of the happiest times in my life. Hard at times, but one of the happiest. I met many good men.'

As the war was drawing to a close, Ian Hammerton and his comrades in the Dragoons began to look ahead at the next stage of their lives. 'We all said it's going to be a great deal harder to win the peace than win the war, and that has been so true. I think we've lost out a lot since. But I did feel in 1946 that I wanted to do something constructive as a result of what I'd seen.' He dedicated himself to teaching, and believed that he was aided in this career by his time in the service. 'I've never lost those seven years in the army. It's been in me all the time. I think it made me a better teacher than I might otherwise have been. I think the experience was useful. One learns a lot more about oneself (in war). I think I emerged as a much more confident person than I'd ever been before. I had a much wider appreciation of life generally, and of people.'

William 'Bill' Dunn suffered life-changing wounds on Juno Beach, including the loss of his arm, which had to be amputated. 'I don't think I've ever recovered really, to a degree . . . (but) I've never been beat . . . I've tried to overcome my disability ever since I first came home.'

He agreed that there was a psychological cost to D-Day. 'I think there was, because for years afterwards, I used to get these dreams . . . Seeing me own crew shot down beside me . . . my crew members were closer to me then than what my family were. Because we all had a job to do. We all depended on each other. You work together, you sleep together, you went out together. You weren't parted. You could more or less read them before they did them(selves), you're so used to them. You knew that they were going to fight for you as well as you're going to fight for them.'

While he was wounded and waiting on evacuation from Juno, Bill saw a man burned to death. Often he relived the terrible moment in his sleep. 'It's a nightmare to me. It's where he's screaming for people to help him. They were throwing water on him, but it was no good. And, I think the nightmare more or less stops, when you, in your own mind, are shouting for them to get him out.'

Although Bill was never formally counselled, he believed that the doctors and nurses who treated his physical wounds played a large role in helping men overcome their mental injuries. He was also helped by his family. 'I think the best counselling one gets is one's family. My wife's done a hell of a lot for me.'

As well as painful memories, there were many good ones. Bill and his best friend were separated when they were evacuated from Juno, each one told that the other had died. For years they sought each other out. Bill recalled the moment of reunion. 'I recognized him when I turned the bottom of the street, and he's feeding his chickens. And all of a sudden, when he glanced up again, I saw he recognized me. He threw the tin of corn up in the air. Chickens never had such a good feed. And of course, he came out of his garden and put his arms around me. I see him now at least once a year. And we still have a good reunion when we meet each other.'

Frank Denius, a decorated US artilleryman, recalled a similar lifetime bond that had been forged in Normandy. 'I want to say this. I would never have been able to achieve what I did as a forward observer without my radio sergeant, Goldstein.' At this point in the interview Frank stopped and fought back emotion, a reflection of the love that he carried for his brother in arms. Frank and Goldstein kept in touch after the war and reunited in 2005. 'I hadn't seen him since May of '45,' said Frank, before wiping a tear from his eye.

Like many veterans of the war, Frank did not seek personal glory through re-telling his story. Rather, he did so to immortalize those he had served beside.

'I don't take a great deal of pride, perhaps, and I don't cherish the position. The good Lord has afforded me a good life, and health, and he lets me play football.' He laughed. 'And as long as I can . . . memorialize what American citizen soldiers went through in World War Two, I'm pleased to do so.'

Daniel Chester of the 9th Infantry Division was asked if

people could understand what it was like to fight in World War Two. 'How could they? There's no way you can.'

This does not mean that Daniel is not grateful for those who try and learn as much as they can about the soldier's experience, or those who make that possible. He was very impressed by the job done by the National World War II Museum in New Orleans, and how they detailed the GI's experience. 'You better take one or two full days to slowly go through it, and let it sink in your mind,' he said of the museum.

David Roderick revisited Normandy on the sixtieth anniversary of D-Day, receiving a warm welcome from the French civilians who had 'suffered the most'. 'When we went back on the beach I broke down. That was the only time. I guess everything finally came together and I just broke down.'

Ray Smith, who served aboard HMS *Middleton*, also visited the battle sites. 'I went with the British Legion across Gold Beach and Sword Beach. You saw the crosses and just pictured under all of them the young men that gave their lives so we can live freely. That was the sad thing about it. The youngsters nowadays, I don't think they know the enormity of what it was or what people gave up.'

Harry Billinge was a Commando sapper. He never forgot his comrades, and dedicated much of his life to preserving their memory. 'How could you forget blokes when they were getting killed left, right and centre? A bloke died in my arms in Caen. I was . . . with a bloke called Needs after the RAF bombed the wrong target and he died in my arms. I'll never forget (him). I lay in bed at night and recite all their names. "To live in hearts we leave behind is not to die."'* In the later years of his life, Harry collected more than £50,000 for the construction of the

* From the poem 'Hallowed Ground' by Thomas Campbell.

Normandy Memorial. 'We've got to be consistent [with remembrance]. If you're committed, you won't forget, and I can't forget anyway.'[2]

Harry was asked if he had any advice for soldiers of today's army, but his answer applies equally to us all.

'Help one another. Give one another strength. To the bloke that's losing a bit of heart – give him strength. Know what your mate needs, give him strength and determination. Support one another beyond measure.' Harry's words can be taken in a broader context: to support not only our friends, but our fellow man. One of war's greatest tragedies is that people who would be friends are turned into mortal enemies. This was certainly true for some of the veterans of Normandy.

'One of my best friends here in England, he was one of Major Howard's men,' said Hans Behrens, a German POW who settled in Britain. 'Some of my best friends in the UK were former soldiers.' One of these men had fought on the opposite side in the same battle as Hans. 'We can only have been a few hundred yards apart.'

Hans von Luck, who had led fierce counter-attacks against the British airborne in Normandy, spent five years in Soviet captivity after the war. In later years he became friends with John Howard, who had been fighting against him. 'As a professional soldier, I did my duty,' said Hans, 'but as a human being I hold no hate.'[3]

'I wish (the war) had never happened,' said Norman Madden. 'I always think in my mind, there (is) good and bad in everybody. I met some marvellous German people, and they say the same. It wasn't their wish to go to war. You get a certain few people, and it's in England just the same. I don't blame nobody for the war, Germans or England . . . If you're conscripted into an army there's nothing you can do about it. You're all tarred with the same brush, because you were in the army.'

Though Robert Blatnik saw a lot of combat, these experiences made him a more peaceful and compassionate man as he grew older. 'I love my enemies. I don't care who they are. As it says in the Lord's prayer, forgive us our trespasses as we forgive those who trespass against us. And I believe in that now.'

Bob Miksa's hope was that later generations would learn from history, and avoid the suffering that had engulfed the world when he was a young man. 'I wish all the young people growing up today would someday be able to eliminate the insanity of wars from this planet and eliminate all hatred of race, creed and colour and everybody find a place that allows him or her to be successful, and be a valued member of society.

'That's what I'd tell the kids today. Keep away from wars. Try to eliminate wars.'

'Your Peace Is Bought with Mine'

'To the world he was a soldier. To his family he was all the world.'

Inscription from the grave of a British soldier

Drive in any direction in Normandy and you will find a memorial commemorating an aspect of the 1944 campaign. In some villages, like Évrecy, you may find several. On its outskirts stands a column made from Welsh slate, commemorating the soldiers who fought and died during Operation Greenline. In the village centre, surrounded by tricolours, is a memorial to the 130 civilians killed in a single night of Allied bombing.

There are twenty-seven military cemeteries in Normandy, varying by nationality, and in size. More than 20,000 German soldiers are buried at La Cambe, while the Jerusalem War Cemetery, near Chouain, is the final resting place of 49 Commonwealth soldiers. One of them is Private Banks of the Durham Light Infantry, who was killed at the age of sixteen.

No matter the size of the cemetery, the effect of visiting them is the same. On a wet day in December I pulled to the side of the road in the little village of Banneville-la-Campagne. There was a van in the layby, two gardeners working attentively around a set of metal gates through which I passed with my friends. For once we were silent.

Hidden from the road by hedge and trees, two thousand headstones stood in ordered ranks. As the clouds parted overhead, and rays of weak sunlight painted the graves, my friends and I drifted in different directions, walking the rows, and thinking about the men who lay there.

Some of the headstones would stop and hold us. Often, this was the soldier's young age. Other times, an inscription. One in particular will stay with me always.

'To the world he was a soldier. To his family he was all the world.'

I finally moved on and found the graves that I was looking for. They were soldiers of my former regiment, and remembered on war memorials close to my home. Though I live in a rural area, I found ten local men who had been killed in Normandy. Their ages were forty-two, twenty-three, thirty-two, twenty-six, twenty-seven, twenty-six, twenty-three, nineteen, twenty-seven, twenty-five.

Every name on a memorial represents a life that could have been. Think of your own. How many of your most treasured experiences came after forty-two years of life? How many came after nineteen? We say that the lives of soldiers were cut short, but the reality is that for many, they had barely begun.

When a soldier dies in battle, the world is robbed of his promise, and the soldier of his chances. To raise a family. To laugh with friends. To watch a sunset. All of the things that we so often take for granted. That is why their death is a sacrifice. And that is why, at the very least, our duty is to remember them. Remember who they were, remember who they could have been, and remember why they were called upon to die. Remember this, so that we never have to ask it of others.

I have endeavoured, so much as possible, to tell the story of Normandy in the words of the men who fought there. These accounts have, of course, come from those who survived the battles that so many did not.

'Their stories went with them, and so have never been told.'

These were the words of Canadian soldier Alex Kuppers, who landed on Juno, and while it is true that we will never know the stories of the fallen, some of them did leave behind insights into their thoughts and feelings at the time. Oftentimes in letters, and sometimes in poetry.

David Rhys Geraint Jones, known as Geraint, read law at Trinity Hall, Cambridge, before joining the army. He was an accomplished poet, with a volume of his work published in 1944.

In June of that year Geraint landed in Normandy as a liaison officer in the 159th Brigade, 11th Armoured Division. On 28 June, during Operation Epsom, he left Mondrainville in an armoured car to find C Company of the 3rd Monmouthshires, who were suffering heavy casualties. While coming to the aid of his comrades, Geraint was struck in the head by a sniper's bullet, and killed.

He was twenty-two years old. One of his poems is entitled 'The Light of Day is Cold and Grey' and seems to foretell his own loss of life and all that he will miss. It ends with the lines 'Your peace is bought with mine, and I am paid in full, and well, if but the echo of your laughter reaches me in hell.'

NOTES

INTRODUCTION

1 George MacDonald Fraser, *Quartered Safe Out Here* (HarperCollins, 2000), p. 10.

CHAPTER ONE: THE EYES OF THE WORLD UPON THEM

1 https://queenmary.com/history/
2 Surviving D-Day/Memoirs of WWII #41 from www.memoirsof worldwarii.com
3 Veteran State of Mind podcast, episode 94 remembrance special

CHAPTER TWO: ALL AMERICANS, SCREAMING EAGLES, AND RED DEVILS

1 Stephen Ambrose, *Band of Brothers* (Simon and Schuster, 2001), p. 65.
2 Stephen Ambrose, *Band of Brothers* (Simon and Schuster, 2001), p. 76.
3 'A Tribute to Major Dick Winters' 5 part video series by long-time friend State Representative John Payne.

CHAPTER THREE: 'WE'LL START THE WAR FROM RIGHT HERE'

1 Bedford's population in 1944 was 3,200. Today, it is home to the National D-Day Memorial. The numbers of Bedford Boys who died often vary. This book has used the lowest estimate, taken from https://www.warner.senate.gov/public/index.cfm/blog

2 Alistair Horne, 'Defeat at Normandy! Our Near-Loss on D-Day – And What the World Would Look Like if We'd Failed', *Washington Post*, 5 June 1994

CHAPTER FOUR: TO WIN OR LOSE IT ALL

1 HMS Belfast Association.

2 https://www.iwm.org.uk/history/ 8-things-you-didnt-know-about-hms-belfast-and-d-day

3 www.royalhampshireregiment.org/about-the-museum/timeline/ d-day-1944/

4 Juno Beach Centre Legacy of Honour collection, video interview with Havelyn Chiasson.

5 http://www.6juin1944.com/assaut/juno/tables.pdf, p22

6 https://warchronicle.com/winnipeg-rifles/

7 Surviving D-Day/Memoirs of WWII #41 from memoirsofwwii.com

8 Juno Beach Centre Legacy of Honour collection, interview with Jim Parks.

9 Juno Beach Centre Legacy of Honour collection, interview with Jim Parks.

10 Surviving D-Day/Memoirs of WWII #41 from memoirsofwwii.com

11 M. Zuehlke, *Juno Beach: Canada's D-Day Victory, June 6, 1944* (Vancouver: D&M, 2005), p. 142.

12 https://theddaystory.com/juno-beach/

13 https://www.junobeach.org/canada-on-d-day-by-the-numbers/

14 *Le Jour J au Commando No.4 – Les Française du Débarquiement* by Rene Goujon, published by NEL in 2004 and quoted in 'The 177 French Soldiers of D-Day' *France-Amérique*

CHAPTER FIVE: GO TO IT!

1 https://screenrant.com/band-brothers-private-blythe-death-true-story-change/

CHAPTER SIX: LODGEMENT

1 https://assets.publishing.service.gov.uk/media/5a78d775ed915d07 d35b2d91/ww2_dday.pdf

2 'Danger Zone' by Robert Citino, July/August 2016 edition of *World War II* magazine and available on https://www.nationalww2museum. org/war/articles/danger-zone

3 Surviving D-Day/Memoirs of WWII #41 from memoirsofwwii.com

4 https://www.junobeach.org/canada-in-wwii/articles/the-normandy-campaign/account-of-personal-experiences-in-action-on-sunday-11-june-44/

5 https://heritage.canadiana.ca/view/oocihm.lac_reel_t12657/154

6 https://heritage.canadiana.ca/view/oocihm.lac_reel_t12657/155

7 https://heritage.canadiana.ca/view/oocihm.lac_reel_t12657/155

8 https://heritage.canadiana.ca/view/oocihm.lac_reel_t12657/156

9 Juno Beach Centre Legacy of Honour collection, video interview with Roly Armitage

10 https://www.normandywarguide.com/war-diaries/1st-bn-south-lancashire-regiment-june44

CHAPTER SEVEN: DEATH IN THE HEDGEROWS

1 J. Wertheim, *The Ritchie Boys* (New York: CQ Roll Call, 2022).

CHAPTER EIGHT: THE KEY

1 https://www.thehill112.com/

2 https://www.theguardian.com/world/1999/nov/14/firstworldwar.uk

3 https://www.ncbi.nlm.nih.gov/pmc/articles/PMC3181586

4 John Buckley, ehttps://www.dday-overlord.com/en/battle-of-normandy/Allied-operations/paddle/d. *The Normandy Campaign 1944: Sixty Years On* (Taylor & Francis Group, 2006).

5 See Stephen Hart, *Montgomery and Colossal Cracks: 21st Army Group in Northwest Europe 1944–45* (Praeger, 2000).

CHAPTER NINE: THE BREAKOUT

1 https://www.americanairmuseum.com/archive/person/harold-graham-shook

2 https://www.dday-overlord.com/en/battle-of-normandy/Allied-operations/paddle/

CHAPTER TEN: AFTER NORMANDY

1 https://www.independent.co.uk/news/obituaries/leonard-bud-lomell-us-ranger-who-led-a-successful-attack-on-german-clifftop-machine-guns-during-dday-2237426.html

2 Veteran State of Mind podcast episode 93

3 https://eu.onlineathens.com/story/opinion/2022/06/03/remembering-sacrifices-d-day-77th-anniversary/7457407001/

ACKNOWLEDGEMENTS

This book would not have been possible if not for the tireless work of my editor Ingrid Connell. I am very grateful to her for the opportunity to work on a subject that is so close to my heart, and I would like to extend that gratitude to the entire team at Pan, including Nicholas Blake, Holly Sheldrake, Lindsay Nash, Jiri Greco, Neil Lang and Alex Fowler.

Thank you to Morgana Pugh, Anne-Marie Byrne, Wall to Wall, Simon Young and the BBC for having me onboard to write the accompaniment to their incredible documentary series *D-Day - The Unheard Tapes*, and to the staff at the National Word War II Museum and The Imperial War Museums who have, over many decades, chronicled the accounts of our soldiers, sailors, and airmen. This book also used references from several other sources, and I would like to express my gratitude to all, including Alex Fitzgerald-Black at the Juno Beach Centre, Jim Parks and Roly Armitage for giving permission for us to use their interviews, and Joshua Scott at www.memoirsofworldwarii.com. Thanks too to the many authors who have written so brilliantly on the Battle of Normandy, some of whom I have read since childhood, and others I have had the recent fortune to discover.

As ever I would like to thank my friend and agent Rowan Lawton, and the Soho agency at large. A big thank you and 'well done mate' is owed to Charlie Robinson, who was of great assistance, and has proved that army subalterns are indeed capable of reading maps. Thanks to Phil and Matt for joining me on a visit to Normandy (less so for the introduction to the region's brandy), and to my family for the continued support.

Finally I would like to thank the veterans of the campaign who not only braved war, but the re-telling of it. To them, and to those who continue to honour their memory, I am eternally grateful.

We will remember them.

Geraint Jones

PICTURE ACKNOWLEDGEMENTS

Page 1 *top* © Archive Photos/Getty Images

Page 1 *bottom* © Keystone / Stringer via Getty Images

Page 2 *top* © IMPERIAL WAR MUSEUM/AFP via Getty Images

Page 2 *bottom* © Glasshouse Vintage/Universal History Archive/ Universal Images Group via Getty Images

Page 3 *top* © Wall/Stringer/MPI/Getty Images

Page 3 *bottom* © HUM Images/Universal Images Group via Getty Images

Page 4 *top* © AFP via Getty Images

Page 4 *bottom* © James Mapham/No 5 Army Film & Photo-graphic Unit/Keystone/Hulton Archive/Getty Images

Page 5 *top* © Sgt. G Laws/ Imperial War Museums via Getty Images

Page 5 *bottom* © Popperfoto via Getty Images/Getty Images

Page 6 *top* © Keystone-France/Gamma-Keystone via Getty Images

Page 6 *middle* © IWM (B 5525)

Page 6 *bottom* © Pictorial Press Ltd / Alamy Stock Photo

Page 7 *top* © piemags / Alamy Stock Photo

Page 7 *bottom* © Keystone-France/Gamma-Keystone via Getty Images

Page 8 *top* © Archive Photos / Stringer via Getty Images

Page 8 *bottom* © Photo12/UIG/Getty Images

Page 9 *top* © Major Stewart/ Imperial War Museums via Getty Images

Page 9 *bottom* © IWM (B 6045)

Page 10 *top* © Associated Press / Alamy Stock Photo

Page 10 *bottom* © IWM (B 6852)

Page 11 *top* © IWM (B 7441)

Page 11 *bottom* © IWM (B 7570)

Page 12 *top* © IWM (B 7517)

Page 12 *bottom* © IWM (B 5803)

Page 13 *top* © Photo12/UIG/Getty Images

Page 13 *bottom* © Photo12/UIG/Getty Images

Page 14 *top* © IWM (B 8886)

Page 14 *bottom* © Keystone/Hulton Archive/Getty Images

Page 15 *top* © Associated Press / Alamy Stock Photo

Page 15 *bottom* © piemags/archive/military / Alamy Stock Photo

Page 16 *top* © New York Times Co./Getty Images

Page 16 *bottom* © Fred Ramage/Keystone/Hulton Archive/Getty Images

THE TESTIMONIES

Voices from THE IMPERIAL WAR MUSEUMS

Excerpts from the following interviews are taken from the IWM Sound Archive. All © IWM unless otherwise stated.

Bader, Ramsey (10593)
Bashford, Anthony (12907)
Behrens, Hans (14228)
Benbow, Hilaire (25199)
Bendix, Michael (18570)
Blinkhorn, James (13263)
Blizzard, Arthur (17979)
Bradley, Norman (19077)
Branson, Philip (13266)
Bryan, Thomas (21188)
Buchanan, John (19867)
Budzik, Kazimierz (12135)
Cammack, Harold (18832)
Carlill, John (34427)
Christie, Cecelia (13121)
Clubley, George (16628)
Collins, Frank (18334)
Coombs, Aubrey (21106)
Cordery, Ted (33378)

Court, Alfred John (16059)

Crane, Roy (16437)

Donnelly, John (19799)

Dunn, William 'Bill' (12938)

Dunnett, Amy 'Pam' (18784)

Eberling, Ernst (11389)

Edwards, Trevor (20736)

Elliott, George (10602)

Fitzgerald, Robert (18464)

Follett, Ronald (12402)

Franklin, Maurice (27797)

Fursland, Arthur 'Larry' (26746)

Fussell, Peter (10242)

Gautier, Leon (34425)

Geloso, Andre (10068)

Golley. Ernest 'John' (12039)

Gosling, Richard (21290)

Griffin, Norman (18615)

Grimaux, Michel (34426)

Gueritz, Edward (17394)

Hammerton, Ian (8939)

Hann, Ronald (20812)

Hanna, William (13949)

Hooper, Eric (11208)

Jeltsch, Fritz (20598)

Jones, Arthur (18346)

Kelly, James (11281)

Kirtland, Herbert (17594)

Kuppers, Alex (34428)

Krupinski, Walter (11388)

Leatherbarrow, Richard (8253)

Lewis, Patrick 'Bill' (18479)

Lough, Ernest (12381)
Madden, Norman (18567)
Majendie, John (22925)
Martin, Harry (21105)
McGovern, Francis (17825)
Meredith, Berkeley (18577)
Millin, William 'Bill' (11614)
Minogue, Joe (2955) © Fremantle
Mogg, Herbert John (30505)
Morris, Arthur (17840)
Nicolson, Joan (12075)
Nield-Siddall, Warwick (19672)
Oliver, George (28897)
Painter, Gordon (26747)
Parr, Walter 'Wally' (11073)
Peace, Thomas (18048)
Penter, Gordon (19769)
Phillips, Richard (31401)
Powter, Kenneth (16648)
Rayson, George (18004)
Rosewarn, Douglas (17500)
Siegel, Siegfried 'Hans' (34433)
Smith, James (18253)
Smith, Robert (18575)
Snell, William (13580)
Steffen, Klaus (12577)
Thompson, Arthur (13370)
Tondowski, Maurice (26742)
Trott, Kenneth (30393)
Vallance, Royston 'Roy' (19074)
Vaughan, John (11548) © The Rights Holder
Von Luck, Hans (34430)

Warren, Cecil (15605)

Waskowsi, Gunter von (19767)

Welch, Godfrey (20610)

White, Ronald (17581)

Wilkinson, James 'Jimmy' (18508)

Wilson, John (17985)

Wood, William (15427)

Wright, Cyril (10662)

Voices from the NATIONAL WW2 MUSEUM

From the collection of The National WWII Museum and the Eisenhower Center Peter Kalikow World War II Collection, University of New Orleans. With special thanks to the Stephen E. Ambrose family. Reproduced by permission of the National WWII Museum.

Bielec, William

Blatnik, Robert

Chester, Daniel

Chester, Daniel

Clark, Russell

Coleman, Harper

Davis, Jack

Denius, Frank

Duffy, Gowan

Dymnicki, Francis

Ehlers, Walter

Evans, Donald

Fiore, Dominick

Fontana, Frank

Ford, Richard

Franzky, Gerhard

Gast, William

Greer, William
Guisewite, Myron
Harkness, Henrietta
Howard, John
Jaber, Anton
Jeffrey, Wallace
Kerner, John
Klimas, Irvin
LaRose, Bruce
Lesniewski, Joseph
Lomell, Leonard 'Bud'
Lowry, Robert 'Bob'
Martin, James
Meier, Hebert
Miksa, Bob
Myers, Julia
Nacey, Edward
Nannini, James
Parley, Harry
Peardon, Eveline
Porcella, Tom
Raaen, John
Roach, George
Roderick, David
Rodgers, John
Schafer, Leon
Schultz, Philip
Shook, Harold 'Hal'
Smith, William
Stern, Guy
Stovroff, Irwin
Thomas, Chuck

True, William 'Bill'
Tweed, Earl
Uttero, Cosmo
VanDuzer, Raymond
Wichterich, George
Williams, Robert
Windisch, Lutz
Witmeyer, John
Zuras, Nicholas

Voices from THE JUNO BEACH CENTRE
From the Juno Beach Centre Legacy of Honour video collection, set up to capture veteran's voices and experiences.
Armitage, Roly
Chiasson, Havelyn
Parks, Jim pp 142–143

OTHER VOICES
Billinge, Harry – his interview appears on Geraint Jones's *Veterans State of Mind* podcast, episode 93
LeBas, Jacqueline – Calvados Archive
Nance, Ray © Fremantle
Parks, Jim – additional material from Memoirs of World War II, a short film series to be found online and dedicated to preserving the history of the Second World war and those who served.
Smith, Ray – his interview appears on Geraint Jones's *Veterans State of Mind* podcast, episode 94
Winters, Dick – his story can be found in his autobiography, *Beyond Band of Brothers*, as well as *Band of Brothers* by Stephen Ambrose and in A Tribute to Dick Winters video series by Representative John Payne.

Geraint Jones is a *Sunday Times* and *New York Times* bestselling author who served as an infantry soldier in Iraq and Afghanistan. His first work of non-fiction, *No Way Out* with Major Adam Jowett, was a *Sunday Times* top 10 bestseller. He has also written a memoir of his final Afghanistan tour, *Brothers in Arms*, and co-authored *Escape from Kabul* with Levison Wood, using first-hand accounts to describe the dramatic military evacuation of the city in 2021. He has published several novels, including titles with James Patterson. His podcasts, Veteran State of Mind and The War Story Podcast, include interviews with D-Day survivors.